TRADE CENTERS AND TRADE ROUTES

The Century Earth Science Series

KIRTLEY F. MATHER, *Editor*

TRADE CENTERS
AND
TRADE ROUTES

By

EUGENE VAN CLEEF

THE OHIO STATE UNIVERSITY

D. APPLETON-CENTURY COMPANY

INCORPORATED

New York   *London*

347

PRINTED IN THE UNITED STATES OF AMERICA

TO THE MEMORY OF MY MOTHER
WHOSE ENTHUSIASM AND OPTIMISM
DURING MANY YEARS OF RESIDENCE IN
CHICAGO PERSONIFIED ITS "I WILL" SPIRIT

EDITOR'S INTRODUCTION

It is becoming increasingly apparent that the one fundamental problem which man must solve if he is to make himself secure as an inhabitant of the earth is that of the distribution of the materials upon which his existence depends. The natural resources provided abundantly by the earth are unevenly scattered through its geologic structures, topographic features, and climatic elements. There is apparently enough and some to spare if available techniques for discovery, recovery, and utilization with a minimum of waste are used. The real issue is that of ways and means for organization of society so that the essential materials and products can be efficiently and equably distributed among all its members.

The facing of this issue is essentially a function of sociology and political economy, but it involves an understanding of earth science. No stable superstructure can be established upon any other foundation than knowledge of the earth processes and their products, combined with an adequate comprehension of the relationship between human beings and the physical environment in which their lives are set. The modern geographer with his research concerning such relationships is providing the groundwork and preparing the way for the discovery of effective programs designed to advance mankind one step farther along the road toward lasting security as a creature of the earth.

This broad survey and critical analysis of Trade Centers and Trade Routes strikes at the very heart of the complex problem of distribution. It gathers information and suggests correlations which are of great value to all who are concerned with plans for the material and æsthetic welfare of the race. It merits a prominent place in the literature of geography, sociology, and economics. Designed primarily for students in collegiate departments dealing with those branches of learning, it is also preëminently adapted to the needs of "city planners," chambers of commerce, "men of affairs," and the general reader interested in the future of human society.

KIRTLEY F. MATHER.

PREFACE

Public interest in national, State, and local planning combined with vast impending monetary expenditures for the realization of these plans certainly make desirable and probably essential a study of the problems associated with planning. In this book attention is focused upon the city, town, and village as *trade centers.*

Investigations of the structural forms, functions, and patterns of trade centers are by no means new. This is evidenced by city maps dating from the seventh century B.C. These maps in themselves indicate that some one directed attention to patterns and perhaps other aspects of urban design in order to delineate properly the distribution of trade-center parts. It is not, however, the author's purpose to trace the history of trade centers, but rather to consider present-day problems, referring to historic times when necessary for interpretation of modern situations.

Trade centers can be accurately interpreted only if their integral relation to the physical and functional environment be recognized. The means of integration, whether material such as highways or intangible such as ideas, are viewed as trade routes. Hence, the trade center and trade route together constitute a unit. They are analyzed separately in order to avoid confusion, but always with the thought that in the realm of reality they are inseparable.

The writer hopes that this presentation, while not exhaustive, may prove of assistance to those who have an immediate interest in urban and rural problems and that it may perhaps attract the attention of those who heretofore have given relatively little thought to these intriguing biological phenomena of our modern civilization.

Grateful acknowledgment is made to those whose writings may have influenced this presentation. However, most of the interpretations here recorded are based upon the writer's personal experience, direct observation and research, more especially during the past fifteen years.

EUGENE VAN CLEEF.

CONTENTS

PART I

TRADE CENTERS

PART II

TRADE ROUTES

LIST OF FIGURES

xv

PART I
TRADE CENTERS

TRADE CENTERS AND TRADE ROUTES

CHAPTER I

TRADE CENTERS AND THEIR CLASSIFICATION

Trade centers are dynamic elements expressive of the world's cultural and economic structure. They are an index to the level of a nation's civilization. As such, trade centers may be viewed as organisms of society, rooted in the earth, reflecting different moods, varying in intensity of activity, and reacting sensitively to both internal and external influences.

These organisms are not passive mechanical phenomena contributing to a geometric pattern spread out upon the earth's surface, but rather active, aggressive, biological centers which originate ideas, which initiate movements to take advantage of nature's offerings or adjust themselves to nature's limitations.

The world's major business is conducted in trade centers. Some trade centers, like New York, London, or Chicago, exert an influence international in scope, while smaller centers transact an amount of business insufficient to make an impression outside of their locality. Size, however, is not necessarily a criterion of importance in the world's total trade, for, without the smaller centers, the larger ones would have difficulty in surviving. In this day of rapid and low cost means of communication there exists an interdependence among trade centers which gives to every center a position of consequence. No city may justifiably ignore another because of a sense of superiority in size, quality, or influence; none may wisely believe itself to have a better opportunity to share in the world's trade if a neighboring center could somehow be eliminated. Munro says:

The demeanor of the city is not, therefore, a matter of concern to itself alone. It is of vital concern to all who desire high national aspirations to be established and maintained, for the ideals of a nation are determined by the most influential among the various elements of its population. Being so determined they are constantly in process of change. Hence, the saying that although men may make cities, it is equally true that cities make men. He who makes the city makes the nation and indeed it is the cities of the future that will determine the character of the world.[1]

[1] William B. Munro, in *Encyclopedia of the Social Sciences*, Vol. VII, pp. 481-482.

The Rise and Fall of Trade Centers.—Like the life within them, centers of trade activity are born, develop in varying degree, and face the possibility of extinction. No trade center may rest upon its reputation and long maintain its position in the competitive struggle. That this is true becomes evident when we scan the public press. Civic Industrial Bureaus, groups of public-spirited citizens, and other organizations, either permanent or temporary, advertise the qualities of their respective cities to millions of readers in the hope that some of them may be enticed away from their present location in favor of a supposedly better center. Before elaborating upon the rise of cities, our understanding of the problems involved may be clarified if we first cite evidence of the fact that cities do decline.

The Fall of Ancient Cities.—The decline of cities is a very real phenomenon centuries old. The "Fall of Rome" is an expression which the populace well recognizes, but, because it occurred so long ago and because the city still exists, even though without its former world power, the phrase has seemingly acquired the status of fiction. In southeastern Asia the cities of Tehran, Merv, Bukhara, Samarkand, and others along the caravan route from Europe to India and China grew vigorously for hundreds of years, until, in 1498, Vasco da Gama circled the Cape of Good Hope, establishing an all-sea route to India. The death-knell of these towns was sounded and, although they did not altogether disappear from the map, they dwindled to almost an inconsequential status.

Sidon and later Tyre, commercial ports of ancient Phœnicia, commanded the respect of the entire Mediterranean world, but to-day they are historic memories. Carthage, a Phœnician outpost on the north African coast near the present site of Tunis, grew to be a power within itself, surviving the period of the decline of Phœnician supremacy, from about 700 B.C. to the rise of the Roman Empire. It attained a population of over 200,000 about 150 B.C., but as the power of Rome ascended, that of Carthage diminished. To-day Tunis, twelve miles southeast of the original site of Carthage, after an existence of 1,500 years, has a population of a mere 170,000 persons.

The Fall of Modern Cities.—We need not look alone to ancient cities for cases of decline or sudden extinction. Witness the trail of ruins in the wake of the lumber centers in upper Michigan, northern Wisconsin, and Minnesota. Not even the names remain in many instances, and where the railroad station still displays the name, no significance is attached to it except as the passer-by may have his attention directed to the fact that here once stood a thriving center. Among towns better known, one can point to Quebec, which relinquished its supremacy to Montreal, 150 miles up the St. Lawrence River, when this body of water was made navigable to the latter point; between 1881 and 1891 Montreal increased in population by 41.4 per cent while Quebec added less than 1 per cent. Cincinnati, in about 1860, was larger than Cleveland or Chicago, but with the change in mode of transportation from river to rail, with the movement of immigrants from abroad and residents along the Atlantic Seaboard to the fertile plains of the Upper Mississippi Valley and the Northwest, Cincinnati could no longer hold its own. It has grown, to be sure, but only at a retarded rate as compared with the other two centers.

Since the World War we have witnessed the spectacle of two major European cities doing their utmost to survive but apparently struggling against the inevitable. These are the cities of Danzig and Königsberg. Both were thriving centers before the War. However, in the case of Danzig, its severance from Germany to become a free city and to accommodate Poland with an outlet to the sea via what is known as the Polish Corridor has spelled its probable permanent decline. The Poles have seen fit to create a new city, Gdynia, in the vicinity of Danzig. Gdynia has risen from a village of 300 fishermen in 1923 to a modern port city of over 36,000. It is pure Polish, is in direct competition with Danzig, and is connected by rail with the Polish hinterland in a manner to circumvent Danzig. In these circumstances there is little hope for Danzig to maintain its present population.

Königsberg, before the war Germany's northeastern military outpost against Russia, is now a depressed city in detached East Prussia. Polish territory obstructs its hinterland, preventing direct access to the U.S.S.R. Within East Prussia there is insufficient economic activity to serve the needs of the city. The population was dispersed in part by the exodus of military men immediately after the war and of great numbers of merchants and others who not only served army needs but also shared in the former port activities between Königsberg and oversea centers on the one hand and interior centers in Germany and Russia on the other. Its future is obscured by that disconcerting element —uncertainty of international policies.

Thus we see that trade centers are in a constant state of flux. They are either just getting started in life or have attained full maturity or are in process of decline. The little settlement at the junction of two or three main railways or country roads, to-day known only as "Stop 18," may develop into an important collecting and distributing center to-morrow. Another agglomeration of people may have just attained a population of 5,000 or 10,000, entitling it to incorporate and pass from the village to the town or city stage. Still others are seeking only to maintain their status in the firmament of progressive cities.

CLASSIFICATION OF TRADE CENTERS

Classification According to Dominant Function.—Numerous classifi-

TABLE 1

THE ACTIVE ORDER OF URBAN GROUPS, TABULATED ACCORDING TO
Dominant Functions [2]

CLASS I ADMINISTRATION	CLASS II DEFENSE	CLASS III CULTURE	CLASS IV PRODUCTION
Capital cities Revenue cities	Fortress towns Garrison towns Naval bases	University towns Cathedral towns Art centers Pilgrimage towns Religious towns	Manufacturing towns Craft centers

CLASS V COMMUNICATION			
Group A *Collection*	*Group B* *Transfer*	*Group C* *Distribution*	CLASS VI RECREATION
Mining towns Fishing towns Forest towns Depot towns	Market towns Fall-line towns Break-of-bulk towns Bridgehead towns Tidal-limit towns Navigation-head towns	Export towns Import towns Supply towns	Health resorts Tourist resorts Holiday resorts
"Entrepôt" Cities			

[2] M. Aurousseau, "The Distribution of Population," The *Geographical Review* (1921), Vol. XI, No. 4, p. 572.

cations of the world's trade centers have been set up. Whether they are good or bad is largely a matter of opinion. Here we present four groupings, the first (Table 1) is based upon function and is quoted from Aurousseau who offers an admirable arrangement.

The terms in Table 1 are self-explanatory, and illustrations of each type are easy to locate, but, by way of insuring clarity, a few illustrations may be cited. Washington, D. C., and many of our State capitals are dominantly Administration centers. Verdun, France, represents the Fortress type; Salt Lake City, Utah, is a Cathedral town; Gary, Indiana, is a Manufacturing center. Among centers listed under the heading of "Mining towns," Hibbing, Minnesota, may be cited because of the dominant function of mining iron ore. Duluth, in the same state, is a Break-of-bulk city, while Portland, in Maine, represents an Export center whose exports are the dominant factor in the city's welfare. It is the winter export port for Canadian products, primarily grains. Health and Tourist resorts are numerous, but Colorado Springs, Colorado, Hot Springs, Arkansas, and Atlantic City, New Jersey, may be noted in passing. The "Entrepôt" city is best illustrated by London, that is, a center which collects goods from points without the country for redistribution to foreign lands.[3]

Classification According to Fact of Location.—Trade centers may be classified according to location (Table 2). This classification contains some of the elements which appear in Table 1 but omits much detail and has the virtue of offering simplicity. It lacks, however, the economic elements except those that the location may imply, such as port functions. But implications must be distinguished from facts.

TABLE 2

TRADE CENTERS CLASSIFIED ACCORDING TO FACT
OF LOCATION

CLASS I. INTERIOR		CLASS II. COASTAL	
Land	*Water*	*Continental*	*Island*
Plain	Lake	River mouth	
Valley	River	Embayment	
Highland	Sea		

[3] A city which collects goods for "redistribution" within the country might be referred to as a "centrepôt" for purposes of distinguishing its functions from those of an "entrepôt."

The items in Table 2 might cause one to inquire into the reason for the locations indicated. Rather than to include in this classification the element of reason, another one has been set up based entirely upon the latter factor (Table 3).

TABLE 3

TRADE CENTERS CLASSIFIED ACCORDING TO REASON FOR LOCATION

Class
  I. Junction of routes

  II. Head of Navigation
      A. Along rivers
      B. Along embayed coasts

  III. Change in direction of traffic routes
      A. River bends
      B. Water bodies, highlands or other natural features impeding transportation

  IV. Change in mode of transportation
      A. Water and rail
      B. Mechanical vehicle, pack animal, or man

  V. Arbitrary or accidental selection of locality

The mere fact of location has less significance than the reason. Assignment, however, of a single reason for a location is hazardous. If historical records are not available to enable us to establish with certainty the reason for the location of a particular center, our best conjectures may be impossible of verification and may of course be wholly in error. Yet, when trade centers have acquired considerable stability and have shown progress dominantly along certain lines, the primary reason for their *survival,* if not for their location in the first instance, usually can be satisfactorily determined, and not infrequently the survival element may be identical with the initial cause for the selection of the location.

Figure 1 on page 9 offers concrete examples of several of the most common reasons for the location of trade centers as listed in Table 3. Indianapolis, at the junction of railroad lines whose axes are essentially at right angles to each other and at the meeting point of rail and river which likewise form large angles with each other, presents a situation reproduced many times. These joining routes penetrate radically different territory. In the case of rail lines, trains generally slow down

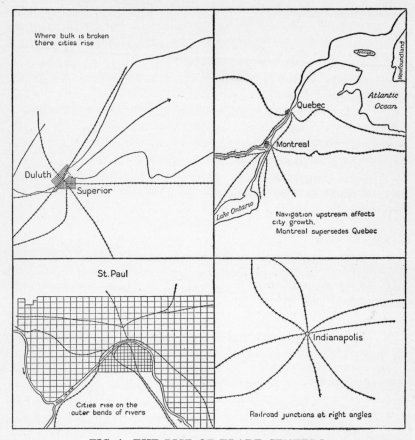

FIG. 1. THE RISE OF TRADE CENTERS

Four geographic conditions under which most trade centers grow with vigor are depicted here. If relief were shown in these diagrams we would observe that the sites generally are upon relatively high land and well drained. They allow for considerable areal expansion.

when approaching important intersections. A complete stop does not consume a great deal more time than slowing down, and, by offering the opportunity to exchange freight, "pays" for the time consumed in stopping. Such exchanges require personnel to handle them, and herein lies the nucleus for the beginning and for the development of a trade center. The same principle applies to the intersection of water routes or of water and overland routes.

The effectiveness of location at the head of navigation can again be illustrated by Montreal. While the selection of the actual site of Montreal was no doubt largely determined by its defensive qualities in the days when Indians were unfriendly and long-range guns unknown, yet the growth of the city was undoubtedly fostered by its favorable position at the head of navigation on the St. Lawrence River, dating from the improvement of the river channel above Quebec.

Class III, including most cities of consequence located upon rivers, can be well illustrated by St. Paul, Minnesota. The great bend in the Mississippi River forces traffic to choose between attempting to cross the river at great cost and inconvenience, or going around the bend. Following the outer side of the bend is customary. At the point along the river where the route changes its direction, traffic slows down and eventually stops. There a point of transfer may arise and a city may be born.

Chicago at the southern end of Lake Michigan presents an excellent case of the effect of change in direction of traffic. Chicago was evolved largely during the era of east-west trade development, particularly between the Northwestern States and the Eastern Seaboard. Had there been no lake, the route between the latter two regions probably would have been a short cut well to the north of Chicago. As it is, freight and people have had to make the turn around the head of the lake. There a city was destined to be established and to grow rapidly.

Where bulk is broken (Class IV), that is, a mode of transportation changes, workers are necessary, and, as a consequence, cities such as Duluth come into being. Rail to water, water to rail, pack animal to automobile, or coolie's back to camel—it makes little difference what the combination may be. At the point where the shift in load is effected, owing to a necessary change in the type of transport medium, or for any other reason, trade centers may rise.

Under Class V in Table 3, that is, arbitrary or accidental selection, many different kinds of cases might be listed. Some cities like Canberra, Australia; Washington, D. C.; Berlin, Germany; Leningrad, U.S.S.R.; or Littoria established in 1932 in the drained Pontine marsh area of Italy; and Sabaudia inaugurated in 1934 in the same region were located by legislative or royal decree. They were either consciously founded or given preferred attention to the end that they might become important centers. Manchester, England; Glasgow, Scotland; and Bremen, Germany, have dug themselves into fame by building canals and locks to overcome natural handicaps.

Classification According to General Activity.—The classifications thus far presented show the possibility of assorting trade centers in accordance with the individual's particular viewpoint. Still other tables could be set up, but it is not essential to exhaust the list of conceivable arrangements. However, for the purpose of convenience in the consideration of trade centers in succeeding chapters, we present a classification even more simple than any of the preceding. It is based upon *general activity*.

Just as quickly as we attempt to characterize a center by a descriptive term which in itself implies a restricted scope, we expose ourselves to severe criticism because rarely does a trade center function in a restricted manner. As it matures, its life becomes complex and numerous elements enter into its maintenance. Nevertheless, convenience justifies a general classification provided we recognize its limitations. The terms in this last classification border upon the all-inclusive and are indicated in the following table:

TABLE 4

TRADE CENTERS CLASSIFIED ACCORDING TO GENERAL ACTIVITY

CLASS I. COMMERCIAL	COMBINATION CLASS	CLASS II. INDUSTRIAL
A. Exchange	Commercial and Industrial	A. Production

Most trade centers are in part or wholly commercial, that is, are engaged in the exchange of commodities or services, the latter in large variety, including even the exchange of spiritual uplift for the monetary support of a religious institution. St. Paul, Minnesota, aside from the fact that it is the state's capital, derives its sustenance mainly from engaging in the collection of commodities for redistribution. Numerous centers concern themselves primarily with the production of raw materials such as coal, iron ore, or building stone. Bluefield, West Virginia, depends upon coal; Chisholm, Minnesota, lives because of iron ore. Bedford, Indiana, gives thanks to the presence of superior limestone deposits.

One may readily challenge this classification because it seems inconceivable that a commercial center should produce nothing, or an industrial center have no commerce. The challenge undoubtedly is fair, but we must not overlook the fact that the classification calls for commerce or industry as a *general activity* not to the absolute exclusion of every other possible function. The table recognizes the duality of major activities in trade centers by indicating a transition column under the heading "Combination Class" wherein neither commerce nor industry dominate. Chicago and New York City typify such centers, in fact, the latter city ranks first in the United States both as a commercial center and as an industrial center.

Location vs. Accessibility.—In all these classifications the qualities of location and accessibility are implied if not specifically stated, and

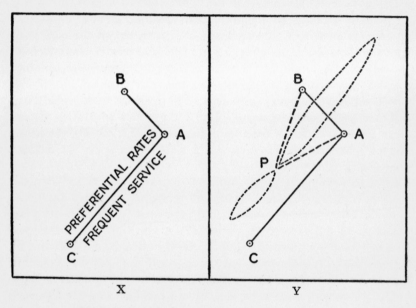

FIG. 2. LOCATION VERSUS ACCESSIBILITY

(X) Trade center *A* is closer in miles to *B* than to *C*, but in terms of accessibility, owing to preferential freight rates and better service, is nearer to *C* than to *B*. (Y) Trade center *A* is nearer *B* than to *C* as the crow flies, but owing to the barrier and the necessity for using pass *P*, it is farther in terms of accessibility from *B* than from *C*.

both are closely associated with an element of transportation. Transportation facilities generally determine the degree of accessibility of a given center. Since trade itself means an exchange of commodities, it is logical to conclude that easy access to a trade center is paramount to its vigorous growth. Consequently, most developing trade centers are located where transportation conveniences are of a high order. A pure and sufficient water supply is fundamental, of course, but given these elements, we may be certain that as between a location fairly easy of access and another difficult of access, the trade center falling in the first category holds the greater promise for successful development. One geographer has effectively said, "Accessibility is the economic crystallization of location." [4]

Accessibility should not be confused with mere distance. It does not necessarily imply nearness. A trade center A (Fig. 2 X) may be twenty miles as the crow flies from one center B and fifty miles from another C yet be more accessible to C than to B. The road to B may be unpaved and in wet weather so muddy that it becomes almost impassable, whereas the road to C is paved and always usable on the wettest of days. On the other hand (Fig. 2 Y), a highland may separate B from the major trade center A, necessitating going around the eminence at pass P, a distance of seventy-five miles to reach B, or, if low enough to be crossed, may have such steep gradients as to make travel slow and dangerous. Again, airplane service may give B a distinct advantage over C. In all these instances it must be clear that the major center is more accessible to C than to B although its immediate distance from C is greater than from B.

Since accessibility is largely a matter of transportation facilities, the elements of time, cost, and quality of service enter. Costs being the same, the center which can be reached most quickly is in a better position than all other competing centers. On the other hand, the *time element* favoring a given city may be entirely offset by the high cost of transportation. These varying relationships call for vigilance upon the part of all centers desirous of progress to the end that they secure freight parity with competitive centers or a freight rate advantage over their competitors if they enjoy shorter distances to given focal points of economic activity. In some instances the time and quality of service factors may discount slight differences in transportation costs.

Many Chambers of Commerce and Industrial Bureaus recognize, probably unconsciously, the significance of accessibility if one may judge by the nature of their literature advertising their respective advantages as trade centers and as places where people may earn a satisfactory and more or less Utopian living. Not all of them, however, seem to be cognizant of the fact that location and accessibility are not synonymous terms. Hence they not only confuse them but often mistake location for accessibility. Concrete illustrations will make this clear.

In a market analysis, published by an aggressive southern city, atten-

[4] Dr. A. J. Wright, Department of Geography, The Ohio State University.

tion is directed to the fact that, within a circle having a 500 mile radius extending from the city as a center, the population numbers 59,327,433 people. "Place the circle in any other position on the map and you at once include the waste area of sea or gulf, foreign land or the sparsely settled districts of the Mountain States." To be sure this location has its virtues, but its enthusiastic supporters overlook the fact that it possesses disadvantageous peripheral qualities when referred both

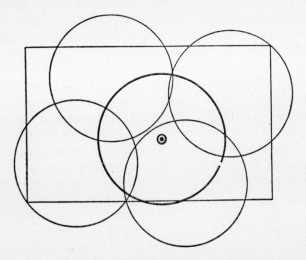

FIG. 3. THE 500-MILE CIRCLE

This map is characteristic of the type issued by Chambers of Commerce, Industrial Bureaus, and other similar civic organizations to illustrate the trade territory and population numbers within 500 miles or a "night's ride" of a particular trade center. The purpose is to demonstrate the superior qualities of the geographic location of the center. In this diagram the rectangle replaces the actual map which appeared in the original presentation. The heavy circle is supposed to include less waste area than any of the other circles and, hence, includes more favorable territory tributary to its central trade center than could be circumscribed about any other trade center on the map.

to population and to transportation network. The population is not symmetrically distributed about the trade center, but rather the trade center is located upon the outer edge of the population mass. Similarly the railway and highway network do not focus upon this city, but the city lies on the outer side of a quadrant of transportation lines to which access is possible in many cases only by indirect approach. This lack of accessibility, comparable in quality with that of competitive trade centers, accounts in large part for that city's present rank.

The Chamber of Commerce of a large city in New York State points to the fact that there lie within a 500-mile circle focusing upon it "ten of the twelve counties having industrial purchases of $500,000,-000 each." These counties are scattered from Suffolk County, containing Boston, to Cook County, containing Chicago. Such trade centers as Gary, Indiana; Lowell, Massachusetts; and Jersey City, New Jersey, are among the others shown upon the Chamber of Commerce map. The implication is that the central location of this city gives to it a distinct advantage over many other centers. Only the offering of special buying advantages such as uniqueness of product, price, or quality will offset inaccessibility. The element of accessibility can not be ignored. Would Gary trade mostly with a city 500 miles distant rather than nearby Chicago? Would Lowell trade with a far distant center rather than its neighbor, Boston? Would Jersey City, a part of the metropolitan area of New York City, trade with a remote community in preference to its local economic fraternity? Clearly the claims of this particular trade center to the unique value of its location fade almost into oblivion as the light of accessibility is turned on.

The number of trade centers which draw a circle about themselves to show the all-inclusiveness of their respective hinterlands and the consequent superior qualities of their locations is almost as great as the number who advertise. The failure to differentiate between location and accessibility is common to practically all of them. On the other hand, too much can not be said relative to the significance of the element of accessibility. Probably no single phase of a trade center's characteristics is as important to itself as the possession of the highest degree of accessibility.

Location versus Site.—The term *location* [5] is used in this chapter to convey the idea of regional position whereas the term *site* may be employed with reference to topographical position.

The location of a city involves its relation to other points detached from it. For example, we may locate a center with mathematical precision by determining its latitude and longitude, or we may locate a community with reference to its position on two or more routes. We might also refer to the location at the head of a bay or upon a peninsula.

On the other hand, site has reference to topographic exposure. Thus

[5] Sometimes a distinction is made between *location* and *situation*, in which case *location* is used quantitatively involving latitude and longitude and *situation* is used qualitatively. For our purposes this technical distinction is unnecessary, *location* and *situation* being used synonymously.

a city may occupy a piece of terrain at a particular point upon a bluff overlooking a river valley. The site of another center may be upon a flood-plain or terrace or hill slope.

Both site and location may imply the inclusion of similar or even identical natural phenomena, but not necessarily so. The confluence of streams may, in a given instance, have been potent in determining both location and site of a city, but the locational influence may have involved ease of transportation and access to neighboring centers, whereas the purity and abundance of the waters at a particular point or the drainage may have served as the determining factor in the actual place (site) of erection of homes, public buildings, and streets and avenues.

Conclusion.—In all of the considerations leading to the classification of trade centers we must not lose sight of the fact that, as the centers evolve, the original reasons for their being may easily become obscured. Their growth to-day may be due to elements entirely different from those which were associated with their establishment, as for example, improvement in transportation highways, changes in modes of communication, or realignment of political boundaries in the hinterland. Their classification, as we have seen, may vary greatly, for it may be based upon their original location, or their first site, or their present function, or still other elements.

In our further analysis of the trade center we shall be more interested in its present activities and future possibilities than in its history. We have elected to look at trade centers as present-day phenomena; to examine them for their composition and structure, particularly with respect to the manner in which their economic and cultural qualities fit into our civilization; to note their reciprocal and inter-relations with special reference to trade, employing the term trade in its broadest connotation; to view their probable future and to venture an occasional suggestion as to the most effective direction which that future may take.

CHAPTER II

WORLD DISTRIBUTION OF TRADE CENTERS

A map of the world delineating all trade centers reveals great irregularity of distribution. While the centers show certain group tendencies with respect to location, there seems to be not the slightest indication of uniformity in space relations even for relatively small portions of the earth. The reasons for this situation have already been indicated in some detail in the discussion of classifications. They may be summarized in general as (1) uneven topography of the earth's surface, (2) irregular distribution of natural resources, (3) great diversity of climates, (4) the element of accidental circumstance, and (5) the peculiarities of man himself. Nevertheless, in spite of this irregularity, it is possible to classify distribution into three types: (1) scattered, (2) clustered, and (3) lineal. Since there occur, within each of these classes, centers of varying size of population, the larger centers are more likely to be located closer to other large centers than to be isolated. There seems also to be some relationship between the sizes of these centers and their actual location.

Examination of the distribution of trade centers by continents brings to light three major "urban" or trade-center regions, namely, (1) the Northeastern quarter of the United States and adjoining southeastern Canada, (2) northwestern Europe, and (3) east coastal Asia. As secondary regions, South Africa, southeast Australia, southeast South America, and India may be noted. South Africa has but four centers with 100,000 or over and India has only thirty-five such centers in a region of some 350,000,000 people. Examination of a map of these latter areas, however, brings to light a large number of smaller centers. These, as we have already stated, may possess qualities identical with those of urban centers having a population in excess of 100,000. Their influence in economic and political or cultural circles may be equally as important.

Trade centers ordinarily are classified into sizes according to arbitrary numbers. We might throw into one group all centers below 50,000 inhabitants, or begin as low as 2,500 which the United States Census

Bureau uses as the critical number distinguishing urban from rural groups. Then, too, as Mark Jefferson has done,[1] we may select the number 100,000 to distinguish "great cities" from those which, presumably, are not great. The adjective "great" has nothing to do with fame or particular attainment, but is purely quantitative. The number 150,000 might have been chosen as well, but apparently 100,000 is a more attractive figure.

Although there are between 500 and 550 trade centers with a population of 100,000 or over (the number is not given with exactitude because of inaccuracies in the censuses of many countries) the total population of all these "great cities" does not exceed 10 per cent of the world's population. On the other hand, there is reason to believe that more persons live in trade centers having a population of less than 100,000 than in those of 100,000 and over. In the United States 30.4 per cent of the population live in the centers between 1,000 and 100,000, whereas 29.6 per cent live in centers with a population of 100,000 and over. Since the trend toward urbanization has been exceptionally strong in the United States as compared with most parts of the earth, we can safely assume that in most other regions the bulk of the population likewise lives in the smaller centers. Thus we see that if we limit the expression "urban population" to those people occupying "great cities," we give undue emphasis to the large centers whose fate, we shall note later, rests largely upon the activities of the small centers which occupy their hinterlands.

The Topographic Factor.—A world physical map showing distribution of cities within these trade-center areas would not only emphasize a continental peripheral and hence lowland location but would also reveal that among centers away from the great seas and oceans the lowland site is dominant. Only where space is limited or the lowland climate is unfavorable or where resources are a particular influence do we find large or economically significant centers at high altitudes. Quito reaches an altitude of 9,350 feet, Mexico City 7,730 feet, La Paz 12,139 feet, Denver 5,270 feet. These and a few others are the exceptions.

Most of the earth's population lives below an altitude of 2,000 feet. The development of trade among these people depends largely upon the quality of the accessibility of their centers, that is, upon the means of communication. These means usually are more readily developed in regions of low relief and low altitude than in regions of high relief and

---

[1] Adapted from Mark Jefferson, "Distribution of the World's City Folks," The *Geographical Review* (1931) Vol. XXI, pp. 446-465.

high altitude, and only very special circumstances, generally of an economic nature, or occasionally military, make it possible for trade centers to prosper in the face of poor accessibility.

Climatic Distribution.—As civilization has advanced, accompanied by the spread of population over the earth's surface, man has shown greatest activity in intermediate climatic regions, that is, in those regions in which variability in temperature and precipitation throughout the year are marked. "The spur of the seasons," as has been said, has been the most stimulating element in the rise of civilization. Therefore, it is not surprising to find our largest trade centers in the regions of intermediate climates. The tropics have few large centers, and regions with Arctic climates are devoid of them.

Large tropical trade centers are located either upon plateaus where the climate simulates the intermediate, and where there is a port city in the lowland, as in the case of the Mexico City-Vera Cruz couplet, or located at sea level with a couplet center in the highland hinterland for those who can afford to commute between the hinterland and their places of business. The Manila-Baguio couplet in the Philippines or the Rio de Janeiro-Petropolis couplet in Brazil illustrate the latter type of distribution.

Many are the persons who do not wish to acknowledge a climatic influence upon man, but rather to credit man with good judgment in adjusting himself to the world's distribution of climates. There can be no doubt in either case, influence or adjustment, that in the course of the centuries of man's struggle for existence his gregarious habit has resulted in the development of large common centers and these have risen most often in the regions of stimulating intermediate climates. Ellsworth Huntington, of Yale University, for years an investigator of climate in relation to man, has often pointed out the close correlation between the regions of high civilization and those of stimulating energizing climates, climates in which variability is an outstanding characteristic and in which certain ranges in the elements are dominant.[2]

Scattered Trade Centers.—By "scattered" we mean those centers whose distances from each other are distinctly irregular. In some instances these distances are so great that communication between any two is infrequent; in other cases they are so close to each other as to be highly interdependent. Then, there are those whose distances apart and orientation with respect to each other place them in an inter-

[2] Ellsworth Huntington, *Civilization and Climate* (Yale University Press, New Haven, 1915). See also other writings and lectures of Ellsworth Huntington.

mediate relationship. The isolated types are most common in semi-arid plains, in deep valleys or rugged mountains, in pioneer lands and slightly settled portions of the humid regions. The second type occur in the readily accessible areas of the earth, in the regions of good arable lands, and where sources of power are available for industrial purposes.

The scattering of trade centers, no doubt, has been conditioned by irregularities of the earth's surface and the uneven distribution of its resources. Man's first concern has always been the gaining of a livelihood. Stated even more simply and with less refinement, man's primary objective has been to assure himself of three meals a day. All other considerations obviously have had to be secondary, for without the support of life there could have been no human activity of any kind. Consequently, man has sought to locate himself wherever he has found that he could most easily maintain his existence with the aid of the earth's raw materials.

Trade centers are scattered much more than they would have been had the occupance of the earth been planned in advance of migratory movements. The location of trade centers is largely the consequence of a trial and error method, but with many of the errors of location still surviving. Settlement has been an evolutionary process, a process still going on, but with some slight degree of guidance for the first time in man's history.[3]

Clustered Trade Centers.—Clustered trade centers, sometimes referred to as conurbations, swarms, or grouped cities, are trade centers which develop in such close proximity to each other that their economic welfare largely focuses upon common interests. In some instances the transition from one center to another may be imperceptible, except as signs distinguish them at their coincident boundaries. In many cases, even where discontinuous, the group constitutes essentially a single trade center as though under a single political organization. Such, for example, we have in the Chicago region where the cluster extends across the Illinois-Indiana boundary or in the New York City cluster penetrated by the New York-Connecticut boundary.

Clustered centers are also of the variety in which interests may be distinctly twofold, namely, (1) intensely local with respect to affairs of civic importance and (2) economically interdependent. Such types of clusters are illustrated by the aggregate of communities in the Boston vicinity which constitute Metropolitan Boston. Other clusters

[3] American Geographical Society, *Pioneer Settlement,* Special Publication No. 14 (New York, 1932), 473 pp.

worth citing are the Buffalo area, the Detroit locality, Los Angeles district, and, in foreign lands, the Ruhr Valley of Germany and the Liverpool-Manchester cluster in England.

Clusters are only possible where the natural advantages of a locality are spread over a considerable area. In the case of the Chicago cluster, transportation facilities combined with a focal position in a remarkably productive lowland region are available to a district extending from Waukegan on the north to Michigan City on the south, and from Chicago itself to Elgin and Aurora on the west. There are those who would even include Milwaukee in the Chicago cluster. Each small center

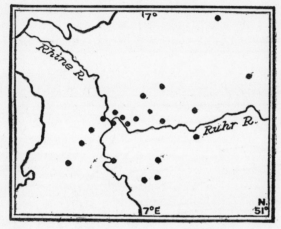

FIG. 4. A CLUSTER OF TRADE CENTERS—
THE RHINE-RUHR VALLEY

This galaxy of trade centers is outstanding for its number within so small an area. Coal, water transportation, nearby iron ore, and a high degree of accessibility have all contributed toward the growth of the cluster. (Scale 1:2,000,000.)

enjoys a percentage, as it were, of the whole advantage which accrues to Chicago proper.

In the Ruhr District of Germany the same set of circumstances, in the main, account for the rise of Essen, Duisburg, Krefeld, Düsseldorf, Wuppertal and many others in that cluster. Local variations occur within the centers themselves, but their major economic activities arise out of the same elements, namely, coal, iron, and a high degree of accessibility.

Lineal Trade Centers.—By lineal trade centers is meant those which occur in relatively close succession along a railroad, river, or highway,

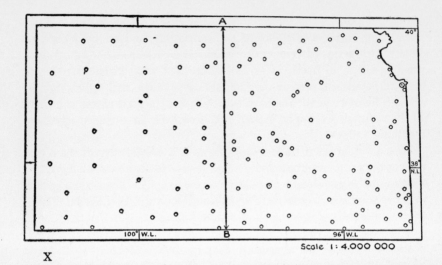

X

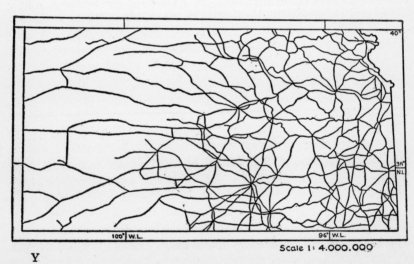

Y

FIG. 5. LINEAL AND SCATTERED ARRANGEMENT
OF TRADE CENTERS

(X) West of *A-B* the lineal sequence of centers stands out in contrast with the scattered effect to the east. If the centers west of *A-B* were connected in an east-west direction by a continuous line, that line would be practically identical with the railroad which ties these centers together. Many of these centers followed the building of the railroad and a few came into being after the establishment of an overland trail or road. This map, compared with the railroad map (Y) below, shows the close correlation between two cultural elements, namely transportation facilities and trade centers.

yet do not possess the interrelations of a cluster. They reflect a direct relationship to the availability of transportation. In fact the delineation of any such series of centers, in the absence of transportation symbols, usually serves, in itself, as an indicator of a transportation route. A detailed population map of the United States shows strikingly a number of such lineal centers. They are especially conspicuous across the Great Plains, and, as we might expect, are prominent in occupied elongated mountain valleys.

This distribution of trade centers suggests a development of the region during the era of railroad growth and to-day is beginning to reflect the building or improvement of modern highways. The lineal arrangement is most common in relatively new countries such as Canada, United States, Australia, Argentina, and South Africa.

Whereas lineal centers along river valleys occur largely in regions occupied prior to the nineteenth century, we find their most active growth associated with the railroad era. Centers in the Mohawk Valley, in the Rhine, in the Rhône-Saône, in the Ganges Valley and elsewhere took on new life and increased stability when railroads supplemented and often displaced the river as a major transportation medium. By stimulating the growth of some centers railroads often caused the decline of others. Those not on new rapid-transit routes could no longer compete with those enjoying improved accessibility. The new route tended to induce an increase in population along its right of way and to emphasize the significance of the growing centers where natural elements had not already started the lineal pattern. Where the pattern was begun under the influence of natural phenomena such as valleys, coasts, or other features, the latter were often reinforced by the coming of the railroad.

The Attraction of Water.—We have already suggested that trade centers were early located along rivers and we know, of course, that they are common on sea coasts and lakes. Generally, we assume that the transportational aspect of such bodies was the attracting force. That has not always been, however, the sole reason nor necessarily the most important factor. Drinking water, water for industrial purposes, derivable from springs, wells, or from surface waters, and thoroughly drained sites are other significant reasons which have led settlers to "gamble" on the future in particular localities. Then too, aesthetic values which some peoples see in the presence of extensive water bodies have received consideration.

Few are the habitations, even the most rural, which are not located either upon a rivulet or larger water body or in close proximity to one. Man, by nature, is a "landlubber," yet he seems always to have had an appreciation of the service which water may render him. So while he has been content to concentrate his energies largely upon the land and its development, he has not been unmindful of the indispensability of the earth's water resources.

Practically all large trade centers are ports. They are either ocean, lake, or river ports. Their trade, as in the case of Chicago, St. Louis, and Berlin, is not necessarily dominated by water transportation. Nevertheless, water shipping has played its part in the rise of these centers. Exceptions to our generalization are found in Mexico City, Denver, Madrid, and a very few others.

Although our present economy is largely a rail economy, the water aspect is still significant. The water influence has given the *continental* distributional pattern of large trade centers a distinctly rim cast, a distribution already suggested. If we describe this distribution with respect to the water areas, then we may say that trade centers tend to encircle the sea. This pattern may be considered as a modification of the lineal arrangement.

Persons who live in centers where the water supply for health and industrial purposes is abundant do not always fully appreciate the good fortune which is theirs. In regions where droughts occur and no reservoirs, which can supply ample water throughout the severest of drought periods, have been provided, the health of the citizens is threatened if not actually damaged. Industrial losses may be tremendous. Centers in drought-ridden areas such as parts of Kansas and Nebraska have frequently suffered great inconvenience. Even a great center like New York City has had to spend hundreds of millions of dollars to provide itself with an adequate water supply. This was attained only after accomplishing one of the world's greatest engineering feats. Recent inauguration of air conditioning in department stores, restaurants, hotels, theaters, and other public institutions has so increased the demand for water that trade centers with adequate supplies in the past suddenly find themselves faced with a possible shortage. Accordingly, their stability is threatened. The ultimate population size of a trade center is proportioned to the amount of water available.

The esthetic value of water bodies has not gone unrecognized. Many resorts of the world have been definitely located with respect to lakes or seas. The beauty of the combined water and land scene and the lure of water sports has been capitalized largely either by a direct appeal of hotel keepers to tourists or of those dealing in the sale of home sites overlooking the water.

But these are conscious efforts. Some centers located upon rivers or lakes have attracted many persons who seem to have an inherent love for the water. In the Scandinavian countries, Finland and elsewhere, enthusiasm for water sites has been the direct urge to settlement in hundreds of localities.

The Consequences.—We may ask, does it matter what the distribution of trade centers is? The centers are where they are and cannot be moved. The trade center in which any one of us earns a living is among those whose distribution we have just discussed. If we would go forward, we must seek to interpret our center in the light of its relation to all other centers. The degree of interdependence certainly differs among the scattered, clustered, and lineal types. To make the most of opportunities afforded by the type of center to which we belong demands careful consideration of that type. Experiences of the people in these various centers certainly differ. Correlative and comparative studies of them should prove profitable.

CHAPTER III

DEFINITION OF THE TRADE CENTER

The trade center has been classified according to function, fact of location, reason for location, and general activity, but has not yet been defined. We have been using "city" and "trade center" interchangeably, although showing some preference for the latter term. In this chapter we shall attempt to show why "trade center," from either an economic or geographical point of view, is far more applicable to our purposes than "city" and in many cases more significant. To this end, we present two definitions, one of a political trade center and the other what we choose to name a geographical trade center.

The Political Trade Center.—To many persons the word city calls to mind an assortment of factories, stores, residences, railroad stations, streets, parks, alleys, smoke, and police. Some visualize a fixed boundary line with perhaps a few suburban areas scattered about. Still others think of the number of inhabitants and the possession of a charter or document of incorporation. People automatically distinguish their own city from smaller ones nearby which may be classified as towns or villages. Then too, such organizations as Chambers of Commerce, Civic Industrial Bureaus, and other similar institutions whose directorates concern themselves to a very large degree with city growth, frequently interpret the word city in terms of population, wealth, and production units. Such persons see only the political city, or trade center, which may be defined as *an aggregation of people sufficiently large numerically to meet the arbitrary specifications established by a sovereign state.*

Generally, trade centers must have attained a certain population before they may become cities in an official or political sense. In Ohio, for example, a population of 5,000 persons determines a city. A community attaining that size must incorporate or, if it is a suburb, may elect to become annexed to the major urban center, provided the latter wishes to accept it.

A community which bases its economic and cultural activities solely upon the conception involved in the definition of a political trade center is likely to suffer from a restricted growth. The viewpoint is pro-

26

vincial, and provincialism usually opposes progress. There are citizens who believe in the isolation of the "home" town, who argue in favor of attending to one's own affairs and having nothing to do with neighboring centers, who even pride themselves in the ability to count the many years during which they themselves have remained at home, who find contentment in local affairs and are satisfied to let the rest of the world go by. Expressions of self-satisfaction such as these do not char-

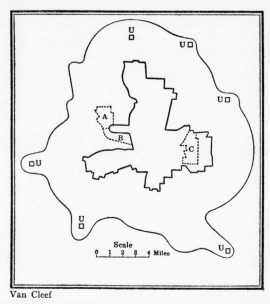

Van Cleef

FIG. 6. THE POLITICAL VERSUS THE GEOGRAPHICAL CITY

The inner figure in continuous line is the *political* city whereas the *geographical* city, sometimes called "metropolitan," includes all the area within the outer line. The small rectangles, urblets, are nearby independent communities and the areas *A, B,* and *C* likewise independent are so close to the major center as to be known as suburbs. Note that suburb *C* is an independent city within the confines of the major city. (Courtesy Allyn and Bacon, Boston.)

acterize the temper of the citizens who recognize themselves as a part of a geographical trade center.

The Geographical Trade Center.—The geographical trade center is *an aggregation of people who derive such advantages as coöperative effort may yield.*[1] In this definition no population limits are set, no legal restrictions are implied, no boundary lines are involved. It matters not whether a trade center has a population of 5,000 or only 4,999;

[1] This definition applies equally well to the popular term "metropolitan city."

geographically considered, both are trade centers and both can function effectively as such, regardless of their political status. It is immaterial if a certain center in Minnesota with a population of some 12,000 persons calls itself a village, because, although it has exceeded the necessary population for incorporation as a city, it refuses to incorporate in order to enjoy the advantages of low taxation. Village or city, it is still a trade center when viewed geographically. The following situation in Illinois would avoid confusion under this definition.

Village and city organization in Illinois has been modified in so many instances and the optional variation carried to such extremes that it is difficult to draw the line of cleavage between city and village types. The presumption that smaller communities exist as villages or towns and that they become cities with expanded population is not supported by the facts. There is the "village" of Oak Park with 63,982 people. . . . But McHenry, which is a city, has only 1,354 inhabitants. In fact, outside of Chicago, there is not one Regional city in Illinois as large as either Oak Park Village or Cicero Town! [2]

A trade center, geographically viewed, is far more concerned with problems involving accessibility than with chalk-line political boundaries. Progressive merchants do not set their delivery zones in accordance with corporate boundary lines, but with reference to the cost of distribution as affected by distance and accessibility. The cost of delivering goods one block beyond a political boundary is essentially no greater than just to the boundary. It is conceivable that costs of delivery to suburban areas can be less than to points within the political trade center limits owing to differences in quality of roads. As absurd as the situation seems, the fact remains that some business organizations regulate their delivery systems by the arbitrary limits of political boundaries. Oftentimes such illogic accounts for the difference between a static and a dynamic business.

The attainments of trade centers, not only in respect to trade but in most other directions, depend upon the adoption by the people of a geographical point of view, consciously or unconsciously expressed. From this point forward we shall use the geographical expression "trade center" in accordance with the interpretation just indicated. Consequently, whether a settlement is a mere crossroad's station, a box-car aggregation associated with the building of a railroad, or a city which

[2] C. E. Merriam, S. D. Parratt, and A. Lepawsky, *The Government of the Metropolitan Region of Chicago* (University of Chicago Press, 1933) p. 29.

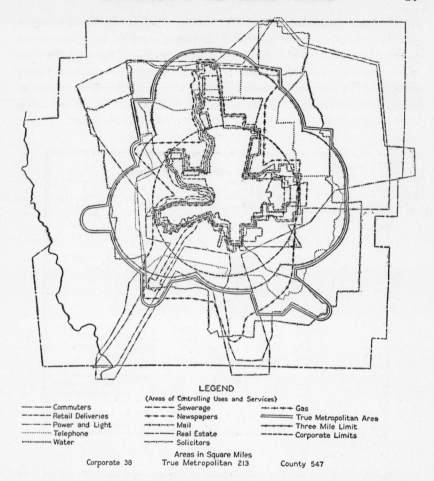

LEGEND
(Areas of Controlling Uses and Services)

——·—— Commuters	————— Sewerage	—+—+—+ Gas
————— Retail Deliveries	—+—+—+— Newspapers	═══════ True Metropolitan Area
——·——·—— Power and Light	—x—x—x— Mail	—○—○—○— Three Mile Limit
·············· Telephone	————— Real Estate	————— Corporate Limits
·—·—·—·—·—· Water	—·—·—·— Solicitors	

Areas in Square Miles

Corporate 38   True Metropolitan 213   County 547

FIG. 7. ELEMENTS CONSIDERED IN ESTABLISHING THE
LIMITS OF A METROPOLITAN CITY

counts its dwellers by the millions, we shall look upon it as a trade center.

Expressed in a different manner, a trade center is a center whose activities involve the exchange of commodities, services, or ideas. These exchanges may be effected in different combinations, such as commodities for commodities, or commodities for services. Thus a purely cultural center, such as a university town or a religious mecca, is as definitely a trade center as an aggregation of people engaged in the exchange of goods. In these centers ideas play an important part in the exchanges, perhaps a more conspicuous part than in the business world. A university or a church has principally ideas available for those willing to pay for them. A manufacturer has material goods for exchange, but he may also pay for ideas, such as his advertising department presents, to further the sale of his products. Generally, however, in an industrial community ideas play a proportionately smaller part in the exchange activities than they do in spiritual or purely educational centers.

Van Cleef

FIG. 8. THE HINTERLAND OF A GREAT TRADE CENTER

While the "I Will" spirit of the citizens of Chicago had much to do with the development of that city, little could have been accomplished without the accessible resources and potentialities of the immediate hinterland. The various items recorded on the map are only a few of the major ones which constitute the total hinterland. Climate, topography, and still other factors have been omitted in order to avoid complications in the diagrammatic presentation. (Courtesy of Allyn and Bacon, Boston.)

THE HINTERLAND OR URBAN REGION

Accessibility and distance with respect to trade centers, already discussed in Chapter I, suggest certain external relationships. Not only is the area of the trade center itself of consequence as a stage for the orientation of its human activities, but what is enacted is profoundly affected by the happenings in the region about, that is, in the *hinter-*

land. The trade center is a focal point upon which environmental factors play. It represents the climax expression of a combination of economic, geographic, social, political, historical and traditional elements or forces focussed upon a single center. In turn, it contributes to the environment or hinterland and with it establishes definite reciprocal advantageous relationships. A trade center plus its continuous hinterland may be referred to as an *urban region*.

Like the geographical trade center itself, the hinterland does not have fixed limits. It possesses a high degree of flexibility and may shift or be shifted according to a variety of circumstances. Consequently, a definition of hinterland becomes a very difficult matter. The concept can be indicated better by a discussion of concrete cases than by generalization.

A Normal Hinterland.—The official seal of Chicago depicts the Chicago River with its two branches in conventional Y form with the motto, "I Will," balanced about the Y. Whenever an opportunity arises for some citizen of Chicago to reveal enthusiastic pride about his trade center, he usually refers to the "I Will" spirit as having been responsible for its remarkable growth from a mere 109,260 people in 1860 to 3,375,235 in 1930. Investigations by geographers have shown that neither man's determination alone nor nature's resources alone can account for the rise of any community, but rather the combination of the natural resources and the will of the people to use them shapes a city's destiny. Chicagoans, then, must grant one more element among the causes of their rapid urban development, namely, proximity to the trade center of a variety of abundant resources.

A map showing the distribution of the resources of the Chicago region reveals within a radius of 500 miles, 40 per cent of the world's annual iron ore production and 80 per cent of that in the United States, 20 per cent of the country's coal production, and 70 per cent by value of the farm crops, with the center of corn production in Illinois within 250 miles of the city. While the timber which was abundant a half century ago throughout the Chicago hinterland is no longer available, the early momentum acquired by the region in the manufacture of wood products still enables Chicago to rank first as a manufacturer of furniture and to be the primary furniture distributor.

In addition to being in close proximity to Chicago, these resources are readily accessible. Due to favorable topographic conditions, country roads and railroads have been easy to construct. The flat sandy and clayey terrain, underlain by Niagara limestone, not too deep for skyscraper foundations, has permitted economical building construction and unlimited areal expansion of the community. These conditions have been supplemented by the presence of the Great Lakes which have afforded an exceedingly low-cost medium (one of the world's lowest) for the transportation of such bulky products as iron ore, coal, grains, and lumber. Not less important in some respects, has been the abundance and excellence of quality of the lake water for local use.

These, in brief, are the major factors in Chicago's rise; they constitute fundamentally the hinterland without which there could be no trade center. Had the resources been far less than they are or had they been scattered over an area with twice the present radius or had the minerals been so deep-seated as to have made them many times more costly to extract or had not the happy combination of an interior continental climate with soils possessing unusual fertility marked the greater part of the Upper Mississippi Valley and Great Lakes Region, Chicago could not have attained its present size. Thrust up a barrier range fifty miles west of Chicago with its major axis paralleling the shores of Lake Michigan and with spurs swinging around an equal distance south of the lake, and this metropolis, fifth in size among all trade centers, would diminish to small proportions if not disappear completely. Such may be the effect of a hinterland upon a trade center's destinies.

A Hinterland Interrupted by Man.—Duluth, Minnesota, at the head of navigation upon Lake Superior, is the principal point at which bulk is broken for cargo destined either for the northwest or for the Lower Lakes. Some wholesalers years ago purposely located at Duluth because of the natural advantages it possessed with respect to cheap water haul from eastern points and its proximity to central and northern Minnesota, North Dakota, and even South Dakota. Much to the disappointment of these organizations, however, they did not reap the benefits which this location, theoretically at least, should have afforded them. They discovered a gradual upbuilding of railroad rates discriminatory against them and in favor of Minneapolis and St. Paul. In other words, the hinterland of Duluth was removed by the establishment of freight rates opposing the flow of goods both from and to this trade center.

Man's Effort to Restore the Hinterland.—The Duluth Chamber of Commerce protested against the rate discrimination before the Interstate Commerce Commission in 1912. The claims were clearly summarized by Commissioner Harlan as follows:

... The City of Duluth is demanding the same position on the rate map that it has on the geographic map of the northwest. ... It is alleged that through the aid of the railroads Minneapolis and St. Paul although inland points 152 miles distant from the lake, have been made the rate breaking point, a position that they have usurped and which rightfully belongs to Duluth, as the latter claims, because of its location at the head of the lakes where water transportation ends.

After a rather lengthy hearing of all parties concerned, the Commission handed down a decision on June 9, 1913, in which the claims of Duluth were justified, and ordered the railroads to make certain readjustments to continue in force for a period of two years. The Commission said:

The conclusion that we have arrived at upon a careful consideration of the whole record is that this rate structure undoubtedly puts Duluth at an undue disadvantage. . . . In spite, however, of the adverse rate conditions under which it has labored, Duluth has now reached a position of commercial importance that has led it to assert its rights, and the record shows that it is entitled to some measure of relief.

The decision also suggested consideration for centers between Duluth and Minneapolis and St. Paul stating:

We have also found that the intervening communities are entitled to some relief, their present rates being based on their proximity to the twin cities instead of their proximity to the head of the lakes.[3]

Accordingly, Duluth regained much of its hinterland, but by no means all. While it has profited by the readjustments which followed, it could not develop as it probably would have done, if discriminating rates had never been established. The Twin Cities acquired so great a momentum and so large a handicap over Duluth during nearly twenty-five years of these rail-rate preferences that Duluth can not hope to overtake them. The case, however, strikingly illustrates the power of man to thwart nature's arrangements in favor of the development of certain trade centers.

Moving the Hinterland.—Manchester,[4] England, some thirty-five and one half miles from Liverpool, had for years imported and exported most of its goods via the port of Liverpool. In 1880 its business men felt that they were paying too large a sum to the interests of Liverpool

[3] Interstate Commerce Commission, Opinions No. 2390, No. 4335; Commercial Club of the City of Duluth—Baltimore and Ohio Railroad Company *et al.*

[4] By Manchester we mean not only the political trade center but the urban region wherein much of the actual manufacture of cotton cloth takes place.

for the service rendered, and conceived the idea of improving the Mersey River on which they were located, making it navigable for ocean ships all the way to their city. Naturally, Liverpool opposed the proposition since it recognized the attraction of penetrating waters for ships and the consequent possibility of becoming a way station in place of serving as a terminus.

Manchester's struggle in Parliament for permission to build a ship canal along the Mersey route was bitter, but it was won after about five years of effort. In 1893, a twenty-foot canal to the sea was opened, and thenceforth Manchester was a seaport. The world's ships come to its very doors and few favors are asked at Liverpool.[5]

If ships were entirely free in their movements, it is doubtful if Liverpool would have survived the extension of the sea thirty-five and one half miles past her doors, but an early start and organized shipping interests saved her from destruction. Certain it is, however, that Liverpool's development was greatly retarded, while Manchester's trade has been decidedly stimulated. Here is a clear-cut example of man's power to bring closer to himself the hinterland which has business to offer. Manchester, whose hinterland extended at least as far as the cotton growing states of the United States, brought this region into direct shipping communication with itself in place of having to operate through Liverpool.

The Continuous versus Discontinuous Hinterland.—In the preceding paragraph reference is made to the hinterland of Manchester extending to the cotton growing states. This suggests that the hinterland of a trade center is not necessarily confined to the territory contiguous to itself. The contiguous territory may be considered the continuous hinterland.[6] The discontinuous hinterland is that territory in the influential environment of a trade center which is detached from the continuous hinterland. It is the remote area in contrast with the adjacent. In the continuous hinterland are trade centers whose dominant interests are associated with the major center. Such centers are referred to as *satellites* of the major center. Thus, we may define the continuous hinterland as the area adjacent to the major trade center in which the latter's satellites are located.

Most trade centers are identified with both types of hinterland. For

[5] J. Paul Goode, *The Development of Commercial Ports,* Report to the Chicago Harbor Commission (1908).

[6] The immediately contiguous territory within the continuous hinterland which in some instances contributes to the formation of the metropolitan city has been termed by the Germans, the "Umland" or country about.

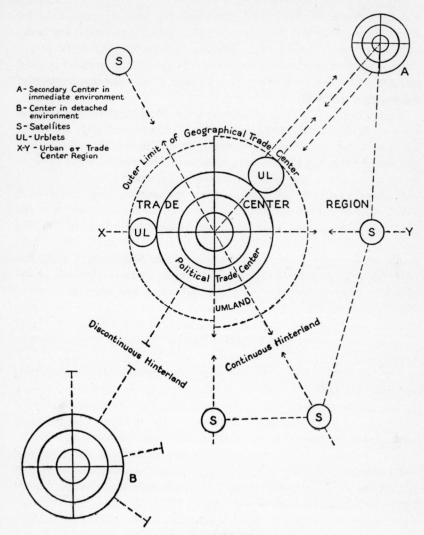

A – Secondary Center in
immediate environment
B – Center in detached
environment
S – Satellites
UL – Urblets
X-Y – Urban or Trade
Center Region

Outer Limit of Geographical Trade Center

TRADE CENTER REGION

UL

UL

Political Trade Center

UMLAND

X

Y

S

A

S

S

S

Discontinuous Hinterland

Continuous Hinterland

B

FIG. 9. THE TRADE CENTER IN RELATION TO ITS
POLITICAL ENVIRONMENT

In this diagram terms of the text are graphically shown. The parts of the
Trade Center Region, sometimes called the Urban Region, are indicated in their
relations to each other.

example, a center such as Indianapolis includes within its trade territory an area roughly one hundred miles or slightly less in radius. The people in this region look to Indianapolis not only for their major material purchases but also for some of their entertainment. Many of them are subscribers to the daily newspapers of this city and, in general, focus nearly as much attention upon Indianapolis as do the residents of the center itself. This is the continuous hinterland of Indianapolis. It lies within the urban or trade center region.

Of course, Indianapolis does not limit its interests and activities to the locality just described, but associates itself with markets in St. Louis, Chicago, New York City and other major centers. In many respects, business men of Indianapolis are as vitally concerned with the happenings in these great metropolitan centers as they are in their own continuous hinterland, yet much of the intervening territory is inconsequential and essentially unknown so far as the people of Indiana's capital are concerned. St. Louis, Chicago, and New York City constitute a part of their discontinuous hinterland. These cities, however, are not parts of the trade center region of Indianapolis.

To determine the exact limits of these two types of hinterland is essentially impossible. The boundary of a continuous hinterland, however, can be closely approximated. This may be done by determining the area in which dealers and farmers depend wholly or almost so upon the manufacturers and wholesale houses of the given center for their source of supplies. This hinterland is practically identical with the trade territory. Caution must be exercised, however, in mapping the region because, obviously, no sharp demarcation can be shown. There will be a transition zone upon the periphery of the continuous hinterland in which the activities of the residents are about equally divided among the competing major trade centers. The latter centers come into competition because they are equally accessible to the people in the peripheral zone or, if not equally accessible, because one possesses attractive features not common to the others.[7]

A map of the discontinuous hinterland is still more difficult to arrive at because data are not readily available or even determinable. Such a map, of necessity, is spotty. By the very nature of the data collected it is

[7] In a recent volume, *Traffic and Trade,* by Paver and McClintock (McGraw-Hill Book Company, Inc., New York, 1935), further light is shed upon this problem. The authors present a method for determining market limits by means of traffic flow. See pp. 58-61. Their philosophy, in brief, is that a market is determined not by the distribution of the permanent residences of the people but by the avenues along which they move, that is, by their distribution in terms of dynamics.

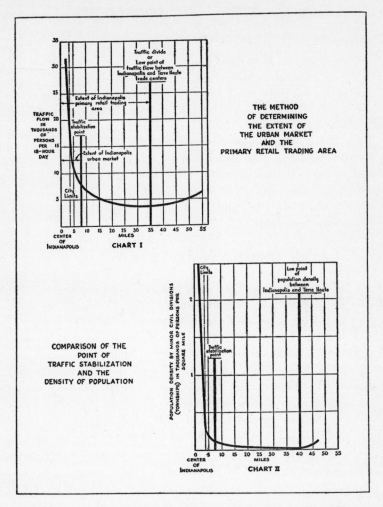

FIG. 10. THE URBAN MARKET, TRAFFIC FLOW AND
URBAN REGION

These diagrams present a method of determining the urban market, that is the equivalent of the urban region of a trade center, in terms of traffic flow. The underlying theory states that trade activity is far more a matter of the characteristics of movement of the population than of its fixed position. The authors of this method were concerned not with "where people live but where and how they go to buy." Traffic stabilization is said to take place "at the edge of or slightly beyond the populated area.... The traffic volume from the center of an urban market outward diminishes at a rapid rate until it becomes comparatively stabilized.... Traffic is said to become stabilized when the rapid rate of declining volume from a market center changes to a lower rate of decline." Thus "the point of traffic stabilization may be used to define the limit of the urban market." And this limit approximates closely to the urban region. (From Paver and McClintock, *Traffic and Trade, 1935,* McGraw-Hill Book Company, Inc.)

evident that the discontinuity of the areas or localities may be far more conspicuous than the hinterland itself.

The recognition of a hinterland, even though difficult to delineate with accuracy, can have much practical significance. If a trade center's welfare depends upon its hinterland, it, in turn, has a direct obligation to that hinterland. Too few trade centers have analyzed their respective hinterlands. All too few have secured the advantages which may be derived from a conscious association with their hinterlands, an activity which a proper civic spirit demands. Here, there is a *sphere of influence,* to borrow an expression from international terminology, which communities should foster. It should be exerted within the area known as the continuous hinterland.

The Sphere of Influence.—The media whereby trade centers may make effective their influence are many. Among them may be mentioned the Chamber of Commerce, civic and trade associations, luncheon clubs, and similar organizations. They may support (a) proposed legislation affecting the welfare of a satellite trade center, (b) assist rural communities in solving some of their local problems, and (c) endeavor to establish a spirit of good will between the respective local organizations and those in the trade territory or continuous hinterland.

A display of interest in a sphere of influence does not necessitate the expression of a domineering attitude, as has been the wont of some nations maintaining spheres of influence in China. On the contrary, all activities must be carried forward with a full appreciation of community sensitiveness. Offers to be of assistance call for tact and diplomacy. Concrete illustrations of ways and means for putting into effect these suggestions will be presented in a later chapter.

CHAPTER IV

TRADE CENTER PLANS AND PATTERNS

Some one has said, "Too many cities follow paths laid out by the patient but wandering cow."[1] Only a few cities have been planned. Washington, D. C.; Canberra, Australia; and Helsinki, Finland, are striking examples of capital cities which have been conceived before

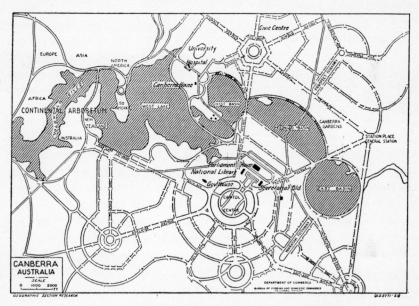

FIG. 11. A TRADE CENTER MADE TO ORDER

In this center where beauty of landscape was as important a consideration as practicability the radial pattern was used. This design was suggested to the prize-winning architect by that of Washington, D. C. (Courtesy of U. S. Department of Commerce.)

construction. Parts of Mannheim and Karlsruhe in Germany; Gary, Indiana; and Longview, Washington, illustrate types of commercial and industrial centers whose founders drafted definite plans before a settle-

[1] Frank Koester, "Civic Unification of a Small City," *The American City Pamphlets,* No. 121 (The Civic Press, New York).

39

ment became established. Some persons gave planning serious thought centuries ago. There seems reason to believe that portions of communities were planned as early as 3000 B.C.[2] The Greeks planned entire cities as early as the fifth century B.C. Roman records point to early contributions to city planning also.

That trade centers have evolved out of initial unplanned shapes, with no particular effort on the part of any one to direct their ultimate design, is not necessarily a reflection upon man's intelligence. For most purposes trade centers have served man's requirements fairly well, but the rapid development of the machine age wakened us with a quick and heavy jolt to the necessity for reform. The current structures of trade centers have suddenly become antiquated. In consequence, most centers are seeking to remodel themselves and to develop according to a well-defined plan. The growing realization of the fact that trade centers are not isolated entities, but integral parts of a social whole has encouraged those persons interested in civic welfare to foster planning. They have come to appreciate the fact that an effective plan contributes toward making citizens efficient.

We need to distinguish here between plan and pattern. By "plan" is meant the physical and economic development of a trade center, not only with regard to its internal functions but also with regard to its immediate *umland,* that is, adjacent territory with which it enjoys mutually-dependent cultural and economic relationships. By "pattern" is meant the physical arrangement of the network of avenues within a trade center. Planning focusses upon the pattern as the physical surface upon which the trade center as a biological organism functions.

Analysis of the street patterns of many centers reveals the pervading effect of the nucleus of their original layout. These nuclei fall into about seven categories as indicated by the accompanying standardized diagrams (Fig. 12). In turn, they can be reduced to essentially three types, the rectangular, radial, and non-geometric design. In most instances these forms grew out of the more or less unconscious evolution of a market square, rectangle, or circle. In fewer cases they started as a protective center such as a fortress or castle at the base of which the peasantry and workers settled, or as a gathering place about a cathedral, where religious ceremonials were held both for the local and distant population. Occasionally the plan shows the influence of the junction of roads, as in the pure radial type, or it indicates the opposite extreme

[2] E. Oberhummer, "Der Stadtplan, seine Entwickelung und Bedeutung," *Verhandlungen Des* XVI *Deutschen Geographentages zu Nürnberg,* 1907, pp. 66-101.

of no junction but merely an elongation which has been expanded where local trade activities have tended to concentrate, leaving its impress of irregularity upon the entire present-day form. Topographic factors such as rivers, hills, mountains, and other features of the landscape have played their part too in affecting the forms of these nuclei.

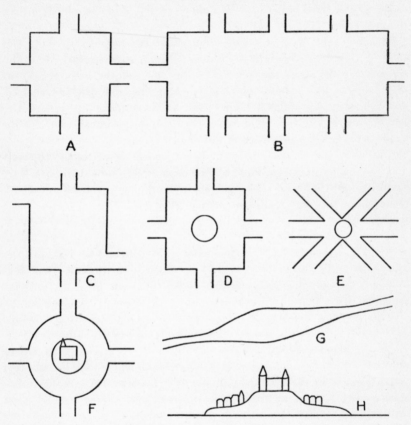

FIG. 12. NUCLEI AFFECTING THE ULTIMATE PATTERNS
OF TRADE CENTERS

A, B, C, and *D* are modifications of the rectangular pattern which have induced a rectangular growth in vast numbers of trade centers, especially among those in the United States. *E* and *F* are nuclei of radial patterns whose ultimate patterns may or may not have grown symmetrically. *G* usually evolves into a rectangular pattern or one of great irregularity, particularly if the reason for its origin is topographic.

H shows a profile or cross-section of a medieval setting which often gave rise to a radial pattern. The castle, cathedral or fortress upon an eminence surrounded by the villagers at the base constituted a normal nucleus for a radial development.

Geographical Aspects of the Planning of Trade Center Patterns.—
The pattern of a trade center may be referred to two planes, the horizontal and the vertical. Differences in relief of the land, generally, are reflected in the design or pattern laid out in the horizontal plane. This design, in turn, frequently affects the heights and character of structures. The vertical plane may be defined in terms of the outline of an urban profile.[3]

Planning may be approached from many different viewpoints. The engineer sees it in the light of bridges, sewers, street paving, or traffic congestion; the social worker approaches the subject with respect to playgrounds, parks, the elimination of slums, and the establishment of well-lighted and ventilated homes; the architect makes an appeal for building harmony and civic beautification; the political municipality itself shows an interest in street lighting or zoning; the merchant seeks improvements in transportation which will enable his customers to reach him easily and quickly, as well as help him effect quick deliveries. The person who views city planning geographically is cognizant of all of these viewpoints and analyzes them in their relationships to the local natural site and the urban region. Such studies are sometimes described as chorographical.

Street patterns of trade centers may, in general, be classified as (1) radial, (2) rectangular, or (3) a combination of both. In a few instances topographic irregularities make for such great irregularity in the pattern that classification within this group is impossible. In certain mountain districts the slopes are so steep and the surface terrain so irregular that roads can be constructed economically only by laying them out along circuitous avenues. Buildings are erected only where level areas may be available. Portions of Trieste and Fiume in Italy and many centers in the Balkans fall in this category. Topographic influences, however, are not the only significant ones. Others will be noted in the detailed discussion of each pattern.

We should understand that the use of the expressions pattern or plan does not necessarily imply that a center has been consciously laid out according to a preconceived idea. We mean that what is now in

[3] The three-dimensional aspect of a city plan was recognized very early as revealed by maps made in the sixth century A.D. Such maps called "perspective maps" [Miss Margaret Fead, *Geographical Review* (July 1933) Vol. XXIII, No. 3] have always met with popular favor. Some of them are not true maps but pictorial representations. Nevertheless, they emphasize the importance which may be attached to the vertical plane as a part of a trade center plan.

existence conforms to or approaches a design which may be interpreted as a pattern within the limits of our classification.

The Radial Pattern.—The radial plan is one in which the pattern

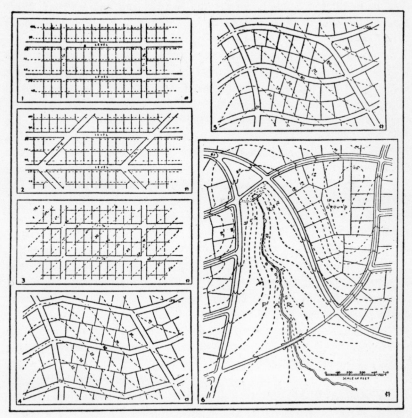

FIG 13. THE TOPOGRAPHIC ELEMENT IN PHYSICAL PLANNING

The topographic element is receiving increasing attention in trade-center designing, but deserves additional careful investigation. In these diagrams the desirable relation between angle of street layout and slope of the land is illustrated. The more irregular the terrain and the steeper the slopes the more "radial" the street pattern. (Courtesy of the *American City Magazine*.)

reveals streets that diverge in straight lines from a common center or from several sub-centers and are crossed by other streets which are arcs or near-arcs of circles. The ideal does not exist, but a close approach is found in the pattern of Karlsruhe, Germany, where the old heart of the city conforms perfectly. The newer sections of the city which represent a more recent development fit the rectangular mold.

Numerous trade centers show a radial tendency by way of an occasional diagonal street. Such streets, however, are more often accidental than planned. Milwaukee Avenue in Chicago and a portion of Broad-

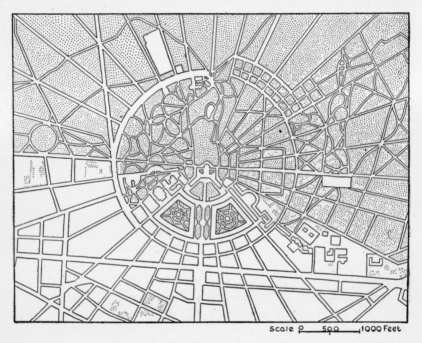

FIG. 14. THE IDEAL IN REALITY

In the heart of Karlsruhe the radial pattern has been worked out almost to geometrical accuracy. While it lends itself to attractive landscape architecture the house and street numbering involve complexity. One can appreciate, on the other hand, the defensive value of this design when in medieval days combat was largely hand to hand.

way, New York, follow old Indian trails and were not laid out with respect to such elements as efficiency or beautification. A few cities in the United States are either introducing diagonal arteries or intending to do so for purposes of reducing traffic congestion. In many European cities the ring or boulevard, encompassing the heart of the trade center, constructed upon the site of former fortifications, is connected with the city center by diagonal streets, thereby introducing a partial radial arrangement.

The radial pattern found favor in medieval times when feudal lords and knights sought power and determined to protect their local territorial possessions by means of walls. The avenue along which one could reach the wall most quickly from the heart of the town, of course, was along a radius. These roads concentrating upon the town center would permit those within to see all persons approaching from the periphery. Numerous trade centers of the medieval period do not show absolute symmetry, but, nevertheless, incorporate the radial idea in principle. Nürnberg, and Tallinn, each retaining the major portion of its original walls, present excellent examples of the radial arrangement. In the latter part of the medieval period the rectangular design occasionally made its appearance in the inner city, as for example, in Krakau.

Topographic irregularity or efficiency are not always the primary reasons for curved roads or the radial pattern. City planners have been among the most ardent enthusiasts for irregularity in pattern, owing to the beauty which curved streets may afford. In many centers the curve closes a vista where the street leaves the field of the observer's vision. If a church, monument, or colonnade of a public building serves as the background for a view along a curved artery, the setting is likely to be picturesque.

Curved avenues provide an ever changing landscape for the pedestrian's eyes, and irregularity in itself avoids monotony.

Sir Christopher Wren recognized the desirability of terminal vistas in his proposed plan for the rebuilding of London after the great fire, although his plan was largely rectangular. In a volume memorializing his great achievements the following pertinent comment is offered:

In his conversion of traffic intersections into important architectural "places" he is exceedingly economical, reserving such features only for the more important occasions. His Royal Exchange Plaza takes an exceedingly interesting shape, for whilst it forms a splendid intersection for main thoroughfares and a site for most important buildings, at the same time it complies with all the requirements of design as regards main thoroughfares, in that it in no way offers any obstruction as traffic passes along. It is to be noticed that nowhere does Wren obstruct a main thoroughfare, yet somehow all his churches and public buildings find sites at the termination of vistas.[4]

[4] *Bicentenary Memorial Volume to Sir Christopher Wren*, A.D. *1632-1723* (published under auspices of Royal Institute of British Architects, London, 1923) pp. 172-173.

The curved road may exert a psychological influence upon shoppers. Take, for example, a portion of Regent Street, London's delightful shopping center; its graceful curve marked by dignified building fronts is most pleasing. As the shopper walks along the street, his curiosity is aroused by just what is ahead around the bend. Thus he continues from store to store until, perhaps, he has gone the entire length of the street. All that the merchants need do is prepare attractive window displays which will entice the potential shopper to step within and then to convert him into an actual buyer. In such circumstances no ugly signs need be projected from the buildings over the sidewalks to induce the passerby to stop. Thus beauty of landscape may create utility.

Disadvantages of the Radial Pattern.—Although both beauty and efficiency may be argued in defense of the radial pattern, certain inherent disadvantages may not be lightly passed over. Perpetuation of the radial pattern is not always a matter of choice. The secretary of the Moscow Party Committee [5] in charge of remodeling Moscow says:

In Moscow a radial-circle scheme of the city has developed historically. There may be different opinions as to the advantages of the checkerboard or the radial scheme, but one must reckon with reality. This is why we make it our task to perfect and improve the existing radial streets and circles. By bringing all the numerous streets into a unified harmonious system, by straightening and widening them, we may obtain a harmonious radial-circle system in sixteen or seventeen radial streets and six circles.

When radii are intersected by straight streets triangular tracts of land are automatically created upon which economical building can not always be accomplished. In fact, such triangles if quite small may be merely waste space. Proponents of the radial pattern are likely to claim that it is these triangular plots of ground and also circles formed at the focal center of the radii, which offer the possibility of beautification through parking or by the erection of monuments or some other structures intended to ornament the site. True as this may be, we cannot ignore the fact that irregularities in street arrangements lead to irregularity in building sites and sometimes in building placement. This contributes to increased cost of land occupance.

With respect to the facility for transportation offered by the pattern we must weigh its supposed advantages over the rectangular pattern against the difficulties which arise in the matter of street and house

[5] *Economic Review of the Soviet Union,* "The Moscow Subway and City Plan" (1934) Vol. IX, No. 10, p. 188.

FIG. 15. THE NEW FAIRMONT PARKWAY, PHILADELPHIA

This parkway, built at a cost of over $800,000, typifies activity in many centers in beautification and also in developing efficiency in transportation. In densely built cities such high costs of improvements have been warranted by the consequent increased values of adjoining property and relief in traffic congestion. (Copyright, 1933, Photo-Illustrators.)

numbering. Diverging streets mean increasing length of blocks as one moves away from the focal center. Therefore, the number of lots in successive blocks cannot be the same, and house numbers cannot correspond in respective blocks, as we shall point out later. Where the streets are irregularly curved the numbering system increases in complexity and is often beyond the ken of the citizens themselves to decipher. While radial streets are supposed to disperse traffic quickly from urban centers, it is equally true that they encourage congestion at the center by concentrating the incoming traffic.

The Rectangular Pattern.—The rectangular pattern includes a checker-board arrangement of straight streets. Although not unknown in pre-medieval times, its major development is post-medieval. It has found its extreme development in the United States. Obviously, the pattern is the simplest geometrical form which can be employed and lends itself especially to level tracts of land.

Examples of rectangular patterns are almost as numerous as there are trade centers in the United States. Trade centers such as Gary, Indiana, in the level Great Lakes Region, and Fargo, North Dakota, in the flat Red River Valley of the North represent the type. Even in regions of irregular terrain, if slopes are not too steep, the rectangular pattern tends to persist, as in Seattle, Washington, or Worcester, Massachusetts. Whether or not steepness of slope limits the rectangular design sometimes depends upon the wealth of the community and the geological structure. The more money available, the more readily may slopes be reduced. Likewise, with few exceptions as in the case of bog lands, the less consolidated the earth materials, the less money required to build roads and public service facilities.

Advantages of the Pattern.—Where topographic conditions permit of streets at right angles to each other, a site may be divided with greater economy of space than is afforded by any other pattern. Triangular shaped buildings are obviated and construction lines are reduced to the simplest forms. Cardinal directions are easily maintained, by citizens and strangers alike, and a simplified numbering system both for buildings and streets can be applied. This latter point plays so large a part in the cost of doing business in any trade center that it deserves special consideration.

Street and House Numbering.—Most trade centers reveal no orderly numbering or naming system. Streets may be named to honor statesmen, civic leaders, or war heroes; or after trees, colors, and anything else which strikes the fancy of the committee on names or fall in with the predilections of individuals. Occasionally a street name has geographic significance, as High Street, South Street, Valley Boulevard, and Riverside Drive. But unless we memorize the sequence of the streets, we are at a total loss to determine locations, distances, and directions from given points without the use of an index or a personal guide. Delivery men from department stores, express companies, and other distributing agencies must spend a certain apprenticeship learning street names and locations. Should an experienced employee resign, much loss of time follows in consequence of his successor having to be taught locations.

Some cities not only fail to systematize the naming of their streets but likewise ignore the orderly numbering of their houses. To illustrate, in one city of about 300,000 population, no accord whatever exists between streets that are numbered and the numbers on the buildings, and no attention has been given to a uniform distribution of numbers in the successive blocks. As a result, 1837 Main Street occurs at the corner of 15th Avenue while along another street parallel to it, the same number is located between 16th and 17th Avenues. The possible complications arising out of faulty numbering are further illustrated by the situation in the Borough of Manhattan, New York City, and noted in Table 5. This is extracted from a street guide issued for tourists and is also widely used by taxicab drivers and others.

TABLE 5

STREET GUIDE—MANHATTAN AND BRONX

This key applies to all streets and avenues above 14th Street

To find the nearest street to any given number on any avenue, cancel last figure of given number, divide remainder by 2 and add number specified below. The result will be approximately street desired.

AVENUES A, B, C, AND D	3
FIRST AVENUE	3
SECOND AVENUE	3
THIRD AVENUE	9 or 10
FOURTH AVENUE	8
FIFTH AVENUE TO 59TH STREET	17 or 18
FIFTH AVENUE ABOVE 125TH STREET	24
SIXTH AVENUE	6
SEVENTH AVENUE	12
EIGHTH AVENUE	9
NINTH AVENUE	13
TENTH AVENUE	14

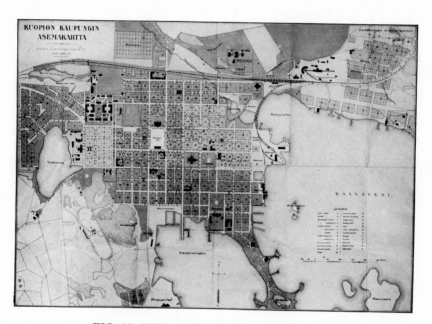

FIG. 16. THE RECTANGULAR PATTERN

The irregularity of street arrangements is so common among European trade centers that the occurrence of a rectangular pattern such as that for Kuopio, Finland, stands out conspicuously. However, many of the centers in northern Europe are of this type either in their entirety or to a very large extent. The simplicity of the rectangular design is self-evident.

ELEVENTH AVENUE 15
LEXINGTON AVENUE 22
MADISON AVENUE 26
PARK AVENUE ....34 or 35
COLUMBUS, AMSTERDAM AND WEST END AVENUES.................59 or 60
BROADWAY ABOVE 14TH STREET (subtract).......................30 or 31
CENTRAL PARK WEST—Divide number by 10 and add 60
RIVERSIDE DRIVE—Divide house number by 10 and add 72

Problem: To find the nearest street to 431 Madison Avenue. First cancel last figure. The remainder is 43. Then divide by 2 and you have 21½. Add the key number which is 26 and the result is 47½, which is between the streets desired.

All avenues run north and south, Fifth Avenue acting as the dividing line, east and west. Numbers on streets begin at Fifth Avenue.

Confusion results from such lack of system.

Systems Now in Use.—Mannheim, Germany, has one of the most interesting systems. In the old town, rectangularly laid out, are one hundred and thirty-six blocks, each block lettered and numbered as per figure 17. In addition, the frontages are numbered successively around the block. So, for example, an address such as 23-P5 means house number 23 in block P5, the block being located five squares from the central dividing line and between blocks O and Q. A system of this sort is good in principle, but, lacking in flexibility, does not allow for city expansion. In the remainder of Mannheim, streets are named.

In one part of Chicago streets are named after trees for which no logical sequence can be argued. In the heart of the business district a few streets are named with some relationship to the succession of our early presidents, as Washington, Madison, Monroe, Adams, Jackson and Van Buren Streets. Even this order is not accurate and hence confuses the person who happens to know the correct sequence of the presidents. In the far western portion of the city highways for awhile are called avenues and, beginning with 40th Avenue, follow in succession to the westward until 54th Avenue is reached when a reversion to names occurs.

Some years ago a few citizens of Chicago recognized the inadequacy and costliness of this naming scheme and proposed to remedy it as far as circumstances would permit. They suggested that, since strong opposition would develop against changes in names of streets, a numbering system could be worked out which might tell a whole story in itself. One hundred numbers were allotted to each city block. Every block begins with a new hundred number, the first hundred starting at a central street in the downtown district. Buildings in these blocks are

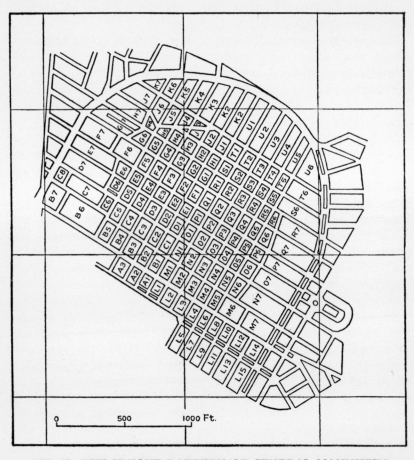

0   500   1000 Ft.

FIG. 17. THE UNIQUE PATTERN OF CENTRAL MANNHEIM

The effort to simplify distribution in this trade center by the use of a rectangular pattern and mathematical index found its limitations when the area of the community expanded beyond the limits of the alphabet. Nevertheless, the original motive was in the right direction. The system might have been extended with a little manipulation such as the use of double letters or the application of letters to streets instead of to entire blocks.

numbered to correspond with each block. Knowing where the division lines are, one can appreciate instantly the distance and location of a structure with reference to the heart of the city. A house numbered

2450 West Maple Street is in the 24th block west from the central dividing line and is in the middle of the block. Since the even numbers on east-west streets are on the north side of the street, we know on which side this particular address is located.

This system possesses one serious flaw. There is no way of determining where Maple Street or any other named street is located except by inquiring or looking upon a map. In the southern division of Chicago east-west streets are numbered, thus greatly simplifying the system. Some day the city will do well to number all the streets. There will be opposition but not insurmountable.

In a part of Duluth, Minnesota, a nearly perfect system is in use, numbers being used for practically all of the streets except those representing reference lines. A cross street, there referred to as a north-south street, divides the central portion of the city into two parts. It is named Lake Avenue because one of its termini marks the head of Lake Superior. The first avenue to the *east* is numbered First Avenue and successive avenues in that direction carry corresponding numbers. The first avenue *west* and successive avenues are numbered in order from one up. These avenues are labeled east or west in accordance with their respective direction from Lake Avenue. The main reference division extending almost the entire east-west length of the city is named Superior Street. All streets paralleling it to the north are numbered in sequence from one up, but are not given the directional adjective, north, because the system breaks down to the south, streets in this direction being named and not numbered. Hence, no need exists for distinguishing north from south streets. In addition to street numbers, 100 numbers are assigned to a block, each block beginning with the hundred which corresponds with the number of the street intersection. Roads in one direction are called avenues and those at right angles are called streets. If the location of a building in Duluth is given as Fourth Avenue East and Fourth Street, one knows instantly that it is at the intersection of the fourth avenue east of Lake Avenue, and the fourth street from Superior Street.

The Perfect System.—If the Duluth plan included the numbering of the streets south of Superior Street as well as north, then the system would be as nearly perfect as one could devise for a rectangular pattern. It represents the acme of simplicity. Only two names need be remembered, Superior and Lake, the numbers being self-explanatory. From the practical business standpoint, any clerk who can count can learn the city locations. No time need be lost through changes in the

delivery personnel of any business house; no time need be wasted
because of the obscurity of some rarely mentioned street.

Objections to the Pattern.—The major criticism of the rectangular
pattern focusses upon its monotony and lack of beauty. The argument
that this type of symmetry does not lend itself to grace and an expression of the esthetic sense can perhaps be best answered by reference to
the boulevard and park system of Chicago, and landscaped portions
of Helsinki, Munich, and many other centers. The question of what
is or is not beautiful is one in which accord would be difficult to attain
under the most favorable circumstances. The most enthusiastic pro-
ponent of the radial pattern must, however, concede that experience has
demonstrated the rectangular not to be hopeless.

The Combined Radial and Rectangular Patterns.—We have indicated
the advantages and handicaps associated with each pattern used in the
pure form. With increased traffic congestion and the necessity for
greater speed, some city planners advocate a few diagonals across the
rectangular net, affording short cuts from the outlying districts to the
business center. A diagonal, as the hypotenuse of a right-angled triangle,
would effect a considerable reduction in distance where the ends of the
hypotenuse are widely separated and the lengths of the other two sides
of the triangle equal or nearly so. Many cities are introducing these
diagonals. Washington, D. C., well illustrates the combination of the
radial and rectangular patterns. The new capital city of Australia, Canberra, has adopted a similar pattern.

The choice of pattern depends upon the purposes to be served and
the nature of the site. The modification of an existing situation must
involve also the feasibility and practicability of eliminating or changing
what is already a fact. Not the least item of importance is cost. This
must be judged, however, in the light of accruing benefits over a period
of time rather than from the point of view of immediate monetary
expenditures.

Opposition of the citizenry is always to be counted upon when any
radical innovation is proposed. In one of our large cities the planning
commission suggested the widening of a prominent street to eliminate a
bottle neck. This necessitated cutting off building fronts. Property
owners fought the move. The city authorities won condemnation suits,
and the job was done. Attractive fronts replaced the old ugly ones;
traffic increased tremendously yet flowed easily; real estate values rose
sixteen fold and the opponents of the original project then walked about
the community boasting of results, singing their own praises of pro-

gressivism. Many similar tales may be collected from other trade centers. They emphasize the desirability of planning commissions which possess the power to act and which may determine whether the plan in existence should be fostered or modified.

The Urban Profile (Vertical Plane).—We have already pointed out that a trade center plan is concerned with three dimensions. We have thus far emphasized the ground pattern, that is, the horizontal plane. Now, let us examine the profile or third dimension.

An urban profile is merely a side view of a trade center. It pictures the outline of the vertical plane. While the profile may be different for different sides or views of a trade center, yet in many of them certain structures stand out conspicuously no matter what the view and, accordingly, identify the trade center unit.

The use of the profile for purposes of expressing characteristic elements in an urban skyline is by no means new. Artists have long since singled out certain structures for conversion into impressionistic forms to represent an entire city. Often these appear as silhouettes. Advertising men have conventionalized towers, spires, skyscrapers, and other edifices to stamp upon the public mind an image symbolical of a particular trade center.

Some of these profiles have been so often repeated that the general public has no difficulty in instantly identifying either their exact location or the location of a general region which their form typifies. The profile of the graceful minarets of the Kremlin suggests Moskva (Moscow) to many and Russia to most persons; the majestic clock tower housing "Big Ben" overlooking the Thames recalls London; the graceful spires of the Köln cathedral towering above the low even roof line of the noted Rhine City are familiar to thousands even though they have never enjoyed seeing them at first hand; the profile of the glorious Taj Mahal requires no label for identification; the Woolworth "Cathedral of Commerce," in spite of high skyscrapers all about, is still a landmark which people everywhere associate with New York City's horizon.

Profiles of Ohio trade centers are shown in Fig. 18 to illustrate different types with respect both to size of trade center and economic interest. Some are profiles of industrial centers and some of distributing centers in agricultural areas. Smokestacks suggest industrial activity; trees, church steeples, water towers, and low buildings in combination point to a probable rural setting. The approximate age of the building era or eras in any center may be derived from the architec-

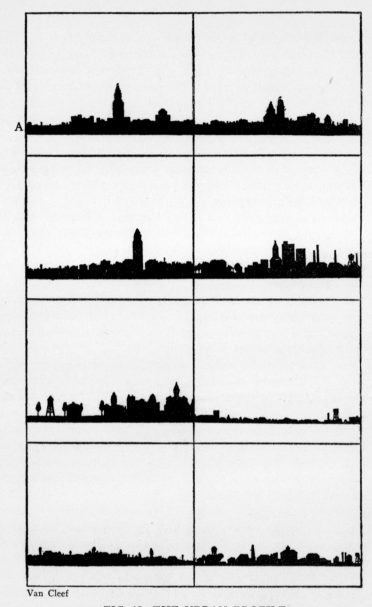

FIG. 18. THE URBAN PROFILE

The profiles of Ohio trade centers ranging in population from a mere 800 (B) to nearly a million (A) suggest the major characteristics of "skylines" which symbolize their respective communities. Architectural forms, economic activities, population size, and an upper and lower horizon may be identified with varying approximations. The even roof line of the mass of buildings marks the lower horizon and the towers, skyscrapers, and other conspicuous features rising well above the roof line constitute the upper horizon. (Courtesy of *Annals of the Association of American Geographers.*)

tural forms. For example, in the profile of Cincinnati there is visible the "block form" of a former day and the "setback" form in tall buildings of to-day. The profile of Troy with its turreted and somewhat domed outlines of buildings recalls the popular architectural style of the 1880's.

The urban profile can emphasize topographic variations although those sketched in Fig. 18 omit this element, since the relief of the land in none of these centers is sufficiently high to warrant its introduction. In some trade centers such as Rome with its seven hills or Tallinn with its lone hill, all capped by striking edifices, topographic contrasts would demand notation.

Probably more important in the profile than topography is the recognition of an *upper* and *lower horizon.* The relatively even roof line of the majority of buildings in the urban area forms the lower horizon and the conspicuous features such as towers, skyscrapers, water tanks, and other phenomena reaching far enough above the average roof line to be distinct from it, constitute the upper horizon line. It is this latter line which is generally selected by artists as the basis for developing conventional interpretations and is the horizon which gives individuality to the trade center form.

We must not expect too much from the profile. From given angles portions of a trade center are hidden from view and the resultant profile may not present a scientifically accurate vertical section for the entire community. On the other hand, the profile in conjunction with the pattern certainly is illuminating. It gives one a better appreciation of the physical structure and form of a trade center than could be otherwise secured. For those interested in the improvement of their trade centers with respect to physical form and economic facility, the profile offers helpful suggestions.

The Trade Center Physiognomy.—If we combine with the pattern all the possible profiles of a trade center, we have before us a relief. If we photograph a center in perspective, we secure another representation which suggests relief or depicts the area in its three dimensions. This we may designate as the trade center's physiognomy. It is a view of the face of the trade center, or, as the German geologist, Edward Suess, might have said, is a presentation of a part of the face of the earth as modified by man.[6]

---

[6] Suess wrote an imposing treatise entitled "The Face of the Earth," but limited himself to a description and interpretation of the physical surface without reference to man's handiwork.

The physiognomy includes, besides the pattern, all of the variations in relief, in different uses of the land and in heights of structures. It depicts also the shape of the outline of the trade center as well as the points of contact of areas contiguous to the political boundary. The sum total of these features characterizes and individualizes the trade center.

Like the pattern and profile, the physiognomy is indispensable to a planning commission, an industrial bureau, a chamber of commerce, a business men's association especially interested in the growth of a particular field of business, and to many public or quasi-public institutions seeking to develop their trade center in the most effective manner. Without the information which it reveals the risk of inaccurate interpretations of the trade center landscape and of its details is very great. Judgment can be rendered with increased facility as to the adequacy of arteries, sufficiency of their width in relation to traffic flow, as to the availability of light and air in homes, offices, and public buildings.

The utility of a study of the physiognomy is revealed by the change in style of architecture which has occurred, especially in American trade centers. The disproportion between width of street and heights of buildings which was brought home to us, largely as a matter of experience, too late to remedy in certain localities, resulted in the setback straight-line type of structure. The virtual narrowing of the streets by increasing numbers of buildings of ever-increasing height obscured much sunlight and air from offices, particularly from those on the lower floors, hence, the decision that working conditions could be improved by setting back the upper floors above given heights.

The new setback has created new profiles and given to a number of centers an appearance strikingly different from that in the days of the skyscraper whose outermost walls were continuous from street level to the uppermost floors. The profile as a part of the physiognomy is impressive for its contrasts and affords interesting and illuminating comparisons between the old and present styles of architecture.

Sub-Landscapes.—The total landscape of a trade center includes, in addition to the physical aspects just discussed, certain more or less intangible elements which we may call sub-landscapes. Sounds, odors, and colors, many of these changing with the seasons, give character and distinction. An excellent description of sounds and odors associated with Japanese centers is worth reproducing here:

No odor can be confused with that of the "daikon" or pickled radish which is so universally prepared and eaten. The night soil carts and the dank waters of the open sewers blend their unpleasant odors with the more pleasing ones of the "miso" and "sake." The clatter of "geta" (clogged wooden shoe) is the sound of Japan. The shrill cries of the fish, cake, and bean curb vendors, the singsong prayers of itinerant priests, the merry laughter of countless small children playing in the streets, and the weird chanting of funeral processions give way toward evening to the tap-tap warning signal of the blind masseurs and the distant boom of temple bells.[7]

Odors may be of such a distinct variety that a trade center may be characterized or identified by them. The stockyard odors of some centers are well known the nation over; a southern center in this country can be detected by tobacco fumes filling the air within a radius of a mile; a German center is associated with the odor of beer and an Ohio community is known by its sauerkraut aromas. Helen Keller once said she could identify many cities visited by their odors.

Thus the sub-landscape of odors is one which has reality and, if it is unpleasant, every effort should be made toward effecting its eradication. This should be done to make the atmosphere more satisfactory for those who are permanent residents and more attractive to tourists or those who visit the center to transact business. The value of eliminating disagreeable odors may be measured not only esthetically but materially.

The noise sub-landscape in which we hear the grinding wheels of antiquated street cars, the shrieking sounds of horns and siren-like accelerations of automobile engines, the rat-a-tat-tat of a steam hammer or an excavating machine, the yelling of enthusiastic newsboys, the music or speeches from a thousand radios, and a hundred and one other sounds, all varying in degrees of intensity according to the size or character of a trade center or the time of year, includes significant elements which planners and developers may not ignore.

The colors of our trade centers in the North change from greens and browns during the summer to a bleak drab gray in the winter or perhaps to a beautiful white snow-bedecked area. In centers located where climates are sub-tropical or where vegetation responds to irrigation the year around the color composite may show more or less variation depending upon the size of the community or the kind of blossoms which the planting may yield. Then too, the materials of

[7] R. B. Hall, "The Cities of Japan: Notes on Distribution and Inherited Forms," *Annals of the Association of American Geographers* (1934) Vol. XXIV, No. 4) p. 182.

which buildings are erected may give brilliant colors, or they may leave an uninteresting neutral effect. Some centers consciously apply color, others avoid or ignore it. No scientific or esthetic planning or building of a trade center can be properly accomplished without due consideration of the sounds, odors, and color in the local total landscape.

CHAPTER V

THE FUNCTIONAL STRUCTURE OF THE
TRADE CENTER

In every trade center, regardless of size and of place, certain elements function in an essentially standard manner as basic parts of the community structure. They may differ in detail in different centers, but, in principle, these elements occur practically everywhere. They are a railroad station, government buildings, public market, hotel district, central retail district, wholesale district, factory area, sub-retail district, residential area, and suburban area.

Decentralization.—The automobile, introduced commercially shortly after 1900, was destined to upset nearly the whole organization of trade centers. Without doubt, it created a revolution in business locations through its speed, convenience, universality, and stimulus to good roads. The activities of social workers have, likewise, exerted a profound influence upon the trade center structure when they convinced employers that healthy and safe working conditions pay. Accordingly, many manufacturers have sought new sites in outlying districts or have changed the architecture of their factories to allow for more light and air, and in still other ways have made readjustments greatly affecting the distribution of business establishments and the plans and patterns of trade centers.

Retail districts have spread from central localities outward along the main arteries to the borders of the trade center. The number of sub-retail centers has increased, and they have grown in relation both to number of establishments and size of individual firms. Industrial plants have forsaken congested railroad terminals in the central district for the pleasanter environment of the outlying areas. Residential locations have not only encroached upon the suburban areas but have moved beyond, forcing the creation of new suburbs at points so far from the main business districts that they have threatened to grow into independent trade centers. Whereas a few years ago a person living eight miles from the heart of a large trade center was considered to be located in a suburb, to-day one often thinks of points at distances of twenty-five

59

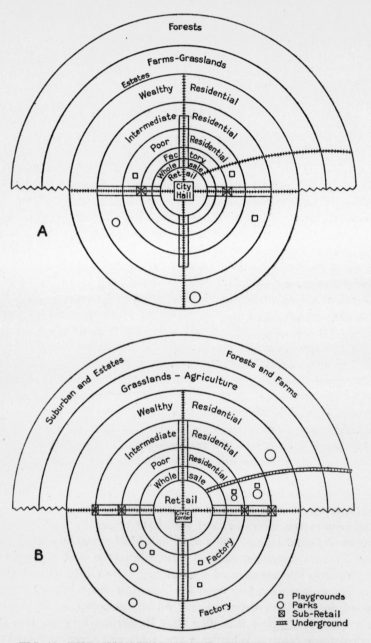

FIG. 19. THE CHANGING TRADE CENTER STRUCTURE

Map *A* indicates the common pattern, generalized, of the pre-war period and *B* represents the present status of the same community. The circles are not intended to portray a radial pattern but merely to mark off the sequence of areas.

FIG. 20. A SUB-RETAIL CENTER

The crowding of the business center or "core" of trade centers has led retailers to establish branches in outlying districts. At the same time independent shops have appeared to serve local neighborhood needs and in some instances to compete with merchants in the central district. For a time traffic congestion encouraged this decentralization. Whether congestion can be relieved and thereby check this outward movement remains in the category of the unanswerable at the moment. (Photograph by Underwood and Underwood.)

to fifty miles as suburban. We are measuring distances as often in terms of time, as in miles.

The Sub-Retail Center.—The development of sub-retail or outlying business centers is causing much concern to merchants of the central district. Efforts to stay the growth have met with failure. Streets never intended to carry hundreds of thousands of automobiles have become so congested as to discourage shoppers from visiting the downtown stores. Proprietors are offering special parking facilities as an inducement to people to patronize their stores, but even that offer is meeting with slight success, for the increasing effort required to reach their establishments tends to discount the proffered convenience. Again, standardization of prices has resulted in fewer bargain inducements on the part of the central stores and has made consumer buying of many commodities equally advantageous in sub-retail districts. The purchaser saves time and energy in the outlying stores. Perhaps the ultimate solution for the downtown merchant lies in establishing branches in the sub-areas, a movement still in the experimental stage. (Fig. 20.)

Industrial Plant Relocation.—With the advent of the automobile and assurance of its probable extensive use, manufacturers began to investigate land values in the outlying parts of their trade centers. Aggressive realtors discovered cheap land for them, low taxes, and economical railroad sidings. The price of automobiles within range of the purchasing power of labor has enabled the worker to own a car. He may live near the plant and still by means of his automobile be quickly accessible to the activities of the center of the city where motion picture theaters and large stores are concentrated. Living close to his place of work, the employee has no carfare to pay and in some instances can eat lunch at home. This gives him and his family a more satisfactory home life than when he lives at a distance from his work. The employer profits by better workmanship, sometimes at lower cost because the employee under the new conditions derives greater pleasures from his daily living, and is therefore willing to accept less pay. As for the manufacturer's customers who might wish to visit him, the automobile again serves, this time whisking the customer from hotel or railroad station out to the factory in a few minutes, thus eliminating the former necessity for a downtown office.

Zoning.—The movement of industrial plants and other types of business away from central portions of trade centers led to their encroachment upon residential areas. Their bulk, their smoke, their odors, their types of workers, their noises, and numerous other elements impinged

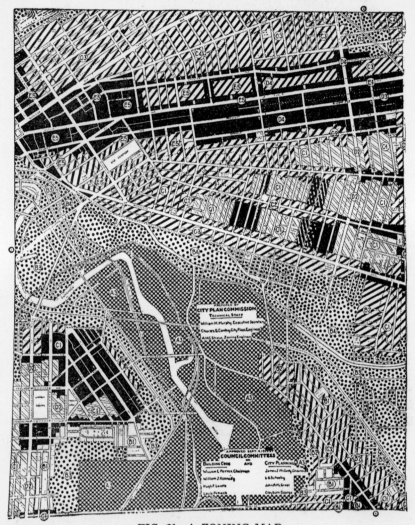

FIG. 21. A ZONING MAP

In this detailed map of a section of a large trade center we see an effort, characteristic of many cities, to delimit the uses to which the land may be put. Naturally, zoning is a much more difficult problem in centers which were established long before the philosophy of zoning was accepted as practicable. However, that the attempt to effect such planning is worth while has been amply demonstrated. For its greater success, we await only the further education of the general public in this direction, for without its support little progress may be made. (Courtesy of the City of Cleveland.)

=KEY=

DISTRICTS

☐ DWELLING HO.

▨ APARTMENT HO.

■ RETAIL BUSN'S

▨ COMMERCIAL

▨ 1st INDUSTRIAL

▨ 2ND "

☐ PARKS

AREA

A- 4800 SQ.FT. PER FAMILY

B- 2400 " " "

C- 1200 " " "

D- 600 " " "

E- UNLIMITED NO. OF FAMILIES

HEIGHT

1- 35 FT. HEIGHT LIMIT

2- 60 " " "

3- 115 " " "

4- 175 " " "

5- 250 " " "

FIG. 21A

upon neighborhoods that were heretofore attractively parked, quiet, clean, and generally pleasing places of abode. This movement aroused strong protests among the residents. A home representing a man's lifetime efforts and savings often depreciated in value almost over night, forcing the owner to accept large losses. Something had to be done to save the situation. The solution of the problem was zoning, that is, the limiting of the lands of a trade center to specified uses and to certain types of structures. (Figs. 21 and 21A.)

Zoning and its Consequences.—Under the stimulus of zoning, which is merely a way of giving notice in advance to all citizens that they can not build what and where they please but must recognize the rights of others, the business activities of trade centers have assorted themselves as never before. Certain districts are now set aside for purely industrial purposes, largely heavy industries; other areas are reserved for industries which emit unpleasant odors; certain portions of the city are set aside for light manufacturing and others for retailing and wholesaling and still other areas for certain types of residential occupance.

As an indirect consequence of such zoning many business establishments have grouped themselves within these larger zones. For example, the sellers of musical instruments in some of the larger cities are concentrated within a few blocks. There was a time when a merchant selling musical instruments preferred to be isolated. He feared the proximity of a competitor. He has discovered, however, that the competition which seemed undesirable actually is profitable. He has found that buyers insist upon value received and shop from store to store, that the concentration of businesses of kind attracts potential buyers to a single center, affording each merchant an opportunity to meet practically all the prospects. Accordingly, each firm may increase its sales because the number of potential customers is larger than when each store is the only one of its kind in a given part of the city. The convenience afforded the buyer, by the grouping of sellers, places him in a better frame of mind to make purchases, fatiguing him less than if he were forced to travel considerable distances from one part of the city to another. Many lines of business have pursued a similar policy with respect to location.

Merchants, manufacturers, and realtors, at first opposed to zoning laws, now are enthusiastic for them. Manufacturers, in particular, have shown an interesting reversal of attitude. Many who shifted their plants to zoned areas where they have abundant land at moderate cost and low taxes, where sunlight and fresh air flood their quarters, urge the public to inspect their installations. They take pride in the attractiveness of the factory site and the pleasant internal and external environmental setting for their employees. They have discovered that the new situation *pays*.

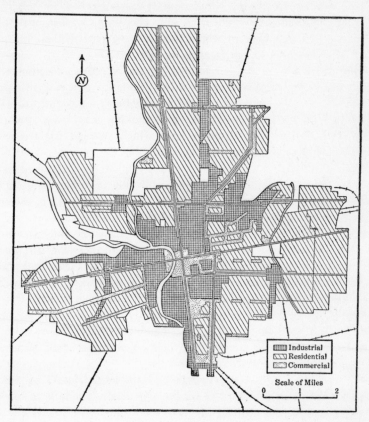

FIG. 22. LAND USE

This map, showing the land use in simplified terms within a trade center of about 300,000 population, brings out clearly the distributional relation to each other of the different sections of the used land. Such a device helps those interested in planning to determine the most effective use to which the land may be put.

Land Classification.—Since city planning and zoning have become accepted modes of procedure in most progressive trade centers, a determination of relative land values has become necessary. That is, when planners have had to decide whether a given block should be reserved for retail business or residential purposes, or for retail stores rather than for manufacturing plants, they have had to decide consciously not only the current but the ultimate value of the land. This, of course, has been one of the most difficult problems in the whole situation. Mistakes have been made and more will be made. Experience will teach us much that will assist in the partial elimination of further errors in judgment.

The United States government is now classifying agricultural lands with respect to best uses to which they may be put, that is, for particular kinds of crops, for pasture, or for forests. This is a proper scientific approach to the attainment of an effective agriculture. A similar approach with respect to urban lands to the end that they too may be most effectively utilized is necessary. In Michigan, Wisconsin, and a few other states, a beginning has been made in urban land classification through laws which provide for the mapping of transitional lands, that is, areas on the periphery of trade centers.[1]

Urban Land Classification.—The classification of urban lands is far more complicated than that of rural lands. Much more detail is involved. In the case of agricultural lands the physical conditions, such as type of soil, drainage, relief, slope, climate, and the market and transportation facilities, are relatively easily determined, and these, in turn, enable us to say for what crops such land is best suited. Once classified, unless it is land immediately contiguous to an urban settlement, the classification is likely to remain good over a long period of time, perhaps twenty-five years, or in some instances permanently, as in the case of many forest lands. Urban lands, on the other hand, are so sensitive to a variety of social and economic factors that their classification must be accomplished in anticipation of frequent changes.

To determine the best use to which urban lands should be put involves an ability to forecast the future. Obviously that is impossible to do with certainty. An element of guess work must creep in. While past experience is valuable, it is not an absolute criterion for the future because the dominant element in a trade center is man, and man is a variable. If it were possible to control man's reactions as we control conditions in a laboratory experiment, we might hope to determine the best use for a given piece of land. The best use to-day is not necessarily the best use a few years hence. In spite of these uncertainties,

[1] Recognition of the close association between urban and rural lands has recently been recorded by the National Resources Committee in its report on "Regional Factors in National Planning," 1935, and also in other reports such as "Regional Planning—the St. Louis Region," 1936.

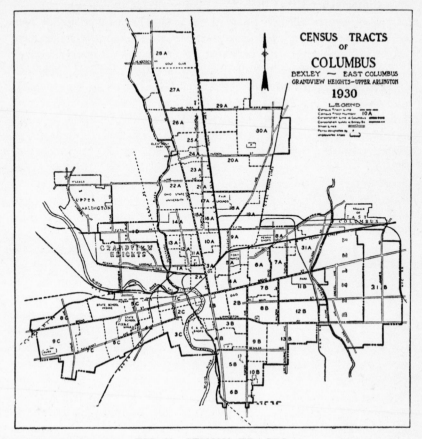

FIG. 23. CENSUS TRACTS

When the United States Bureau of the Census planned the 1930 census it offered to gather data in cities according to tracts, that is, small unit areas whose boundaries are considered permanent. These tracts were set up jointly by the government and local committees in the respective trade centers. In successive decades the census will be taken in each of these units, making the accumulated data comparable. Thus, changes in the various social and economic aspects of the community may be readily observed during succeeding decades and planning adjusted in accordance with them. (Courtesy of Bureau of Business Research, Ohio State University.)

we would be remiss if we did not endeavor to base our forecast of land use on as scientific principles as possible. We suggest, therefore, that the following elements should have consideration in reaching conclusions as to the best use to which urban land may be put:

I. Physical characteristics of the area involved
   A. A topographic survey of the geographical site including such territory as offers any possibility of future inclusion within the trade center
   B. Analysis of the climate

II. Present use of the land in both the trade center and its peripheral area
   A. Business
     1. Industrial
     2. Wholesale
     3. Retail
   B. Public
     1. Administration
     2. Utilities
     3. Places of Worship
     4. Education
     5. Recreation
     6. Health
   C. Residential
     1. Poor
     2. Intermediate
     3. Wealthy
   D. Areal growth of population
     1. Traffic flow
   E. Vacant land
     1. Public
     2. Private

III. Maps showing use of the land at the end of each decade during the past thirty years

IV. Maps of the market value of land at the end of each decade

V. Map of location of resources within the state or outside the state in fairly close proximity, used or likely to be used within the urban center

VI. Areal direction of growth of the trade center

Although the items in the above schedule are essentially self-explanatory, a few of them deserve emphasis. Mapping the actual use of the land at the end of each of four decades, thus giving a cross-section of land use through thirty years, reveals trends and tendencies.[2]

---

[2] An elaborate study of the successive use of the land in an urban center may be found in the monumental work of Homer Hoyt, under the title *One Hundred Years of Land Values in Chicago* (The University of Chicago Press, 1933).

Comparisons are easily made from decade to decade, and frequently the maps bring to light situations not previously appreciated. They call for special investigations and more detailed study. Maps on pages 70 and 71 and Figure 24 suggest the effectiveness of such a survey.

Planning any community, as we have already indicated, involves consideration not merely of physical phenomena but also of the functional.

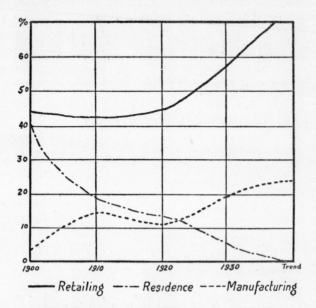

— Retailing   —·— Residence   ----Manufacturing

FIG. 24. FLUCTUATIONS IN LAND USE

In the series of maps (pages 70 and 71) covering a period of thirty years we obtain a vivid impression of changes in character of land occupance in one portion of a trade center. Similar mapping of the entire locality can serve as a basis for judging of trends and consequently for intelligent planning. While the future course of man's activities cannot be exactly predicted, the historical record is indispensable as one of a number of criteria necessary for intelligent planning. The trend of changes in this particular area is effectively indicated by the graph above showing quantitatively the percentage of frontage utilized for different types of activities.

Hence, land values are important, and to understand their variations over a period of time requires mapping by decades. If values have declined or appreciated, there are reasons. These should be understood. When we plan for the future, we must try to anticipate in what way those plans are likely to affect land values. Mapping what has happened often throws light on what may happen.

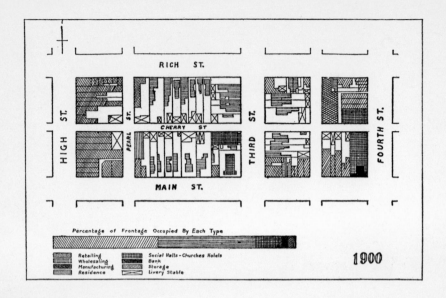

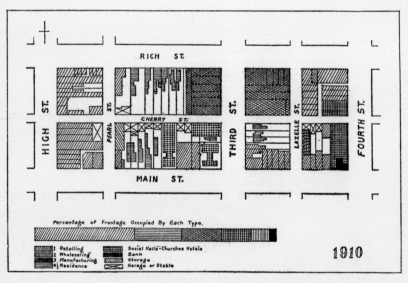

(See pages 68 and 69)

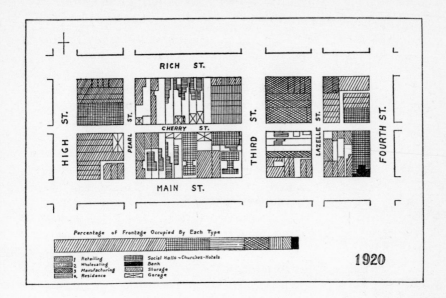

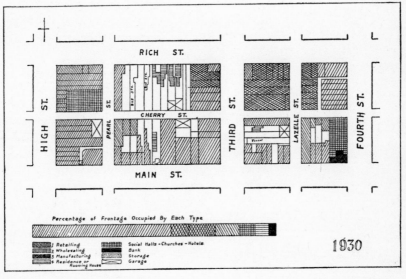

(See pages 68 and 69)

A knowledge of extra-urban elements, such as traffic flow along high-ways entering a trade center or such as the distribution of natural resources, including agricultural lands in areas which serve or might serve a trade center, will help in the planning of highways within centers, and the determination of land use, that is, zoning. These aspects may have a bearing, too, upon the probable areal growth of the trade center and the economic development of the whole urban region. (Fig. 25.)

The day of allowing haphazard trade center growth is becoming obsolete. Progressive business interests no longer tolerate it. Trade has become too complex to allow indiscriminate physical urban development. The struggle for existence, both within the trade center and between trade centers, has grown so keen that only an orderly development of the economic as well as physical plant will make survival possible.

Effect Upon the Pattern.—The direction of growth of trade centers has tended strongly to be axial in the horizontal plane and has been haphazard vertically. Trade centers have tended to become star-shaped or circular. The process has been more or less by concentric expansion much in the manner of growth of annual rings of a tree, but with great irregularity. Until planning was introduced, the outline of trade centers revealed no conscious effort of man toward control of growth, but rather was impressive for its unbalance, or for its inconsistencies even when showing geometric balance.

The pattern of most centers in the United States contains numerous holes of non-occupance, the consequence of an excessive suburban movement during the post-war period. Such patterns also frequently lack adequate economic facilities. Again, such facilities as water-pipes, fire protection, gas, electric light are all built at great cost to be paid for out of taxes which must be sufficiently large to account for the unoccupied portions between the outlying and central or inlying areas. We are now beginning to appreciate the cost of that kind of trade center growth. With scientific planning accepted as a rational mode of procedure by most progressive communities, a repetition of our post-war experience should be unlikely.

Remodeling existing trade centers of large dimensions is neither simple nor cheap. In many instances it may prove to be impracticable. Nevertheless, improvement may be accomplished through a new approach to the problem. We may decentralize more than we have and develop the subcenters with respect to a unit community life correlated, in turn, with the trade center function as a whole. In Germany a plan

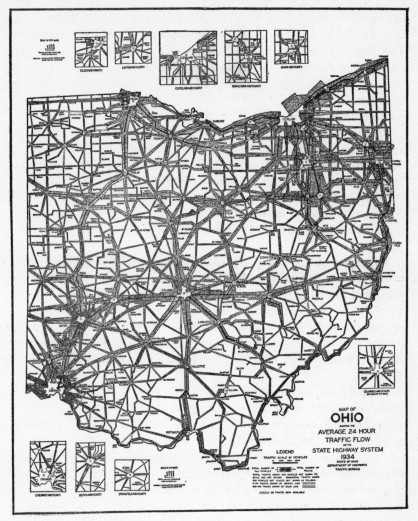

FIG. 25. TRAFFIC FLOW IN RELATION TO TRADE CENTERS

The first step in analyzing the traffic problems of a trade center consists in determining how much traffic is involved. However, it is not enough to have the data for the political area alone. The flow in and out and in relation to other centers is equally important. That the flow is unbalanced is strikingly portrayed by this map of the situation in Ohio.

has been conceived whereby all large industry is located within a single unit wholly detached from the neighborhoods where the workers live. The neighborhoods are limited in population size so that instead of having, for example, 20,000 persons living in one unit, two separate units of 10,000 are provided. Super-roads between these neighborhoods and detached industrial and major commercial areas are planned to provide an easy and swift flow of traffic.

By this plan the individual does not lose his identity and acquire an inferiority complex as he often does in our present congested and depressing neighborhood centers. He is given an opportunity to enjoy fresh air, to develop his esthetic inclinations, and to feel a pride in the privilege of partaking in community progress. There is opportunity for beautification of private and public sites and disencouragement to those who might naturally be averse to the maintenance of clean orderly property.

This type of functional planning, necessarily, is predicated upon a complete survey of the local situation in accordance with the outline presented above. It means the occupance of a greater area than that which now falls within the jurisdiction of some trade centers, but, carried out to its ideal possibilities, it means that in the future, centers of the size of Chicago, New York, or Paris will not be reproduced. Instead, trade center clusters of moderate size may become our new standard.

Recently an engineer,[3] effectively attempting to foresee the future trade center, presented an interesting series of diagrams (Fig. 27) to show how the complexity of a center increases as it absorbs peripheral neighborhoods or suburbs. The series evolves from the simple "Micropolis" to the seemingly manageable "Megalopolis" and the highly complicated unmanageable "Metropolis." Each dot represents a "well-planned neighborhood unit of a given size" with a common density of population. The lines connecting the dots express the interrelationships of the neighborhoods. The growing complexity arising from these interdependent communities constituting a single trade center is readily apparent. In the metropolis the maze of lines expresses most vividly the folly of the urge to make trade centers grow indefinitely. Coördination of interests becomes less and less practicable and further growth merely reacts unfavorably upon that quality of living which the population has a right to enjoy. It is this engineer's concept that business

[3] Eugene Klaber, "The American City: Why the City of Medium Size Will be The City of the Future." (September, 1933.)

FIG. 26. MAN CHANGES THE URBAN LANDSCAPE

Here we see a remarkable transformation within the heart of a great metropolitan center where crowding has placed space at a premium; but the enormous cost of re-modeling the city has paid. Park Avenue, New York City, in the days when the railroad occupied it, was one of the most undesirable areas, whereas to-day, as shown in the right-hand photograph with the railroad submerged, the avenue has become one of New York City's finest. Such reformations are not beyond the ability of any center. Better still is planning in order to avoid such costs. (Courtesy of United States Steel Corporation Subsidiaries.)

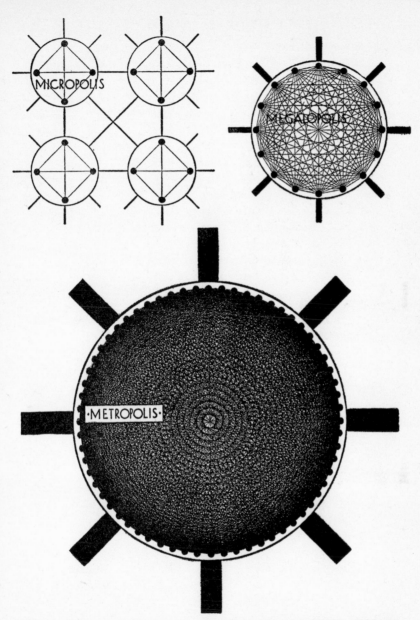

FIG. 27. THE PRINCIPLE OF DIMINISHING RETURNS APPLIED
TO PHYSICAL GROWTH

These diagrams show that as the number of neighborhoods which compose a trade center increase the potential interrelations increase by a geometric ratio. Each dot represents a neighborhood unit of a given size. "Micropolis" contains four neighborhoods, "Megalopolis" sixteen, and "Metropolis" sixty-four. The connecting lines represent the interrelationships among the dots. The manner in which they multiply and their eventual complexity are self-evident. (From Eugene H. Klaber, "Why the City of Medium Size Will Be the City of the Future," *American City Magazine,* September, 1933.)

and industry should be made "a function of the employment and consumption needs of the people and not the cause for which people live."

Planning and the Future.—Probably the greatest handicap to assurance of success in any type of planning lies in man's inability to predict his own economic future. Obviously, conscious orientation of trade centers must incorporate provision for future functioning and that means we must anticipate inventions and changes in social relationships. There are few persons who would claim such capacity. Probably most of us, however, will agree that experimentation is worth while.

Another obstacle, perhaps not so difficult to overcome is the educational factor. Our population is not only ethnically mixed, but we have great numbers of radically different types who are temperamentally different. Their minds must be made receptive to the new order. To this end careful study of these differences is necessary, followed by a psychological approach in each case which will result in winning the support of the entire community. This is no easy task, but would be far more desirable in the long run than to attempt to secure results through the application of force.

Regional Planning.—In recent years the concept of regional planning has gained widespread recognition as it has grown out of effective city planning programs. This has been a development which we might well have expected, inasmuch as investigators into the many different phases of trade center development have, in nearly every instance, found it necessary to recognize the *umland*. In other words, those interested in civic problems have discovered that they could not do justice to their problems in most cases without taking into consideration the entire region of which the particular trade center is a part.

Regions, however, vary in kind. For example, there is the trade region, essentially synonymous with the continuous hinterland, already noted; a resource region, a political region, a physical region; a manufactural region; an agricultural region; a human-use region; and many more. The regional concept recognizes an areal unit throughout which a given element may be found and in which there is a certain degree of homogeneity with respect to that element. Thus, in a manufactural region manufacturing industries constitute the focus of interest. In an agricultural region interest is centered upon major crop or major agricultural use of the land in a given area, upon the economic and geographic conditions under which the crop is grown.

Regions too may be delineated in terms of a combination of several factors of interest to the investigator. The essential requirement, how-

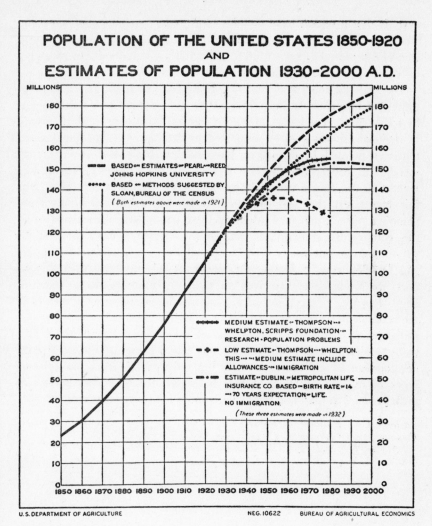

FIG. 28. GRAPH TO SHOW FUTURE POPULATION OF U. S.

No intelligest urban planning can be undertaken without the careful consideration of the probable growth, not only of the trade center under consideration, but of the nation. Hence, graphic expressions such as here presented by men whose calculations may be respected, are of prime importance. (Courtesy of U. S. Department of Agriculture.)

ever, is that a region have definite areal extent, sufficient homogeneous characteristics to give the area an aspect of unity with regard to the elements being analyzed within it, and to be sufficiently distinctive as to differ clearly from adjoining areas.

The regional concept is very old, going back probably as far as Aristotle, but has recently been revived by geographers and subsequently by sociologists, economists, and even political scientists. In 1935 interest in regionalism was greatly stimulated by the National Resources Committee appointed by President Roosevelt to study and make recommendations concerning the best course for the nation to pursue with respect to the future use of its resources. Geographers associated with this board left their imprint upon it by way of urgence that those planning our future take cognizance of geographic differentiation in this country. In consequence, among the several reports prepared by the committee, one treats with "Regional Factors in National Planning and Development." [4] Among the numerous subjects treated in this report, the trade center receives its share of attention. In a series of maps depicting many types of regions the implications with respect to the trade center are many. In fact any broad view of our trade center problems, of necessity, reaches beyond the political boundaries of the respective centers and consequently any one desirous of forwarding the development of a given center will not fail to relate it to the different types of regions of which it may be a part. In other words, city or trade center planning and regional planning hold reciprocal relationships.

[4] *Report of National Resources Committee,* "Regional Factors in National Planning and Development" (Washington, D. C., December, 1935).
See also, *National Land-Use Planning Committee, First Annual Report,* Publication No. V (Washington, D. C., July 1933).

CHAPTER VI

POPULATION GROWTH OF THE TRADE CENTER

We have made reference to the instability of trade centers—their origin, rise, and decline. Attention has been directed to centers which have swept into commanding positions, as did Tyre under the momentum of the Phoenician Empire or as Rome rose to power under the stimulus of a succession of Latin bravados. But many centers have disappeared entirely as has Tyre, while others like Rome no longer play a significant part in the world's exchanges. We have observed the pressure which our rapidly pulsating commercial life has exerted upon the orientation of the parts of our cities where building for permanence is rare and where a continual process of rearrangement constitutes one of the most important activities of the American community.

All of this change has led to attempts at systematic organization of our communities and, equally important, anticipation of their growth. It has forced business leaders to take stock of their respective localities and this in turn has awakened many to the consciousness of the possibilities of helping cities grow instead of allowing them to drift along for better or for worse as the fates of natural environment might dictate. A few Chambers of Commerce at the opening of this century pioneered in the field of forcing trade center growth. The idea that people could be enticed to take up an abode in a given city seemed to fascinate the minds of some men, and the experiment was tried. For many reasons, it has met with both success and failure, mostly failure, and has raised the question as to whether the objective in trade center growth should be more inhabitants or a better community. The U. S. Department of Commerce refers to the objectives of community promotion as follows:

Community promotion in the strictest sense, however, refers solely to efforts to increase the economic welfare and prosperity of a community. It is the consciously directed competition of a city with rival cities. The two basic aims of such programs are to increase the resident and transient population dwelling in the city and its trading area, and to increase its wealth-producing activities. The actual work of community promotion consists in interesting persons from the outside in its economic or recreational advantages. Promotion methods include negotiations with manufacturers or associations wishing to locate industrial plants or conventions, answering the inquiries of tourists and prospective settlers, working for improvements in the agriculture and other wealth-producing activities of the city and surrounding country, and building up the prestige of the city so as to extend its trading radius.[4]

Further light is shed upon this subject by an examination first of the general population tendencies in the United States during the past quarter century and then of those centers which have made a conscious effort to grow.

Population Movement.—That the rural[5] population has steadily moved toward the trade centers during the half century prior to 1880 is now common knowledge. Table 6 reveals a remarkable migration. A ratio of nearly 3 to 1 in 1880 in favor of the rural regions was reduced to a ratio of approximately one to one by 1920.

The end of the decade 1930-1940 may show a different picture, since immigration from foreign regions has practically ceased and the severe economic depression at the opening of the period reversed the migratory movement within the nation. In 1931 there was a "net migration to the farms of over 200,000 and in 1932 a net migration to farms of over half a million." [6] In 1933 the movement again shifted in favor of the trade centers, about 227,000 more going from farm to trade center than in the reverse direction. This may have been due to government employment-relief in the trade centers, other forms of relief, and also to the surrender of farm mortgages which forced farmers to the trade centers for a livelihood. In certain localities there were deviations from the general trend.

All of the increase in total urban population since 1880 must not be ascribed to migration from the rural districts. If this were true the difference in figures would not be so large. A considerable part of the urban increase arose from immigration of foreigners. The latter have

[4] *Advertising for Community Promotion,* Domestic Commerce Series (U. S. Department of Commerce, 1928) No. 21, p. 2.

[5] By "rural" the U. S. Census means all peoples residing outside communities of 2,500 or more. However, the 1930 census divided the rural into "farm" and "non-farm."

[6] O. E. Baker, "Rural-Urban Migration and the National Welfare," *Annals of the Association of American Geographers* (June, 1933) Vol. XXIII, No. 2.

Estimates by Galpin and Manny, *Bureau of Agricultural Economics,* U. S. Department of Agriculture for 1930, 1931 and 1932 respectively are, 17,000, 214,000 and 533,000.

always shown a preference for our larger trade centers even though they were farmers in their native countries. This was due also to the greater ease in earning a living in the city until they could adjust themselves to their new setting. With over 35,000,000 in rural areas in 1880 and only slightly over 14,000,000 in the urban centers and with the excess of births over deaths approximately the same in the two regions, the rural districts might be expected to show a rate of increase essentially equal to that of the urban. A part of the lower rate of increase in the rural population may be ascribed to the growth of villages from less than 2,500 to more than 2,500 which then automatically removes them from the rural classification into the urban.

In some of the larger trade centers such as Chicago, Cleveland, and New York City many Negroes from the south have added to the population, a movement begun during the war and also encouraged since then by industries endeavoring to break strikes among white men. Lastly, the "lure" of the city has been an ever-present attraction, irresistible among both farm and non-farm persons in villages. The excitement of the "big city," high wages, and "opportunity" have been the goal of thousands upon thousands of youths. In addition, Dr. O. E. Baker finds certain elements which "tend to push the young men and women off the farms." [7] These are (1) "the rate of natural increase of population... (2) technical progress... (3) depletion of soil fertility..., and (4) devastation of crops and livestock by pests and diseases." Again, annexations of rural areas by urban centers has helped to create the apparent disparity in rates of growth of urban and rural population.

TABLE 6

URBAN AND RURAL POPULATION OF THE UNITED STATES
1880-1930

CLASS	1880	1890	1900	1910	1920	1930
Urban	14,358,167	22,298,359	30,380,433	42,166,120	54,304,603	68,954,823
Rural	35,797,616	40,649,355	45,614,142	49,806,146	51,406,017	53,820,223
PER CENT						
Urban	28.6	35.4	40.0	45.8	51.4	56.2
Rural	71.4	64.6	60.0	54.2	48.6	43.8

Urban Rate of Growth.—In 1890, 5.8 per cent of the entire population lived in our three largest trade centers while to-day these centers

[7] O. E. Baker, "Rural-Urban Migration and the National Welfare," *Annals of the Association of American Geographers* (June, 1933) Vol. XXIII, No. 2.

attract 10 per cent. In 1930 fourteen trade centers had a population of 500,000 or more and housed 17.1 per cent of the total population. The number of centers with a population of 100,000 or more increased from twenty-eight in 1890 to ninety-three in 1930, representing a gain of nearly 232 per cent, as compared with an increase in population for the country as a whole in the same period of slightly less than 100 per cent and an increase of the nation's rural population of only slightly more than 32 per cent.

Although the urbanward movement continues, the rate has slowed up somewhat in recent years. According to McKenzie, "512 places of 2500 and over in 1920 actually lost population by 1930 as opposed to 375 places of this size that decreased during the decade 1910-1920." [8] Among trade centers with a population between 50,000 and 100,000, a rate of increase of 31 per cent occurred between 1910 and 1920, whereas the rate of increase between 1920 and 1930 was only 23 per cent. In fact, all trade centers with a population ranging between 15,000 and 250,000 experienced an average lower rate of increase in the 1920-1930 decade than in the preceding one. Those below and above this range retained or bettered their rates of increase.

It appears further that the larger the size which a political trade center attains the more likely it is that growth will continue. McKenzie says "no city in the United States has declined in population after once reaching the 150,000 mark," [9] basing the statement upon factual evidence. However, we should not lose sight of the fact that the increase in recent decades has been more in the periphery than in the center of the trade centers. New York City illustrates the phenomenon. The island of Manhattan in the last decade lost population which moved largely to the outlying areas, a small portion having gone entirely beyond the political limits into suburbs. The census returns show a loss of 416,791 persons between 1920 and 1930. Exact data to show the extent of this migratory movement throughout the nation are not available but the 1930 census taken by tracts within ninety-six metropolitan cities indicates clearly that the gain in population in the outlying tracts has been greater than in the inlying tracts. Mark Jefferson has suggested that the decennial census data represent the census of the sleeping hours, and this, in turn, suggests that while the population within a trade center's political limits may show a decline, its population viewed func-

[8] R. D. McKenzie, *The Metropolitan Community* (McGraw-Hill Book Company, Inc., New York, 1933).
[9] *Ibid.*

tionally may not. That is, the day-time census might well continue to show an increase owing to the fact that so many of the persons who take up residence in the suburbs and satellites continue to conduct their business within the political trade center.

To be sure, all of the gain has not been accomplished at the entire cost of the inlying areas. Natural increase and the influx of people from immediately contiguous territory as well as from more remote points have made important contributions. Nevertheless, the major additions seem to have resulted from the outward flow from the heart of the respective trade centers. Furthermore, the curtailment of foreign immigration has eliminated the possibility of replenishing population in the central districts.

The growth of a trade center is something more than a mere increase in numerical figures. It involves areal distribution of that increase and potential sources of supply of population. The outward motion, sometimes called centrifugal, suggests changes in boundary lines, in shape of trade centers as a whole, and in growth of area. The evidence of a former strong expansive influence may be observed on the outskirts of many communities. The staked-out plots of land; the toppling, isolated street-name standards; grass-covered, cracked, and broken cement sidewalks and street pavements in many communities tell the tale of a realtor's boom in the decade 1920-30, which encouraged areal expansion of population and which collapsed just as the decade closed.

Not all the evidence of this horizontal growth is depressing. Many new residential areas were successes. They have been artistically landscaped and suggest the strong attraction of the suburban or "rural" habitat for the urban resident. The post-war period up to 1930 will no doubt go down in history as the "own-your-home" era, the results of which have been both detrimental and beneficial to the public welfare. It was a period of great unrest, with people moving from the center to the periphery, from the periphery to suburb, from suburb to the periphery, and from remote centers to remote centers.

Although the United States was not unique in experiencing post-war building acceleration and subsequent cessation, yet the devastating effects were probably felt nowhere else to the same extent. In European centers some areal expansion occurred but the respective governments seemed to sense the dangers involved and, as a consequence, one traveling abroad does not observe the "remains" of a former over-enthusiastic own-your-home campaign. Too, the natural conservatism of the people undoubtedly assisted in checking excessive trade-center growth, and their inclination to live in apartments instead of individual homes served further as a safety valve against unreasonable areal dispersal of population.

This constant flux of population, with its threat to migrate *from* large trade centers or its willingness to *immigrate,* has challenged the understanding of many chambers of commerce and other civic organizations that have attempted to capitalize the movement. Their approach to an accurate interpretation of its true significance has not always been scientific. Hence, some data relative to their experiences, with special reference to the sensitivity of trade-center population growth to community advertising, is especially illuminating.

Population Increase in Certain Trade Centers.—In a study by R. M. Brown on the effect of advertising upon city growth [10] certain clear cut tendencies have been revealed. One hundred trade centers which showed an increase in population (1910-1920) of 37.5 per cent or over (the average increase for all cities was 24.5 per cent [11] in the decade, 1910-1920) were selected for analysis. Many of these centers grew at an amazing rate, the climax case having been that of Hamtramck, Michigan (48,615 in 1920) with an increase of 1,266 per cent. These hundred urban communities represented largely centers of specialized industry including automobile centers, resort centers, steel cities, oil and gas, cotton and cotton products, lumber centers, and others. The question arises, was their growth due to direct advertising or to the indirect effect of publicity gained by virtue of their industries?

Automobile Centers.—Thirteen of the centers owed their growth to the manufacture of automobiles and accessories. Akron, Ohio, gained by 201 per cent; Flint, Michigan, by 137.6 per cent; and Detroit (993,678 in 1920) displayed a growth of 113.3 per cent. In the entire state of Michigan 84 per cent of the gain in population was accounted for by Detroit, Flint, Lansing, and Pontiac, all automobile centers. These same centers did not maintain the pace during the decade 1920-1930. Akron showed an increase of only 22.4 per cent, Flint 70.8 per cent, and Detroit 57.9 per cent. Hamtramck assumed a more moderate rate, showing an increase of only 38.1 per cent while Highland Park could muster a mere 13.7 per cent.

---

[10] R. M. Brown, "City Growth and City Advertising," *The Scientific Monthly* (January, 1923) Vol. XVI, No. 1. Data brought down to 1930 by the author of this book).

[11] McKenzie, *The Metropolitan Community.*

Resort Centers.—Seven resort centers showed an average gain (1910-20) of 72.7 per cent. Asheville, North Carolina, increased 51.9 per cent while Long Beach, California, jumped ahead by 212.2 per cent. Florida centers show enormous gains in the period 1920-1930. Orlando increased 194.4 per cent, West Palm Beach 207.3 per cent, and Miami 274.1 per cent. On the other hand, Long Beach showed an increase in this decade of 155.5 per cent, a decline in percentage under the preceding decade, although still a healthy growth. Asheville continued to show an increase registering 76 per cent.

Non-advertising Cities.—Among the centers showing growth in excess of 24.5 per cent, the average urban increase for the nation between 1910 and 1920, few were aggressive advertisers. Most of their Chambers of Commerce issued occasional bulletins and some centers, in addition, sought conventions as advertising aids. Asheville, North Carolina, has been a consistent advertiser, somewhat more active since the 1920 census than before. Bethlehem, Pennsylvania; Warren, Ohio; and Lakewood, Ohio, all with substantial increases, engaged in little advertising. Many centers that enjoyed a large increase in population such as Gary, Indiana; Highland Park, Michigan; Tulsa, Oklahoma; and Akron, Ohio, profited from involuntary advertising arising out of the national news quality of their industries. Gary, a planned steel city, with almost magic growth; Highland Park, virtually created by the Ford automobile development; Akron, stimulated by the manufacture of rubber products; and Tulsa, nourished by oil fields fame, have all benefited by free publicity through the daily press. In consequence, they have become well-known without having had to spend much energy in the direction of "conscious" advertising of their individuality.

Advertising Cities.—More light is shed upon the effectiveness of intensive civic advertising by noting the increases in population among those centers which have distributed large quantities of literature or used newspapers and magazines to boast of their achievements, the delights of their climate, or the unparalleled opportunities awaiting those who take up residence within their hallowed domains.

One trade center in the northern part of the country, favorably located for trade, with a population of 78,466 in 1910, quite aggressive in its advertising, attained a population of 98,917 in 1920 and 101,463 in 1930, representing an increase of 28 per cent in the twenty-year period as compared with a 63.5 per cent gain for the urban population of the entire country. It seems fair to expect a progressive center at least to keep up with the average pace for the nation as a whole. Furthermore, it seems equally logical, if advertising "pays," to anticipate a rate of increase higher than the average.

Another trade center, located just west of the Appalachian Highland, quite proud of its assets according to its considerable literature, had a population in 1910 totaling 66,525 and in 1930 113,967, representing a gain of 71 per cent, somewhat greater than the average for the country. Advertising seems to have paid this trade center.

A third center in the far west, well-situated for trade development, accessible to the sea, counted 207,214 citizens in 1910 and 301,815 in 1930, a gain of about 45 per cent, still under the national average. Yet probably no center has been more enthusiastic in its desire to enlighten the nation as to its many advantages, both as a tourist center and a permanent place of residence.

Another advertising trade center, located in the heart of the nation, increased its numbers from 687,029 in 1910 to 821,960 in 1930, a mere 20 per cent, or less than one-half the average for all urban centers. For the period 1920-1930 the increase was 6.3 per cent. During the latter decade this city has launched striking magazine advertising campaigns. Its slight increase as compared with that for the entire country casts some doubt upon the value of its advertising.

These illustrations of centers seeking growth through advertising are too few in number for us to draw generalized conclusions. So many interlocking factors may function, either in stimulating or retarding growth, that an unqualified statement relative to the effectiveness of advertising is dangerous. The fact, however, that so many trade centers of rapid growth, particularly those of specialized industry, have engaged in little or no advertising, while many of slow growth have expended large sums for publicity, raises a serious challenge to the effectiveness of advertising for growth. The question is rightly raised as to whether specialization may not serve as a stronger magnet than merely printed assertions about a community's merits. Researches in this direction may prove of immense value to the public because, if they reveal as a fact that advertising for growth does not pay, expenditures may be directed more profitably into other channels. A survey of expenditures for advertising in 1925 was made by the United States Department of Commerce and revealed that $4,492,001 was spent by 380 cities and probably a total of $6,000,000 by all cities.[12]

Henceforth trade centers interested in adding population will prob-

---

[12] "Advertising for Community Promotion," *Domestic Commerce Series* (U. S. Department of Commerce, Washington, D. C., 1928) No. 21.

ably be forced to take into consideration the recent reversal in direction of migration. It seems to be true that relatively few rural persons have been enticed to large trade centers by virtue of Chamber of Commerce advertising, owing to the fact that little of the literature has reached them directly. Nevertheless, some of the national magazine and newspaper publicity may have wielded its influence among these people. In the absence of statistical data, we shall probably never know how influential this advertising has been in rural districts. The mere fact, however, that the total figures of rural-urban migration reveal the shifting directions of movement must color the entire nature of future advertising campaigns. Advertising for industries and thus indirectly for population will be considered later.

Suburban Growth and Trade Center Expansion.—Among centers of large increase in population some, such as Highland Park, Michigan, and Lakewood, Ohio, may be classified as suburbs. They suggest the fact that the suburban rate of growth has tended to outdistance the major urban rate, just as the peripheral growth of trade centers has moved faster than that of the central areas. The following data for certain suburban areas as a whole are striking.

The census for 1930 shows the rate of growth for ninety-six Metropolitan cities as well as for the political cities of the respective trade centers. The differences between the two sets of data provide an index to the influence of the suburban area upon the whole. Where the rate of growth of the Metropolitan area is greater than that of the political city, obviously, the suburbs must have grown more rapidly than the city. Figure 29 tells the story. The rate of increase of New York City from 1920 to 1930 was 23.3 per cent, but of the Metropolitan district 28.2 per cent; of Boston proper 4.4 per cent, but of the Metropolitan district 14.9 per cent—a tremendous difference. Philadelphia, long reputed to be the "city of homes," has bowed to the "inevitable," its urban increase having been but 7 per cent, while the Metropolitan district increased 16.1 per cent. All these figures, of course, mean that the suburbs have increased several times as rapidly as the adjoining or neighboring political center.

This rapid suburban growth occurs about large centers, and it seems to be true that the larger the center, the higher the rate of increase of the suburban population. That is, suburbs of trade centers in the group of 500,000 and over, with few exceptions, tend to show a more rapid growth than suburbs of groups below that population size. The logic of this situation is clear, for, if a considerable part of suburban

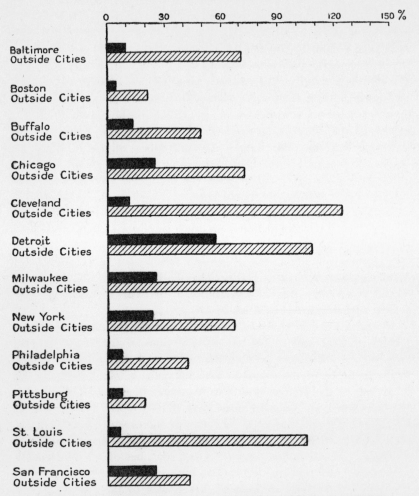

FIG. 29. SUBURBAN GROWTH EXCEEDS URBAN GROWTH

In this group of trade centers having a population of 500,000 or over the rate of growth of suburbs is an index to the decentralization of population which has occurred during recent years. Growth has resulted largely in accretion from other centers, from rural districts, and from the major trade center itself. Percentage increases for "outside" cities do not agree in every instance with those cited in the text, p. 87, for metropolitan districts because they are more inclusive. (Data based upon U. S. Census, 1930.)

growth has been at the expense of the central city, then, the larger the latter, the larger the source of supply for the suburb. On the other hand, suburban growth, like urban growth, is sometimes due in part to annexations or consolidations and, in consequence, suburbs enlarging under such circumstances may easily show as great rates of increase when located close to major trade centers of moderate size as when located near those in the group with the larger population figures.

Another source of population has been the rural districts. Many farmers and village residents, upon migrating to urban centers, locate in the suburbs where they still may enjoy something of the rural or village atmosphere and yet indulge in the activities of the major center.

The phenomenon of rapid suburban growth is closely associated with urban areal expansion. As the population of the suburb increases and also that of the outlying districts of the political trade center increases, the two units approach each other areally. Then the question invariably arises, shall these be consolidated? This question, in turn, raises two others, namely, shall the suburb maintain its political autonomy but enjoy the economic advantages of proximity to the major center or shall it surrender its independence, subject itself to a different political régime, and lose much of its individuality?

While the latter two questions are those in the minds of the suburbanites, the citizens of the major center are also confronted with important questions. Shall additional area be included within the city limits at the risk of increased taxation? Will the larger center become less wieldy and, in consequence, suffer certain losses due to a scattering of energies and attentions? Can the zoning and planning system now in effect be made to accommodate the larger area without undue injury?

These questions involve in the last analysis the welfare of both the "urb" and the suburb. The ramifications are many as they affect political organization, industrial concentration versus decentralization, distribution of residential sites, retail business competition and other elements.

Accordingly, we need to examine the methods used by those who put forth conscious efforts either to make trade centers grow or to prevent their decline. We need to determine what criteria the people of any community should use as a guide when about to launch a campaign pointing toward the improvement of their local political unit. We should distinguish between the practical approach and the ideal. These aspects are considered in the next chapter.

Urblets and Satellites.—Expansion of the urban area, involving, as it does, so close an approach to the suburban area that absorption of the latter becomes a possibility, directs attention to the areal relation of the suburb, or the urblet, and satellite to the major urban center and to each other. The urblet may be distinguished from the satellite in its intermediate location between the satellite and the major center. The urblet is more closely associated with the major center than is the satellite. (Fig. 9.)

Rural-urban migration affects population growth in the urblets and satellites much as it does in larger trade centers, although, in the main, the rate of accretion is slower. Increases in population tend, however, to induce areal expansion as truly in small as in large centers. This means a continued approach toward each other of these various types of organizations and a consequent reduction in inter-trade-center space. This may have far-reaching effects.

As inter-trade-center spaces become smaller and the demand for food grows larger because of the larger population in the total trade center region, these spaces may be brought out of extensive into intensive cultivation and lead to the eventual evolution of what may be termed an *agri-trade*-center region. Such a region may attain a state of equilibrium in which growth of population becomes practically static. On the other hand, it is conceivable that the cultivated land can be so occupied as to form either one vast cumbersome urb or an agglomeration of urbs, dependent for their agricultural support upon more remote lands.

The future growth of trade centers may be favorable to permanent detachment of both urblet and satellite. "Village" life may increase even at the expense of major trade centers. Many factors may guide their destinies. Among them no doubt will be continued development in communication efficiency. Probably, the more effective the means of communication and the lower the cost, the less the urge will be for people to leave the farm, urblet, or satellite and certainly the less the urge to become a permanent resident of the large trade center. Similarly, many now living in a congested trade center will be tempted to move to its periphery or to the urblet or even to a nearby farmstead. When the population of the United States becomes static, as some experts in the field of demography predict will happen by 1950 or 1960, the shuttling of population from urban areas may become a very slow movement, so slow as to be essentially imperceptible in many regions. (Fig. 28.)

These are all contingencies which leaders in forward looking trade centers will ponder carefully when examining ways and means for making their centers grow.

CHAPTER VII

THE TRADE CENTER AND THE CHAMBER OF COMMERCE

Probably the two most representative organizations in any trade center are the "City Council" or its equivalent and the Chamber of Commerce, if one exists. We may safely assume that a Chamber of Commerce [1] is in operation in all of the larger trade centers. Of the two organizations, the latter undoubtedly is the more aggressive with respect to the encouragement of growth in population and in trade. Certainly its efforts are generally of a direct nature whereas those of the government are at best indirect.

The membership of the Chamber of Commerce is derived from nearly every type of business in the locality and includes most of the financial leaders. Although this organization carries no official status, by the very nature of its composition it wields a large influence, if not real power, in connection with problems affecting the destinies of its local community. Because of this relationship between the Chamber of Commerce and the citizens as a whole and because the records show that since the beginning of this century the Chamber has played an outstanding rôle in the growth and vicissitudes of the cities in the United States, it deserves detailed study. We shall look at its actual performance and then consider the potentialities of the functions which it is attempting to perform.

The Traffic Bureau.—Most Chambers of Commerce have a traffic bureau either as a distinct department or incorporated among the general duties of some individual. It is the purpose of this division to secure railroad, bus, and other rates favorable to the trade center and to prevent the levying of rates which seem to involve unfair discrimination.

We have already differentiated between the elements of geographical location and accessibility. The existence of a traffic bureau implies a recognition of the differences between these elements, that is, (1) loca-

[1] We shall understand this term to apply to associations of Commerce, Industrial Bureaus, or Foundations and other organizations with similar names whose essential functions correspond with those of the Chamber of Commerce.

91

tion in terms of geographical distance alone, and (2) location in terms of freight rates. If a center is located upon the main trade highways, the problem of physical accessibility may not exist, but the problem of equitable freight rates among a group of centers, all in competition for the same trade, may be very real. Trade center A may have a geographical location entitling it, theoretically, to a fair share of the total business of a given area, but the freight rate structure may be such as to exclude it from much of that trade.

A concrete example will illustrate how freight rates may affect location.

Suppose, for example, city A pays freight rates of 2 cents per pound on a commodity shipped to city B, 150 miles away. Suppose city C which heretofore has paid a rate of 2½ cents on the same commodity, now is granted a new rate of 2 cents on the route to B. Assuming service to be equally as good as that of A to B, C immediately is placed upon an equal competitive basis with A. If the rate is dropped still farther to 1⅞ cents, C's location has changed again, for now this rate, lower than that between A and B, has virtually moved C closer to B. It is such shifts that an alert traffic bureau will watch, opposing them when disadvantageous to the local situation and supporting them when favorable.

Every trade center is entitled to the advantages which its natural location affords. Theoretically, freight rates are based upon length of haul but in practice, until recently, the Interstate Commerce Commission and other rate-making organizations have taken into consideration many other factors, such as ability to render service, or relation to arbitrarily set base points. The present tendency, however, is in the direction of recognizing geographical location solely, thus orienting all centers with respect to the distance which they are from each other or from any common point. Accordingly, unfair competition should not arise through forcing a shift in position by reason of disproportionate freight rates.

The traffic bureau's duties do not cease with freight-rate problems. Passenger-train service requires equal vigilance. The movement of human freight can be quite as important as package freight. People frequently visit a city for the purpose of buying. If they can not make good connections, even in this day of the automobile and auto-bus, they remain away, giving their patronage to some other center more readily accessible. A generalized case to illustrate many real instances of passenger service discrimination follows.

Suppose a passenger train schedule between trade centers X, Y, and J is such that Y can be reached easily by a morning express run from X, but J which is the same distance from X as is Y can be reached only late in the evening, necessitating an overnight stay if any shopping is to be done. Obviously Y receives most of the shoppers from X. The case seems somewhat extreme but is by no means so. The X and J traffic bureaus, tolerating such service, are unfit to function further. Certainly any community which accepts such service admits its lack of influence in the trade area and can not entertain much hope of either business development or population growth.

Another problem is that associated with partial or complete abandonment of railroad, trolley or bus service between a trade center and its continuous or discontinuous hinterland. This type of curtailment in service may be the equivalent of shifting a trade center from a main line to a secondary route. Above all, a trade center must maintain its accessibility if it hopes to retain the convenience it has acquired. The Chamber of Commerce may properly assume this responsibility.

Advertising Literature.—Chambers of Commerce have sought to bring to the attention of the world through the printed word advantages to be derived by persons selecting their respective centers as places of business and residence. Their advertisements commonly take the form of booklets or displays in magazines and occasionally in newspapers. The subjects generally treat with location, history, climate, transportation, natural resources, markets, labor, and future possibilities. Three of these aspects most frequently emphasized are location, climate, and the market.

Examination of the literature reveals that all too often sweeping generalizations are made without regard to the truth. Again, the discussions sometimes indicate a sincere desire to be truthful, but the editors apparently possess insufficient knowledge to handle the subject effectively. A few quotations selected from among scores of booklets offer supporting evidence.

One trade center lists among its assets "geographical location" and then proceeds to cast itself as the hub of a half wheel. It claims "Nature has set it in the direct path of commerce and made this city the hub of demand for this vast territory." The map implies that such centers as Cleveland, Buffalo, and Pittsburgh are quite secondary to this city of less than 150,000 population. Again, what trade center is there that does not possess geographical location? Such statements do not gain public confidence.

Another trade center refers to its climate in these glowing terms: "She knows little of the *extremes* of heat or cold; and for the *major part of the time* God's sun shines, and the air is balmy and delicious." Yet the facts are that temperatures in summer commonly exceed 90° F., approach close to the zero mark in winter, and many times in the year range through 20 to 30 degrees in a twenty-four to forty-eight hour period. The average daily range of temperature is 18 degrees.

A third center, discussing its markets, refers to freight transportation and concludes with the statement, "This package-car service combined with the extensive facilities for handling freight, is the great factor which has made this city the preëminent distribution center for southern markets." It ignores Memphis, New Orleans, Houston, Fort Worth, Dallas, and other centers which, rightly so, would hardly acknowledge second place. The boast would be better if it used the modifier, Southeastern, in place of Southern, and located the markets.

The Slogan.—Slogans have long adorned the stationery of many Chambers of Commerce, Industrial Bureaus, and Convention Committees or have been incorporated in their special advertising copy. Just when the slogan came into use is unknown. The city or town seal on the coat of arms, common in medieval days, may well have served as a forerunner to that of the present day.

The seals of some of our newer cities carry epigrams which are employed also as slogans. Chicago takes pride in its motto "I Will" inscribed about a conventionalized Chicago River. The "I Will" spirit is always held responsible when the citizens of that city can boast of some outstanding achievement, or it is cited as a spur to accomplishment when a new project is proposed.

Slogans undoubtedly have their psychological value, but when their meaning is rather doubtful or actually represents exaggeration the constructive value may be nil or, in fact, negative. One of the most common slogans and perhaps least significant is "The City of Opportunity." Lacking distinctiveness and used by numerous trade centers, it claims little and may have all the elements of truth in it. On the other hand, "Where Enterprise was Invented" assumes so much that the person of average intelligence can hardly be impressed except by the absurdity of the assertion. The "City of Magnificent Distances" or "The Gate City of the South" fall within the realm of reason, convey some concreteness in idea, and assume sufficiently distinctive character as probably to leave no unfavorable impression upon the mind of the average reader. A slogan for the sake of a slogan only, wholly devoid of the

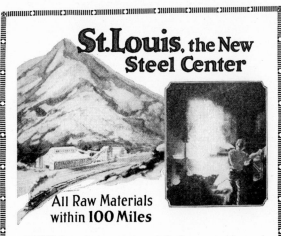

FIG. 30. A CHAMBER OF COMMERCE CAPITALIZES
THE GEOGRAPHIC SETTING

reasonable and without at least a large modicum of truth, can only bring damage to a trade center. It must bear some definite relation to the realities of the center.

Informational Advertising.—One finds it difficult to understand why business men persist in placing their stamp of approval upon some of these types of advertising, when in their own organizations they insist upon accurate representation of goods because their experience of years has demonstrated this policy to be most profitable in the long run. Fortunately, less and less of this kind of advertising covers the printed page.

We have held that a trade center cannot hope to excel in every direction and that, since the man of average intelligence appreciates this fact, the best efforts of any Chamber of Commerce should be directed along channels representing its best qualities. Prospective settlers want facts and not fancied pictures painted in magnificent colors to represent what does not exist. Since the element climate is misrepresented more than any other, frequently expressed as "the ideal climate," "the most delightful climate," "the healthiest climate," we single out this item as the basis for suggesting how a Chamber of Commerce can present one of its urban characteristics in a manner to convey intelligible meaning to those persons and industries that would best fit into the local conditions.

Climate bears a direct relation to human efficiency in factory and home and to the cost of living. The salability of a variety of commodities such as wearing apparel, both cold and hot refreshments, electric fans, heaters, and numerous other elements are definitely related to climate. Road construction, road maintenance, and road usability are affected by climatic conditions. The character of a climate largely determines whether or not the people can convert their center into a garden city or whether every pound of food must be imported. It has a bearing upon the water supply with respect to purity, quantity, and power possibilities. Construction costs, labor income, and hence purchasing power are all influenced by the climatic factor. The climate of any trade center is a matter of interest to factory hand, out-door laborer, clerk, industrialist, housewife, and tourist.

Chambers of Commerce that would inform the country about their respective city's climate will have copy covering climate prepared by those who are experts in the given field. At least one Chamber of Commerce adopted this policy and found it so successful that the bulletin telling the story of the local climate went into several large editions. An attractive booklet was devoted to the facts presented in detail and approved by the U. S. Weather Bureau. Comparative data were included so that the reader could make his own intrepretations if he wished. Statements were convincing and the entire work reflected credit upon the Chamber and was eminently worth while.

New Industries.—Many Chambers of Commerce have been careless in their advertising for new industries and, in consequence, have wasted enormous sums of money in addition to causing losses upon the part of industries brought to their centers and by those local persons who may have been induced to invest in the new enterprises. Bringing industries to a city is hazardous business unless it is done with scientific care and accuracy.

Available evidence seems to show that little has been accomplished in proportion to the energy and money spent by way of causing the establishment and growth of new industries or in enticing industries from other localities. The failures are conspicuous and the successes negligible. What are the prospects for enticing new industries?

In a study of the tendencies of manufactures toward concentration or dispersion [2] a number of interesting items have been brought to light. Industrial expansion has largely followed population growth, although other factors have played a part such as the rise of the automotive industry or the rapid development of mineral resources, or improvements in transportation. We do not mean that industries themselves actually moved with population, but rather that new establishments were created, while the old ones remained where they were or even in some cases disappeared. Unfortunately no exact data are available to enable us to differentiate between physical removal and the establishment of new plants.

The census data referred to indicate that "the large centers are rather more than holding their own in relation to the less populous areas," so far as industrial activity is concerned, measured in terms of *wage jobs*. The number of wage jobs in rural areas increased, however, from 1919 to 1929, a fact which suggests the possibility of some slight dispersion of industry from smaller cities. This, however, may not be the case, but may reflect merely the "back to the land" movement. Most significant of all is the notable increase in wage jobs between 1899 and 1929, in industries in the areas of "secondary concentration" just outside the large cities.

[2] *Location of Manufactures 1899-1929,* Bureau of the Census (U. S. Dept. of Commerce, Washington, D. C., 1933).

TABLE 7

PER CENT OF INCREASE (+) OR DECREASE (−) OF WAGE JOBS IN THE
UNITED STATES IN AREAS OF CONCENTRATION 1899-1929 [3]

	AREAS OF PRIMARY CONCENTRATION	AREAS OF SECONDARY CONCENTRATION	ALL OTHER AREAS
1899-1929	+ 83.8	+ 114.9	+ 78.4
1899-1919	+ 92.6	+ 126.3	+ 77.0
1919-1929	− 4.5	− 5.0	+ 0.8

Areas of secondary concentration are defined by the Census Bureau as composed of those portions of a country lying outside of the corporate limit of cities of 100,000 inhabitants or more. If detailed statistics were at hand we would probably find that the increase in wage jobs in this secondary area occurred in close proximity to the political limits of the cities rather than in the more remote intervening localities. The Bureau of the Census says, "The dispersion which has occurred consists principally of expansion into *areas adjoining* the dominant population and industry centers, rather than into the thousands of smaller cities and towns throughout the country." Presumably, detailed analysis of the data for the "areas adjoining" would support our initial theory that the relocation of industries has been primarily a movement toward the suburb or urblet rather than into distant trade centers.

In addition to wage-job data, the 1929 census reveals for the first time some definite data relative to the relocation of manufacturing plants. An analysis of 287 that relocated, points to "a general movement away from the cities of 100,000 inhabitants or more," but does not reveal how far they moved, that is, whether merely to suburban areas or greater distances. "Seventy per cent of the total number represented intrastate relocations" and the rest interstate. This conclusion in itself suggests the probable futility of attempting to pull industries away from far distant centers. The assertion often made that industry is decentralizing seems not to be supported by the facts if by decentralization we mean dispersal from one part of the country to distant parts. That there is a movement from the heart of trade centers to the periphery appears to be substantiated.[4]

---

[3] *Location of Manufactures, 1899-1929,* Bureau of Census (U. S. Department of Commerce, Washington, D. C.).

[4] In an investigation of the subject of decentralization by Daniel B. Creamer, "Is Industry Decentralizing?" the conclusion is reached that with few exceptions industry has shown a tendency to "diffuse" somewhat and that there has been no

Certain industries have shown a stronger tendency to relocate than others. Manufacturers of tin containers have moved closer to canning centers while shoe manufacturers seem to have followed new markets. There is no assurance, however, from the experience we have had in general, that such relocations constitute a continuing movement or even an intermittent one with a high frequency.

We may properly ask, what are the principal sources of supply of industries? They may be considered in general, as three in number, namely, (1) industries which have failed to prosper elsewhere, (2) branch factories, and (3) new industries. Most failures apparently are due to mismanagement; hence, industries not progressing well elsewhere are not likely to succeed locally unless the management is changed. Branch factories are exceedingly few and, in consequence, a community can not hope to secure many such industries if it secures any at all. New industries require considerable local capital, have an uncertain future, and, therefore, are not likely to provide an important source of possible supply to be drawn upon by an industrial committee.

Clearly, this business of attracting new industries involves hazards. The committee should first make a survey of the hinterland with respect to raw materials, labor, climate, and other elements to be noted and then ask itself numerous questions such as: What industries ought to be established which are not already in the trade center? What commodities sold in the trade territory are manufactured from raw materials available to the trade center? Is the market sufficiently large to warrant a local factory, or can the nearby demand be amply and more profitably cared for by existing industries at other centers? Could a local industry expand its organization to include the production of the new item more effectively and hence more profitably than a new factory built for the sole purpose of manufacturing and marketing the particular commodity? These and other pertinent questions must be answered before any Chamber of Commerce honestly dare to invite a new industry to its domain.

Natural Resource Survey.—The survey of the hinterland just suggested is important because, as we have already shown, a trade center is largely the product of its natural environment. A committee on resources is quite as vital as one on Parks and Playgrounds, Membership, Traffic, and other phases now represented.

marked "dispersion." This work reviews that of the Bureau of the Census covering the period 1899-1929 and considers additional data down to 1933. (See Bibliography.)

An inventory of the mineral deposits easily accessible to the city and a survey of the crops produced forms the basis for determining for any trade center the extent to which it is profiting from available resources. Such a survey should include not only a statistical record of the quantities of the products yielded by the earth but the proportion of the total which is brought into the city. It should likewise trace the remainder to its destination. Following upon the construction of a map or several maps, showing the distribution of raw materials, an inquiry into the causes for their movement should reveal to the trade center whether or not it is securing its due share. If it is not, then further tracing of the materials may help to reveal the reason therefor.

Also as stated, a study of the local climate in relation to agriculture, to recreation, to labor efficiency, to cost of living, and to the manufacture of products sensitive to atmospheric conditions will prove invaluable. The quality of the soils, the character of the landscape especially with respect to its scenic beauty and the pattern of land use are other elements in the environment which should not be overlooked.

Labor.—A survey of the type of people in the region may properly be included under a natural resource survey. There are industries requiring a special type of labor which may not be resident in a trade center, which should not be imported, or which would be virtually economically impossible to import. This lack of a given type of labor might be good enough reason in itself to discourage the attempt to establish a particular industry. The clothing industry, for example, mostly engages a considerable amount of eastern European labor. A trade center boasting a seventy-five to one hundred per cent American-born population would hardly be conducive to the growth of many clothing industries.

Consider an agricultural development in the near environs of a trade center. A survey may disclose that certain crops can be grown locally and would be desirable. For example, root crops might be in question. The climatic conditions combined with a large expenditure of human energy might be the requisites for the successful introduction of such crops. A careful investigation of the best type of people fitted for the particular kind of agriculture under the given conditions would be the first requisite. If the type could be located and could be properly financed, the Chamber would be justified in proceeding with that development.

A few years ago, an effort was made to settle the land in the vicinity of a certain northern Minnesota trade center. Only after the costly trial and error method had been pursued, did some success begin to accrue. This method could have been avoided had those involved in the development given the matter the same concentrated and logical thought at the outset which they were forced to give in the end. They discovered that for their agricultural project more essential than money was the type of people who understood how to farm the particular kind of land and had the patience and courage to tackle the problem. The Finns and Poles and some Czechs met the situation. Americans, French, Germans, and others were unequal to the task.

The Sphere of Influence.—Correlation between a trade center and its hinterland, that is, the territory of its sphere of influence, probably can be most effectively brought about through the Chamber of Commerce. Committees such as the Agricultural Extension, and Good-Will Tour Committees are expressive of sphere of influence activities.

Some Chambers of Commerce still sponsor the provincial notion that they must function only in the interests of their membership. Their objective involves direct aid to members. Happily, the number of such organizations grows smaller as their leaders come to appreciate that advantages which accrue to the entire community must also reflect benefits upon the parts.

Some major trade centers have within their sphere of influence many small trade centers, ranging in population from a few hundred to as many as 5,000 or even 25,000, which often have taxation controversies, road-building projects, bridge construction problems, annexation questions, freight-rate adjustments, and other problems which require state legislative action, federal approval, or merely the development of local sentiment sufficient to carry a bond issue. Proposed changes may involve the prospect of either encouraging more business for the major trade center or of taking away business. Chambers of Commerce fully alive to their responsibilities will keep in close touch with these problems and diplomatically offer such assistance as they believe may contribute to the mutual advantage of their neighboring communities. The consequence of such efforts may not only result in an immediate monetary return to the major center but in the upbuilding of invaluable good-will between the two centers.

Consider for a moment the local township, county, or village fair. Some wide-awake Chambers of Commerce in the larger centers make a point in always having representatives present at these fairs and take an active part in the preliminaries to help make them a success. Agricultural fairs, particularly, are not only sponsored by these Chambers, but in some cases permanent agricultural committees whose membership includes representatives from the entire nearby agricultural territory are supported by the Chamber to function the year round in the interests of improved agriculture, as well as for the staging of the annual fair.

The Good-Will Tour, an excursion of Chamber of Commerce business men, to small centers in the continuous hinterland is for purposes of developing an harmonious spirit between the major center and smaller centers. Its primary objective aims at an increase in sales by the business interests of the center sponsoring the tour. The spirit of the tour, however, should be reciprocal. No community can be self-sufficient and none can continually sell without buying. Good-Will tourists should appreciate that their hosts, like themselves, are interested in selling, and hence they should indicate a willingness to buy from the community in which their prospective customers are located. Here is recognition of the fact that Good-Will works in two directions and is an aspect of trade relations between major and minor trade centers too long wanting on the part of major trade center representatives.

Foreign Trade.—A few Chambers of Commerce sponsor a Foreign Relations Committee, support a coöperative office of the U. S. Bureau of Foreign and Domestic Commerce, or follow some other plan for keeping their membership in touch with trade opportunities abroad.

Certain of these offices display commendable aggressiveness while others act merely in the capacity of bureaus of information for those who seek data. The latter rarely act upon their own initiative to supply local manufacturers or importers with information which might return them profits and still less often endeavor to arouse an interest among the business element in the profitableness of the world market. Just as a national market offers more opportunities than a local one, so an international market invites more business opportunities than the national. No urban center is too small to share in world trade. The Chamber of Commerce with a world outlook will foster the spirit of foreign trade among local manufacturers.

Foreign trade, however, is a two way affair. Imports as well as exports are involved. Therefore, the local Chamber has an opportunity to assist industries in scouring the earth for sources of supply of raw materials as well as in fostering sales abroad. It is not unpatriotic to purchase supplies wherever one can do so to advantage. We do that in national markets; we should do likewise in international markets. In fact, if we refuse to buy from abroad, foreigners cannot buy from us. Thus we restrict our outlets, reduce our output, and to that extent fail to provide labor for many who wish to work.

Quality or Quantity.—Permeating many of the activities of a Chamber of Commerce, one may find a spirit seeking to increase the community's business through increasing the number of industries and through population growth. Therefore, we ask whether or not it is desirable that trade centers attain to large populations?

According to European city planners, large size is not essential to comfort and may conduce only to much misery. Some persons have argued that when a community has reached a size which enables it to afford its members the normal amenities of life it has fulfilled its purpose and the addition of numbers beyond this point contributes nothing. Too large additions may actually remove the pleasures of life from some citizens. The law of diminishing returns operates in population and areal growth as truly as in business. When so many persons seek the same pleasure that they create discomfort for each other, then the original objective is defeated. For example, it is conceivable that a given residential area enjoys the quiet of small numbers and an atmosphere not seriously polluted with smoke. The numbers may be such as to enable the residents to have friendly relations with most members of the community. Because of these favorable conditions plus the enthusiasm of realtors, increasing numbers of persons move into the locality. Soon the community spirit disappears and suspicions of a metropolitan folk replace the former friendly atmosphere. Closely-built homes, perhaps interspersed by apartment buildings, contribute their smoke to pollute the air and by their physical presence obstruct the light from each other. The crowds that congregate upon the streets, the lack of personal pride in keeping the highways clean and the homes in good repair further contribute to the destruction of all that was originally attractive in the delightful small suburban community. The objective of those who sought this locality has been defeated by the rush of numbers seeking the same end in the same place.

Just what the population number should be depends upon the location, the environment, the purpose, and the times. In England, Letchworth, a garden city, was planned to house a maximum of 35,000 people. In the United States some have set the ideal at from 300,000 to 500,000. Only the experience of years of planning will enable us to specify exactly the ideal size.

Several hundreds of planned projects have been attempted in this country in recent years, ranging from mining towns such as are located

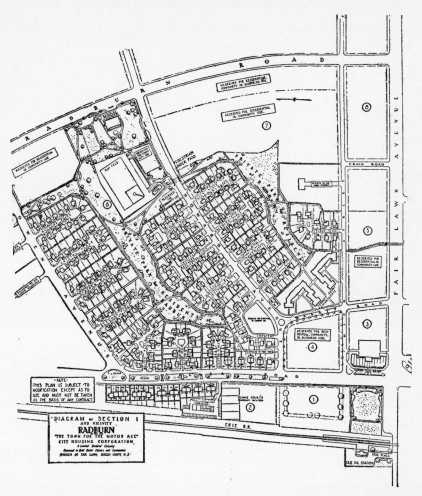

FIG. 31. A COMMUNITY PLANNED FOR QUALITY AND SIZE

A portion of Radburn, New Jersey, thirteen miles as the crow flies from central New York City, represents probably the first serious attempt in this country to build a trade center according to a carefully preconceived plan. The concept was influenced by the work associated with Letchworth, England, the first community in England in modern times to have been built according to plan and for a limited population. Although Radburn is not perfect, its experiences have been of immeasurable value to many other centers throughout the nation. Apartments are separated from single dwelling areas; streets are built for safety; recreation facilities are easily accessible; and the business district is concentrated. All structures are architecturally attractive.

on the "Iron Range" of northeastern Minnesota to suburban centers like Radburn, New Jersey, just outside of Paterson. Mariemont, Ohio; Forest Hills, New York, and numerous centers in Florida and southern California have met with varying degrees of success. They are, however, neither old enough nor complex enough to serve as a satisfactory basis for determining the best approach to the solution of many intricate problems.

On the assumption that growth means progress, shall the growth be forced through extravagant advertising claims or shall a trade center adopt a policy of improving its living conditions so as automatically to attract people from elsewhere? Seemingly, adoption of the latter policy would not only contribute greatly to the center's welfare but would tend to assure wholesome growth. The problem, of course, is not one solely of commerce, nor of physical conditions, but of profound social significance as well. It ought to enlist the best brains of the community.

A Local Analysis.—The most reasonable procedure in the competitive efforts of all centers seeking either quantity, quality, or both, is to emphasize and develop those aspects of the commercial life for which they are best adapted. Trade centers should be able to prove to others that they are endowed with certain advantages not attainable elsewhere within the given trade territory or even within the entire country. To be prepared to do this necessitates not alone a survey of the environment but an analysis of the confines of the trade center itself. This function lies within the province of the local Chamber of Commerce. A check-list for testing the analysis has been admirably set forth by Dr. Ralph Heilman [5] in a list of fourteen points which he believes an ideal trade center should possess. His "Fourteen Points" are:

1. Economic and industrial life to provide employment
2. Clean government
3. Good schools
4. Recreation facilities
5. Churches, non-antagonistic and truly Christian
6. Library with branches
7. Public utilities well-managed
8. Health department
9. Good industrial relations
10. Thrifty but not miserly citizens
11. Neighborly relations

[5] Dean of the School of Commerce, Northwestern University, Chicago.

12. A Chamber of Commerce with vision
13. An aspiring people
14. A civic spirit
A fifteenth point may be added, namely, a world outlook

No interpretation of the meaning of each point is necessary because the expressions themselves seem to be clear. Point fifteen, however, deserves a word of elaboration because few citizens conceive of their trade center internationally. International exchanges, particularly in commerce and industry, are growing so numerous and the means of international communication are reducing distances both in time and cost so effectively that the trade center which ignores its relation to the rest of the world must soon suffer adverse consequences. Isolation is only possible if we are satisfied to return to a primitive existence.

Civic Future.—Some persons may feel that placing the major responsibility for the development of a trade center upon the membership of a Chamber of Commerce discounts the local government too much. We repeat, however, that the Chamber of Commerce has within its numbers the major portion of the business men and civic leaders who, either by self-appointment or otherwise, have assumed a leadership which calls for just such responsibility. If they fail to live up to it, the community suffers, for they exert the bulk of influence in political affairs, in industry, in commerce, and upon the public press. The influence is not always expressed publicly, yet it exists none-the-less. Therefore, the future of a trade center can and, in some instances, must lie largely under the direction of the Chamber of Commerce.

For the Chamber to make the most of its opportunity to lead a community toward the better things in life it needs (a) to maintain that community upon the direct highways of trade, (b) to possess a full knowledge of the natural resources of its environment and (c) to endeavor to realize the Heilman points just listed.

CHAPTER VIII

THE OCEAN PORT AS A TRADE CENTER

Analysis of the most influential variety of trade center, the ocean port, includes a description of the nature and functions of numerous types of trade centers. Ocean ports serve as the doorways of the nations. Through them the major international physical activities pass. A port in many respects gives character to a nation and often reflects the moods of its peoples.

A Port Defined.—A port is a harbor plus the facilities for handling trade. While all ports, with negligible exceptions, are harbors; all harbors by no means are ports. In a port the mechanical equipment for carrying on trade and handling passengers is of the utmost significance for no matter how favorable for navigation a harbor may be, ships often do not enter if equipment is inadequate. The physical aspect and the hinterland of the harbor play a large part in port development, but usually, given the mechanical facilities for handling cargo, the probabilities are that a harbor will be navigated by numbers of craft, and the port will develop accordingly. In order better to understand a port we set up the ideal conditions for a harbor and a port respectively.

The Ideal Harbor.—Ten physical conditions may be recorded which if realized, would give us an ideal harbor. They are:

1. Deep water but not too deep for anchorage
2. Bottom favorable to good anchorage
3. Spaciousness
4. Tide-less water
5. Absence of currents
6. Absence of strong winds
7. Absence of silting
8. Easily negotiable entrance channel
9. Ice-free and fog-free
10. Low shore line of unconsolidated materials

The ideal harbor is a coastal reëntrant safely navigable in which ships may find protection from storm waves. It should be carefully noted

106

that a harbor does not imply trade. Hundreds of harbors have neither trade nor people along their shores.

The Ideal Port.—Add the following four points to those just listed for the ideal ocean harbor and we have the conditions for the ideal ocean port:

1. Mechanical facilities adequate for handling commodities and passengers
2. Location upon or close to the main world trade routes
3. A productive and easily accessible hinterland
4. A consuming hinterland

Recognition by business men of the critical importance of these factors in port development is well illustrated in a newspaper advertisement of the Port of Jacksonville, Florida. It is reproduced below, as typical of the newer attitude toward the utilization of fundamental facts in advertising ports. (Fig. 32.)

Types of Ports.—Ocean ports may be classified into four types according to their natural physical setting, namely, (1) open roadstead, (2) bay, (3) river, and (4) bay and river. The port of Valparaiso illustrates type one, Rio de Janeiro, type two, London, type three, and New York, type four.

The open roadstead may sometimes be converted into a good port by the construction of breakwaters, as has been done at Cherbourg and Trieste. It rarely offers the same opportunity for development found in the other three types. Invariably, it is more susceptible to storm winds. The maintenance of deep channels generally presents a difficult, not to say costly problem. The bay type may prove quite satisfactory, particularly when well enclosed and when protected from both storm waves and winds. The river type has numerous advantages over the first two, especially if the river may be ascended a considerable distance as in the case of the rivers on which London, Hamburg, and Stettin are located. These ports, however, frequently suffer from lack of spacious turning basins, from silting, from a large tidal range, from early ice formation, or from lack of space for dock and warehouse construction. The bay and river combination, best exemplified by New York City, offers the advantage of both the river and bay types and at the same time relief from their respective handicaps. This type may not be without some disadvantages, of course, but the ideal port does not exist.

Mechanical Facilities.—The post-war period has seen a greater growth of aggressive port competition than has any other period in the world's modern trade era. New countries came into being with new or revived

FIG. 32. NEWSPAPER ADVERTISEMENT
(*Ohio State Journal.*)

ports while in long established countries old ports assumed new vigor and significance. In all of them the mechanical equipment for effective handling of cargo and quick dispatch of ships has been advertised to prospective port users. Probably at no time in international trade rivalry has this phase of port development received so much attention or has it been given so much publicity. The number of five-ton or fifty-ton cranes, the arrangement of quays, tracks, and warehouses with reference to each other, the capacity of warehouses for a variety of goods, as well as their facilities for quick handling of commodities appear foremost among the characteristics of the ports which the port authorities or others in charge emphasize. In a handbook published by one of our Atlantic port centers one may read important headings such as "Discharging and Loading Cargo," "Wharves and Warehouses," "Railroads Serving the Port," "Communications," and other subjects indicative of the recognition by this port of the part which facilities play in attracting trade. Again, in a special pamphlet descriptive of a European free port the illustrations and text treat of "Cranes," "Warehouses," "Railway tracks," "Warehouse for Customs Clearance and Dispatch of Goods by Rail," and other phases of the port's equipment.

Location.—The importance of location with reference to the main trade routes, both sea and land, can not be overestimated. While it is generally true that ships go where they can get cargoes, they go usually when they can get them at a profit. To operate profitably, ships must be assured of freight. To carry goods in one direction only, returning in water ballast to the original point of departure or proceeding with an empty bottom from the port of delivery to another one far removed, soon lays up the ship, for under these circumstances profits vanish. Hence, a port in hope of development must lie upon routes which ships find profitable to traverse and which are frequented by ships from many parts of the earth.

A striking instance illustrating the locational element is associated with the Russian port of Alexandrovsk at the base of the Kola peninsula on the Arctic Ocean. This port, constructed during the War as an emergency port in the hope of getting supplies into Russia just before the fatal revolution (1917), has attracted a negligible trade. It is far removed from the trade centers of northwestern Europe and its poor access to a still poorer hinterland not only precludes a return load for ships that bring cargoes, but the environment, devoid of a consuming population, can consume only small quantities of goods. Prospects for development here are slight.

A Productive Hinterland Easily Accessible.—A harbor may possess ideal physical conditions, but unless the surplus products of its hinterland can be brought economically to it, the harbor cannot develop into a port of consequence. The importance of an easily accessible hinterland is illustrated by the ports of Boston and New York City.

Both ports are equidistant from the products of the Upper Mississippi Valley reckoned in miles via Albany and Buffalo. With respect to time, however, New York City is nearer, particularly in winter, because of the topographic differences between the trans-Massachusetts and the Hudson Valley routes. Across Massachusetts the 2,000 foot Berkshire highland must be crossed if the southern route is followed, or the five and one half-mile-long Hoosac tunnel penetrated if the northern route is sought. Numerous curves and deep cuts, the latter frequently choked in winter by heavy snow drifts, reduce speed and materially increase the time between Albany and Boston over that between Albany and New York City.

Granted, however, that the inconvenience to the railroads of the highlands in the immediate hinterland of Boston is not sufficient to favor New York, there is the all-water route from the interior to New York City. Canal boats may make the entire distance to the latter port without transfer of cargo, whereas the nearest points to Boston which the canal route serves are Troy and Albany. This connection with the hinterland has not only provided New York City with freight for which Boston could offer no competition, but it has influenced freight rates in favor of New York City and has undoubtedly contributed freight, through its psychological effect upon shippers who mentally follow the New York State Barge Canal-Hudson River route to New York City without consideration for Boston.

One might suppose that the location of Boston 179 miles nearer European channel ports than New York City would prove a distinct advantage for Boston. The time and convenience factors on the land in favor of New York City apparently offset the difference in sea distance. Furthermore, the historical advantage which the port of New York City has enjoyed through the relative ease of communication with the highly productive Mississippi Valley hinterland, first by road, then by canal and lake, and finally by rail and plane has worked to her benefit. Even non-geographic elements such as preferential or equalized freight rates could not offset this geographic setting. Hence, into the port of New York City have poured the products of the rich "Middle West," in preference to Boston, Philadelphia and Baltimore.

A Consuming Hinterland.—Since trade means exchange, obviously people can not confine their efforts to export only. They must also import. Hence, the conception of a consuming hinterland becomes of moment in port development since ships will favor those ports in which they can dispose of full cargoes. To the ship owners as well as the shippers a vessel which can carry cargo on inbound trips as well as outbound means economical operation and, hence, more profits. Furthermore, such exchange possibilities mean better and more frequent service to the ports.

On the other hand, we have hinterlands which do not produce an exportable surplus, but which, nevertheless, import for domestic consumption. The region about Helsinki, Finland, is a case in point. Frequently, ships put in with cargoes for delivery and then move on to nearby ports such as Kotka, Wiipuri, or Åbo to complete their outbound cargo. The value of Helsinki's exports equals about one-fifth of the imports. Helsinki is Finland's principal import center, attracting nearly 30 per cent of the country's total.

Some might argue that a producing hinterland necessarily consumes. That is true in general terms for a nation but does not necessarily apply in detail to the hinterland of a port. For example, Riga in Latvia serves as one of the world's greatest exporters of flax, but her hinterland which produces this product is too poor to purchase much. Consequently, while ships call for a load of flax they cannot always bring a load of something else for exchange. If the people could consume more, more trade would develop and the port could progress at a rate commensurate with its desires. The port is favorably located near many others which can consume partial cargoes, thus offsetting to some extent the handicap of a poor consuming hinterland. Many ports in the United States show a decided excess of exports over imports. In 1929 Portland, Oregon, shipped thirteen times as many tons as it imported, the exports consisting mostly of lumber and grains; Mobile's shipments nearly doubled its receipts; and Houston's exports exceeded its imports by a ratio of nearly twelve to one, its chief exports having been cotton and petroleum.

Thus the phenomenon of unbalance with respect to consumption and production is not at all uncommon. Likewise, we can appreciate that where there is consumption as well as production, especially to the point of balance, the port serving the area is likely to possess a distinct trade advantage over neighboring ports whose unbalance characterizes their hinterlands.

Balanced Trade.—For statistical purposes, the trade of ocean ports is classified into coastwise and foreign or transoceanic. So far as concerns the class of goods exchanged, there may be no material difference, that is, both kinds of trade may involve foodstuffs, raw materials, manufactures, or other products. The character of the particular com-

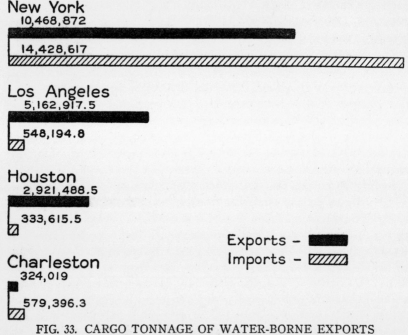

FIG. 33. CARGO TONNAGE OF WATER-BORNE EXPORTS
AND IMPORTS

(1925-1930 Cargo tons of 2,240 pounds)

The unbalance of trade in some ports is strikingly portrayed\ in this graph. Whereas the traffic in the ports of New York and Charleston approaches a balance that at Los Angeles and Houston points to the high productivity of the respective hinterlands on the one hand and their low consuming capacity on the other.

modities will naturally depend upon the country of origin and the parties concerned in the transaction.

In some countries "entrepôt" trade is singled out from the rest. For example, England lists the entrepôt trade of its ports separately from its foreign trade. Again, "colonial" trade is occasionally distinguished in port statistics in order to emphasize the part which a country's colonies play in its total commerce. In pre-war days Germany listed its colonial trade; France and England continue to list theirs separately.

A survey of our own ocean ports reveals that those with hinterlands of densest population and maximum productivity in a variety of commodities approach closest to a balanced trade. For the year ending June, 1929, the last outstanding foreign trade year, the Atlantic Coast ports of Portland, Boston, New York City, Philadelphia, Baltimore, Charleston, Savannah, and Jacksonville, showed an approach to a balanced trade with slightly over 60 per cent of their trade represented by imports. The Gulf ports Houston, Galveston, New Orleans, Mobile, and Pensacola combined, record imports approximating 43 per cent of their total trade. In contrast, the major Pacific coast ports, including Los Angeles, Seattle, Portland and Tacoma, showed imports equal only to about 20 per cent of their total trade in which such bulky goods as petroleum, lumber, and grain figured as the dominant exports.

These trade figures for the three groups of ports are just what one might anticipate, viewed in the light of the hinterlands which they serve. The Atlantic ports serve a hinterland of about eighty-nine millions of people, the Gulf ports about twenty-two millions, and the Pacific ports about eleven millions. A certain amount of overlap in population groups exists, but these figures probably approximate closely such totals as might be arrived at if a detailed determination could be made. The values of the manufactures in these districts show the following ratios: 87 per cent of the total value in the Atlantic, approximately 7 per cent in the Gulf ports region, and about 6 per cent in the Pacific district. Of further interest is the location of the center of manufactures, of the major agricultural crops, excepting cotton, the center of total number of farms, and the center of population. All are in the hinterland of the Atlantic ports. (See Fig. 34.)

These data make clear the close relation between the port trade balance and the elements of the area served, more particularly the size of population and diversity of production. Examination of ports in other lands in relation to their respective hinterlands brings to light a similar story. Evidently, any port desirous of expansion must first look to the quality of its producing and consuming hinterland. A survey of this nature will throw light upon the possibilities of a balanced trade if there is no balance now. It will show whether or not the hinterland can be made more inclusive through freight-rate adjustments, so as to bring to the port either population or products or both to the end that port trade expansion may be possible. An investigation of this

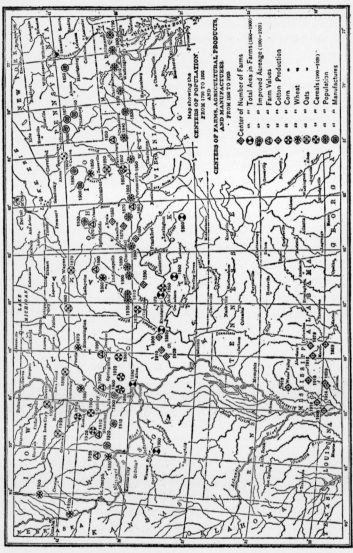

FIG. 34. CENTERS OF FARMS, AGRICULTURAL PRODUCTS, MANUFACTURES, AND POPULATION

The distribution of these critical centers illustrates an apparent correlation between the rise of cities and the productivity of their respective hinterlands. Likewise the reciprocal relation between population concentration and producing areas is evident. These economic elements are of prime importance to ocean ports as well as to interior trade centers. (Courtesy of Bureau of the Census, U. S. A.)

nature scientifically made should enable the citizens of the port center to determine the direction in which they can spend their energies most profitably: whether advertising trade possibilities, expanding the mechanical facilities of the port, or urging ships to come to the port; or whether they should spend time and money in pursuing any of these aggressive avenues.

Freight Rates and Port Growth.—Thus far the geographical aspects of port trade development have been stressed with an occasional incidental reference to freight rate influences. This is not the place for a presentation of the complicated subject of freight-rate structures or the theory of rate making, but it is important that we at least glance at the significance of rates in export and import trade. Oftentimes these through-rates place ports in relatively the same locations with respect to foreign trade, whereas their respective rates on domestic freight recognize distinctly different locations. Then too, such rate adjustments are influential in affecting the degree of balance which the ports may experience.

The special student of the subject of port development will do well to study the theory of rate making and its application. For the purposes of this volume we shall merely cite a single case to illustrate our point. In 1933 the class rates for domestic freight between Chicago and New York City were as follows:

Classes	1	2	3	4	5	6
Costs in cents per 100 lbs.	152	129	106	76	53	42

Between Chicago and Boston they were:

Classes	1	2	3	4	5	6
Costs in cents per 100 lbs.	154	131	108	77	54	42

A differential between these two sets of rates ranged from two cents down. On goods for export or import, however, the Chicago-New York and Chicago-Boston rates were identical and were as follows:

Classes	1	2	3	4	5	6
	143	122	101	73	52	42

So far as export rates alone are concerned, both New York and Boston have identical locations. Furthermore, the export rate from Chicago is lower than the domestic rate for the first five classes. Accordingly, Chicago is relatively nearer European ports than to New York City or Boston when expressed in terms of freight rates applied to the domestic portion of the total distance traveled by the goods.

South Atlantic ports, specifically those south of Cape Hatteras, are all on a parity in relation to class rates on export goods between points in Central Freight Association territory and themselves, but on domestic freight, great variability occurs in the rates. Thus, the hinterlands of these ports may have a dual nature, that is, a foreign-trade and a domestic-trade hinterland, their differentiation determined entirely by the non-geographic element of arbitrary freight-rate setting.

Rank of Ports.—Frequently comparisons are made among the world's ports to emphasize rank. The rating often is based upon value of commerce, sometimes upon cargo tonnage, again upon ships' tonnage, or upon number of ships. Each of these bases presents defects. Little doubt exists in the minds of most persons interested in the ranking of the ports as to first and second place, but the farther down the list the less the certainty in conclusions. First place generally is clear because of the sum total of activities rather than because of leadership in any single direction.

Ship's Tonnage Versus Cargo Tons.—No one would question the rank of the port of New York among those in the United States. The total tonnage of ships in foreign trade entering and clearing in 1929, the last prosperous year before the depression, was 48,830,000, as compared with 45,867,420 entering and clearing the lake port of Duluth-Superior. The cargo tonnage [1] for these ports for the same years was 73,161,000 and 60,386,000 respectively. Thus the discrepancy between ships tonnage and cargo tonnage is readily appreciated in this comparison. Again, among world ports in pre-war days, London was conceded first place by many, and so far as value of commerce was concerned this was true, for it totaled $2,003,986,000 whereas New York's total was $1,966,257,000. On the other hand, the total entrances and clearances at London were 25.1 millions of net registered tons as compared with 28.9 millions at the port of New York.

Ship's tonnage is a poor criterion for comparative purposes because it does not indicate what is in the hold of a ship. It is not an index to actual trade. A ship may enter a port with water in ballast, in which case its registered tonnage is just the same as though there were cargo in the hold. Consequently, the significance of such a ship with respect to the port's trade can not be of the same quality as it would be if it held

---

[1] The commodities handled at Duluth-Superior are primarily coal, iron ore, lumber, and grain while at New York City they are multitudinous in type.

cargo instead of water. To be sure, such a ship may be calling for cargo, but one-way traffic does not possess the value of two-way traffic.

Cargo totals represent a better basis for port rank than ship's net registered tonnage. We meet, however, the difficulty of determining total weight, and even so, since commodities vary in unit weight, unless we compare the total weight of similar commodities, the comparative figures still remain unreliable. Many kinds of goods are measured by volume and some by the piece. This fact still further complicates the problem.

Value of Commerce.—If dollar value is used as the basis for comparisons, conclusions will be subject to error since all goods do not possess corresponding unit values. A cargo like coal may have a low unit value while package freight has a notably higher value. Coal may play just as significant a part in the welfare of the community as package freight or even a greater part, but in terms of value it would not give a port high rank as a trade center. Yet value among ports characterized by a decidedly mixed freight throws some light upon rank. Value, however, in successive years changes, owing to varying prices and exchange rates; therefore, the comparisons of value for a series of years must be made with caution.

Number of Ships.—The number of ships entering and clearing a port, provided those of a purely local character are not counted, indicates to a degree the extent to which a port may be busy in handling ships but not necessarily the amount of trade transacted. In the case of a port like Los Angeles from which nearly all the exports are petroleum, no return cargo appears. Petroleum ships are not suited to the carriage of other products nor can the port hinterland absorb much. So, while the number of ships entering and clearing is sizeable, it reflects neither the trade activity nor its nature. Further, the fact that a ship enters with cargo does not mean that the ship has a full cargo. Again, the number of ships entering and clearing generally are equal, owing to the fact that the ships that put into a port to secure cargo are also the ships that clear port. Hence, the number of ships plus size does not give an accurate statement of total freight.

Standard Classification.—No satisfactory basis has yet been arrived at for determining the rank of ports. Some attempt has been made by an international congress (Brussels, 1913) to standardize the method of determining values and to agree upon the kind of ton (2,240 pounds) to be used for measurement in order to make possible a reasonable comparison of the foreign trade of world ports. Perhaps two elements should enter into the ranking of ports as trade centers which do not now receive recognition, namely, domestic trade and size of population served. These figures combined with those just discussed should furnish fairly conclusive data relative to the ranking of the ports.

We have pointed to the fact that trade is a two-way affair. Commodities, with few exceptions, in foreign trade are merely domestic goods going out of the country or goods coming in to become a part of the domestic flow. Therefore, it must be true that, unless a port is engaged in entrepôt trade only, and that is hardly possible, its foreign trade is an integral part of its domestic trade and in proportion to the activities of its combined foreign and domestic trade it holds high or low rank among the ports of the world. The size of population served is helpful in determining a port's rank because population gravitates toward a port which attracts ships and goods from diverse countries. A large population in itself, however, does not necessarily imply a large trade activity, because the purchasing power of the people is a critical factor. Bombay, for example, with its hinterland containing a vast, poor population is not to be compared with New York City whose population hinterland is smaller in numbers but richer in purchasing power. A small population with few exceptions, may be interpreted as indicative of slight trade, especially in respect to a variety of commodities handled. A small population would not, however, necessarily imply an inefficient port. Port efficiency must not be confused with the volume of total trade handled.

Ports and National Growth.—We have suggested that a port often reflects the climax achievements of a nation, for in it may be gathered not only its most modern private and public structures, and its best shops, but also homes of its leaders in business, in politics, in arts, in literature, and in the sciences. While all ports of a nation can not be equally well equipped in every direction, yet most of the active centers share in the elements of leadership. It is significant, however, that trade usually "blazes a trail" for cultural development, and in proportion to the amount and nature of a port's trade the country in which the port is located reflects the attainments of the finer things in life.

The port provides for contact with all parts of the world. For this reason, no aspiring national people can feel content if it must use a foreign port for the conduct of its trade. A nation is dissatisfied if the utilization of its port necessitates passage through foreign territory. Such arrangements, encouraging unrest and irritation, have frequently precipitated trouble among nations and at times have led to wars.

Among the prizes sought during the World War were seaports. Poland was promised an outlet upon the Baltic if she would cast her lot with the Allies. The creation of the Danzig Corridor was the reward after the war ended. Italy was promised Trieste, and, although the promise was not kept immediately after the cessation of hostilities, she acquired the port through the patriotic fervor of D'Annunzio, whereupon her allies and the associated powers permitted her to retain it. Lithuania, without a good seaport, sought Memel, formerly German owned. While the League of Nations and allied powers took the matter of the disposition of Memel under advisement, patriotic Lithuanians wrested it from temporary French possession and placed it under Lithuanian sovereignty. Subsequently, the action was approved by the interested powers. Ambitious Czechoslovakia, without sea contact, has been temporarily satisfied with the internationalization of the Elbe and a long term lease on docks at Hamburg, while mountainous Switzerland, with whose name the word "navy" has often been humorously associated, has insisted upon the preservation of its rights upon the Rhine River where it operates a fleet of barges to the North Sea.

Not all the nations, however, have fared equally well by way of seaport property. Isolated Hungary and Austria can not reconcile themselves to their present status and even Czechoslovakia would much prefer ownership of a port than her present arrangement. The U. S. S. R. has seaports, but they are far removed from the main trade routes and are likewise poor strategically. Old Russia struggled for years to better her condition in this respect, and it is said her war with Japan was caused by a desire for an ice-free port. Her position to-day is worse than ever, for many good ports such as Tallinn, Riga, Libau, and Windau, all on the Baltic, have been lost to her.

Nations without ports may feel like persons in straitjackets. They can maneuver somewhat, but have not complete freedom of activity. Since trade constitutes the very life blood of a country, any obstacle to its easy circulation militates against the rate as well as amount of progress.

CHAPTER IX

TYPES OF OCEAN PORTS

Most ports differ from each other not only with respect to their approach to the ideal but also with reference to the nature of their business, their traditions, and their special problems. We cannot discuss here all of the earth's great ocean ports, but we can investigate four of them, each of which incorporates features distinct from those of the others and which together represent practically all the earth's assortment of port trade centers. They include respectively a terminal port, an entrepôt, a free port, and an inland port.

New York—A Terminal Port

When Hendrick Hudson visited the site of New York City in 1609, he was so favorably impressed that he remarked, "Its soil is the finest for cultivation that I ever in my life set foot upon and the situation is well adapted for shipping." The history of the harbor and port development bears testimony to Hudson's vision. Few ports have shown a corresponding rapidity of growth in commerce, albeit they have in many instances forged ahead of New York with respect to modernity of equipment. That it has been able to hold its own in the face of inadequate equipment in some of its parts is indicative of the presence of certain fundamental influences upon commercial growth greater even than port equipment.

The Natural Environment.—New York City's supremacy may be attributed to several causes, (1) its location opposite Europe where the North Atlantic begins to narrow rapidly, (2) its accessibility to the Mississippi Valley via the Hudson River-Mohawk Valley Pass, (3) its superior harbor.

New York City's location upon the Atlantic at a place where the continent swings rapidly to the eastward toward Europe gives it a distinct advantage over ports to the south. Combined with this favorable location is the Hudson-Mohawk Pass already noted. Competition of other Atlantic ports with New York has met with little success except as freight-rate adjustments equalized to some extent the trade

120

basis of all the ports. But even with adjustments of this sort New York has remained supreme. In normal years the vessel tonnage in foreign trade entering and clearing the harbor equals 25 per cent of the total tonnage at all ports, the value of its imports and exports ranges from 40 per cent to 50 per cent of our entire foreign trade, and immigrant entrances into the United States passing through this port total between 50 and 60 per cent of all entrants.

Critical Influences in Growth.—The effect of the Hudson-Mohawk Pass which invited the building of the Erie Canal, opened in 1825, is revealed in the population statistics for New York City. The decennial increase between 1810 and 1820 was 37.3 per cent and for the United States as a whole it was nearly the same, 33.1 per cent. But between 1820 and 1830 the gain for New York City rose to 63.8 per cent. From 1830 to 1840 it was 61.5 per cent, and in the period 1840 to 1850 it was 64.9 per cent. The increase in the last decade probably was due to the combined effect of the Canal and the gradual penetration of the railroad to the Great Lakes, having finally reached Dunkirk on Lake Erie in 1851. The rate of growth for the period 1820 to 1850 was over twice that for the entire United States. The canal made the Great Lakes region more easily accessible than ever before. Valuable forests and cheap fertile lands enticed European immigrants who entered at New York City, the gateway to this easy road to the interior.[1]

For all the activities of the increased population, as well as for the new business transacted upon the waterway connection with the interior, provision had to be made at the Port of New York. The ease of communication via this route as compared with all others was so overwhelmingly in favor of its use that other Atlantic ports felt its handicapping effect. Railroad development after the Civil War, the first successful trans-Atlantic Cable which was laid in 1866, and the overland telegraph and telephone following in quick succession contributed further to New York City's supremacy. While these last facilities benefited other centers too, the momentum which New York City had acquired in consequence of her location on both the interior and transoceanic routes made these elements even more important to her than to her rivals.

Present Status of the Port.—The port district, which includes practically all the local waters, accommodates local ship traffic augmented

---

[1] In 1825, the number of immigrants who entered the country was 10,199; in 1830, five years after the opening of the Canal 23,322 arrived; and by 1835 the arrivals reached 45,374 and were rapidly increasing.

by oversea ships totaling about 44,000,000 net-registered tons annually. Nearly 200 companies operate ships into and out of the port. In 1929 there were 6,978 clearances of transoceanic vessels. Steamship services include 159 foreign routes. Of the forty-four lines engaged in coast-wise trade, thirteen specialize in Atlantic to Pacific Coast business.

The physical conditions of the port very nearly approach the ideal as set up in a previous chapter. On the whole, the port is spacious, deep, and free from strong currents. The mean tidal range of the outer harbor is only 4.6 feet, and that of the inner harbor not over 6.9 feet. The tidal currents range in velocity from as low as .36 to a maximum of 5.40 statute miles per hour. While silting occurs, it is not serious. The bottom offers favorable anchorage and permits of easy dredging to required channel depths and widths. The entrance channel is straight and provides a depth of forty feet. The harbor is generally ice-free but flow-ice occasionally descends from the upper Hudson. Strong winds occur now and then, the maximum ever recorded attaining a velocity of ninety-two miles per hour. Fogs average three days per month from December to March; two days in April, May, October, and November; and one to no days from June to September. Smoke sometimes produces the equivalent of a fog (smog) for a few hours in the early morning on calm days. Few of the world's ports engaged in major operations can boast of harbors with correspondingly effective natural endowments.

The physical arrangement of the port must be viewed from two angles, namely, the land side and the water side. Considering the land first, we find the major activities of the port are transacted upon the island of Manhattan which originally constituted all of New York City, but to-day is only one of five boroughs. The island is thirteen miles long, and its maximum width is two miles. With a population of nearly 2,000,000 people located upon so small an area, congestion is severe. The rectangular street plan with a few diagonals facilitates traffic movement somewhat, but, nevertheless, the space restrictions exert a strong retarding influence. Subways and elevated roads have afforded some relief, and subbasements, thanks to the igneous rock structure of the island, extend to depths of three and four floors, assisting further in relieving the surface tangle. However, as long as the focal center of the trading area is confined to the island, a solution to the problem of reducing congestion can not be anticipated. At best, limited relief may be introduced occasionally.

Several proposals have been made for the physical expansion of

FIG. 35. NEW YORK—A TERMINAL PORT

The crowding of commercial activity is evident. Tall office buildings encroach upon dock frontage and interrupt the free flow of land traffic. The long docks projecting into the bordering rivers restrict the water area. The dense population of the locality and the additional people in the hinterland together absorb full ship cargoes and also provide return cargoes. The port serves as a terminal for the world's ships, but crowding tends to interfere with efficient dispatch of trade. (Photo by Aerial Explorations, Inc.)

the harbor and with it, of course, port facilities. Among them are the utilization of Jamaica Bay; the establishment of a port at the eastern end of Long Island; and the development of the Newark Bay, Passaic River, Hackensack River area east of Newark, New Jersey. Staten Island is being gradually brought under port control and its further use fostered. The filling in of the water area between the southern end of Manhattan and Governors Island has been suggested as a means of providing additional dock sites for the already crowded Upper Bay portion of the harbor.

Arguments may be readily advanced pro and con with respect to these various projects. It seems, however, from the standpoint of the most effective handling of the enormous tonnage originating in the hinterland to the west of the Hudson River, especially the tonnage for export purposes, that the improvement of the Newark territory is most logical. Ships sail as far inland as the waters will allow. If they can reach the Newark area, they will do so. Here they can pick up return cargoes and avoid the extra handling which now occurs by having to transfer freight either to Manhattan or Brooklyn docks.

The tendency of ships to penetrate far into the interior has encouraged the citizens of Albany to develop an ocean port. While this port will undoubtedly attract much shipping, its remoteness from New York, with practically no intermediate trade centers which can provide consequential oversea freight or absorb incoming freight, will take relatively little trade from the port of New York.

The water area (175 square miles) which penetrates into New Jersey territory has until recent years served most of the port needs fairly successfully. But the World War demonstrated its inadequacy in times of stress when peak loads are forced upon it. The navigating channels are narrow, and Manhattan lies along the eastern side of the port whereas the major part of the export freight moves in from the west. These elements make for extreme crowding.

Since bridges may be constructed across the Hudson only under conditions which will not interrupt navigation, just one has been erected—the George Washington Bridge. Because of the excessive cost of such a bridge, few more are likely to be built. This one can bring only a small amount of relief to the total flow of land traffic. The railroad tubes and the new tube for vehicular traffic render some assistance in the handling of the port's business but ferries must for a long time continue to carry the bulk of the freight and passenger traffic in the port.

Water Connections with the Hinterland.—We have already noted the influence of the Erie Canal, known as the New York State Barge Canal, since its improvement by the state at a cost of about $155,000,000. On it seven companies operate barges out of the port of New York. A region of much less economic importance than the Mississippi Valley and Great Lakes Region may be reached via the Hudson River, Lake Champlain, Richelieu River, and Chambly Canal. This route may be construed as possessing greater military than commercial value, inasmuch as the region penetrated is scantily populated and the natural resources are of limited value.

Northeastward from New York City, a water route made up of Long Island Sound waters, Cape Cod Canal, and the open Atlantic provide excellent ship communication with New England, more especially with Providence and Boston. A major portion of twenty local lines operate in this service.

To the southward the Delaware river and Raritan Canal offer possible barge connections with Philadelphia. Easily accessible coastal waters provide facilities for ships of major size to ply between the port of New York and most of the larger ports along the south Atlantic coast of the country.

These numerous water routes, radiating from the port to all of the important inland and coastal regions, contribute to the volume of the port's trade and likewise increase the local problem of effective freight handling. These routes, furthermore, give to New York a position unique among the Atlantic ports and assure its preëminence for all time.

Of importance, too, is the vast world hinterland available by transoceanic routes to New York. It is not a feature exclusive to this port but is of utmost consequence to its trade development. The ease of access from the sea and the low-cost communication with its vast wealthy hinterland are assets of enormous value to the commercial interests of the trade center. This combination of circumstances moderates the intensity of competition of neighboring ocean ports.

Rail Facilities.—While the port of New York ranks among the world's most notable ports, it is not one of the great railroad centers. Twelve lines reach it, not all independently owned, only three actually gaining direct entrance to the city, namely, the New York Central, the Pennsylvania, and the New York, New Haven and Hartford. The remaining nine terminate on the west side of the port. The latter roads provide ferries for carrying bulk freight or the cars themselves across the water to points on Manhattan or Long Island. While this arrangement makes for the ultimate landing of goods at their destination, it introduces both a delay in delivery and a risk involving either loss in goods or damage resulting from frequent handling.

The West Shore Railroad, listed as one of the twelve, follows the west shore of the Hudson River northward to Albany, thence turning west. It is operated by the New York Central. The Long Island Railroad is affiliated with the Pennsylvania; and the New York, Ontario and Western Railroad uses the tracks of the West Shore. The remaining roads are the Erie; the Lehigh Valley; the Delaware, Lackawanna and Western; the Central of New Jersey; the Baltimore and Ohio; and the Reading.

These lines, though few in number, serve the most densely populated area of the United States and likewise that part of the country which contains the major portion of the population. It puts the port of New York in easy and quick communication with both a consuming and producing hinterland—a territory in which the per capita purchasing power ranks among the world's highest, if not the highest, and where the capacity to produce a surplus of goods of almost unlimited variety is second to none.

The Port Authority.—Concerning the expansion of the port to the boundaries of two states, and even a third if those portions in Long Island Sound adjoining Connecticut be included, numerous problems arose whose solution had to be sought in the light of a single physical area. Therefore, provision for some type of management leading toward unification of efforts in port development became imperative. To this end the Port of New York Authority was organized in 1921. As yet, its jurisdiction, highly restricted in many respects, applies only to the properties of New York and New Jersey. The Authority took its cue from the Port of London Authority which we shall describe later. The powers of the American organization are much less extensive, its mechanics of operation much more circumscribed, and, in general, its effective influence curtailed. Nevertheless, it represents a distinct forward step in port development and has certainly justified itself thus far.

The membership consists of twelve commissioners, six from each state, selected by the respective Governors. They serve without compensation and are guided by a code of principles pertaining to the development and government of the port. Although the Authority receives its powers to act from the States, it functions as a self-sustaining public corporation privileged to issue bonds to finance its various under-takings. It has no dictatorial powers applicable to port improvements but may initiate programs and make recommendations to the States, the United States, and to private interests using the port. In proportion to the prestige and confidence which it has established, its suggestions are adopted.

Among the outstanding achievements of the Port of New York Authority may be noted the construction of a Union Inland Freight Station, facilitating freight movement in a manner to remove conges-tion from the water front; the Holland Tunnel under the Hudson River for vehicles; the George Washington Bridge; Goethals Bridge; Outerbridge Crossing; and Bayonne Bridge. In addition, it has worked out a "Comprehensive Plan" for the coördination of the railroads and now has under construction another vehicular tunnel to be known as the Midtown-Hudson Tunnel. We should not overlook the fact that all of this work, accomplished in an amazingly brief period, was financed through bond issues rather than by government funds.

After operating for 150 years under rival political interests, men with vision were able to convince others that, after all, the waters of the port constitute a unit and that efficient use of them was impossible under the methods of the past. Nature does not recognize political divi-sions and as rapidly as man acts in accordance he usually profits.

Terminal Port.—New York functions as a terminal rather than an entrepôt. Its entrepôt trade is negligible. The port is not inci-dental to any other center but lies at the end of transoceanic trade routes. Ships coming into the port come because the port is their pri-mary destination and not because the port is upon their route to some other trade center. Ships put into New York because the cargoes are definitely assigned to this port or they put in to it because they seek definitely scheduled outgoing cargoes. In this respect it differs strik-ingly from Rotterdam, Hamburg, London, and many other outstanding European ports. Careful consideration of these facts must lead one to the conclusion that the free zone, opened in February, 1937, the first in the history of the nation, may not yield the returns anticipated by some.

Although the port is a terminus viewed in the light of oceanic trade, its service to the hinterland is highly important, and from this point of view it is a transfer center for land and water cargoes.

A Manufacturing Center.—The activities of the port are not limited to collecting and distributing finished products. We have hinted else-

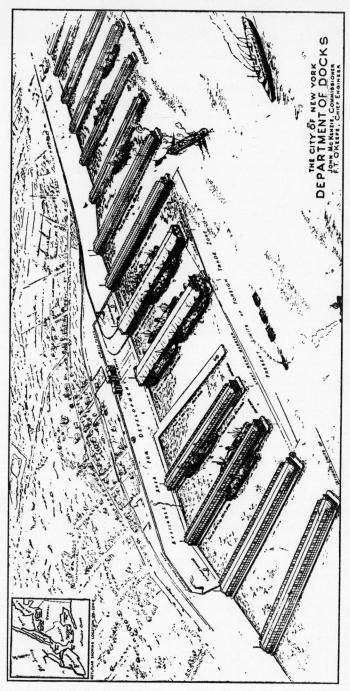

FIG. 36. THE FREE ZONE OF THE PORT OF NEW YORK

Only two of these piers have been converted to free port use for the present. The zone is located along the northeastern shores of Staten Island.

where that here is a trade center which combines commercial and industrial elements.

New York City itself is the greatest manufacturing center in the world. The number of establishments in 1929 was 29,446, employing 563,249 persons. In the "Industrial Area," which includes essentially all the area contiguous to the port, the number of establishments in 1929 was 36,401 and the number of employees 918,206. The variety of commodities is great. The producing units tend to be small, no doubt due to space limitations and high land values. The enormity of the local labor and consuming market is obvious. Add to this fact the ready accessibility of the port to all parts of the continuous and discontinuous hinterland and we can easily appreciate why industrial growth has been so vigorously effected.

London—An Entrepôt Port

The Thames River finds its way into the North Sea through an estuary bordered by mud flats and swamps. At a point upstream where it narrows and flows through a well-drained upland, the stream was crossed in Roman times and here near the site of the present London Bridge, a settlement of "Llyn-din" grew into the world's most important entrepôt—London. The Romans, en route to the tin deposits of Wales, stopped in London and traded there with the natives and others from nearby points.

After the decline of the Roman Empire, the port had to deal with numerous strong European groups such as the Danes, the Normans, the Dutch, and others. In the medieval period, distinguished by the rise of the powerful Hanseatic League, the growth of London was further stimulated, for, although the city never became a full-fledged member of the League, it benefited by contact with it.

Still greater opportunities were ahead when the Americas were discovered. The European world faced about, shifted its interests from the Mediterranean lands, and focused its attention upon trade possibilities with the New World. London's position acquired an entirely new relationship, for, instead of representing a location upon the periphery of the trading world, it now found itself in the very center of activities. This shift, coupled with England's economic policy, assured to London permanence in commercial importance.

London's location upon the Thames whose estuary is opposite the deltaic mouths of the Rhine, Europe's busiest waterway, gives it a commanding position. Likewise, its proximity to the English Channel and direct access to the North Sea, strategic highways that have from early times ranked among the world's primary avenues of commerce, have brought to it trade advantages of which few other trade centers can boast. Even the port of New York does not enjoy a comparable location. London faces the continent of Europe and is sufficiently close to enjoy the qualities of a continental port yet is separated from the mainland by a narrow waterway which affords it a degree of immunity from the military dangers besetting rival mainland centers.

The Great Entrepôt.—Numerous commodities originating in parts of the British Empire are shipped to London for redistribution throughout the United Kingdom as well as to the rest of the world. Tea, spices, cocoa, ivory, and Australian wool are items which find their way to London only. Practically fifty per cent of the entrepôt trade of the United Kingdom is handled at this trade center.

Not all of the entrepôt business is confined to goods of British origin. England possesses a magnet in its excellent bunker coal which attracts to it ships of other nations. Cargo carriers being assured a supply of bunker coal which will serve their own needs and which can also be easily sold anywhere favor English ports. Great Britain, quite willing to sell its coal at a reasonable profit, assumes the risk of purchasing goods for immediate resale or for ultimate sale. Thus, its entrepôt wares are augmented and its trade correspondingly expanded.

To-day the significance of bunker coal as a trade magnet is not as great as in earlier years, for the tramp steamer carries only a negligible percentage of the world's goods. Most shipments have a predetermined delivery point. Then, too, oil as fuel for ships is coming into increased use, but as yet the British are not in a position to offer preferential advantages in this product.

Decline as an Entrepôt.—London has enjoyed her entrepôt service largely because she has been influential in the policies of a nation possessing a world empire. The British merchant marine, directed largely from this port, has been the dominant, if not always the exclusive, carrier of wares from the Orient, from South Africa, from Australia, and other regions. It has favored London as a center of concentration to which many merchants have come whose own governments had not yet effected direct steamship connections with the world's ports. But those days of exclusive trade contacts are fast waning and with them the entrepôt. Other reasons for this change will be noted when we consider the free port.

One of the most influential elements which makes the decline of the entrepôt slow is tradition and the reluctance of traders to relinquish their hold upon long established trading habits. So London continues to be known as the world's largest tea market, the most important ivory-auction center, a wool market without significant competition, and an exclusive meeting-place for buyers of still other commodities. And yet, such products as rubber, coffee, and tobacco are facing competition from other ports.

While an important percentage of London's trade is of an entrepôt character, the port could much more easily forego all of this trade than that derived from its domestic industries. In other words, the first line of trade defense depends upon the strength of the business originating at home.

Even though entrepôt trade dwindles to quite small proportions, its effect upon trade in goods of local origin remains important. Buyers who may come to London to purchase entrepôt wares may become interested in goods made in England. As the port sees its middlemen's services commanding less attention, every effort is being put forth to substitute some features in trade which will continue to attract the world's buyers.

Physical Character of the Port.—London is a river port. The major activities of its seventy miles of frontage are concentrated within about ten miles of London Bridge. Twenty-six miles further down the river are Tilbury Docks, the nearest point to London which the world's largest ships can reach. At the latter docks, a water depth of thirty-eight to forty-two feet is attainable while at London Bridge it drops to fourteen feet at low water. The tidal range is twenty-one feet, a severe handicap to shipping. Special locks and piers have had to be constructed at a tremendous cost to meet this varying water level. These adjustments can never give to the port the same advantages which a tide-free or a low-tidal-range port could give. The port is virtually ice-free. In severe winters thin ice forms, but traffic may be readily maintained. Currents are not bothersome nor is there a high frequency of strong winds. Anchorage is satisfactory but the port lacks that roominess which is desirable to give ships an abundance of turning space. Fogs, especially when mixed with local smoke, constitute a handicap to shipping throughout the length of the port and particularly at its entrance where the shallows of the Thames estuary and the low elevation of the North Sea coast-line increase the hazard. In this locality probably more ships meet with disaster than on any other area of the North Sea.

A Barge Port.—The high tidal range has necessitated the use of

FIG. 37. THE PORT OF LONDON AUTHORITY

In this magnificent structure are housed the offices of that unique board of control of the port of London, known as the Port Authority. Its powers are much more extensive and inclusive than those of the Port of New York Authority. Non-salaried and non-political, it functions efficiently. The development of the port during the past quarter century must be credited to this institution. (From *The Nautical Gazette.*)

FIG. 38. THE PORT OF NEW YORK AUTHORITY

This massive structure houses not only the offices of the Authority but offers warehousing and sales facilities as well as conveniences for shipping. Its major function is to facilitate the movement of freight throughout the land portion of the port.

This terminal is one of a series to be completed eventually, each strategically located with respect to traffic flow. (Fairchild Aerial Surveys, Inc.)

barges. When the tide goes out, portions of the river bottom are exposed. Obviously, ships with narrow keels cannot remain erect under these conditions and therefore dare not venture long in waters which vanish twice during a twenty-four-hour day. Locks along the river banks provide against the receding tide, but do not in themselves allow of continuous loading or unloading.

The barge with its broad flat bottom meets the situation perfectly, navigating until the water depth falls to six or eight feet. In some instances this permits the barge to transfer cargo throughout the entire period of tidal change. Should the barge, however, be located in a portion of the river from which the water recedes entirely, it comes to stable rest and upon the return of the tide floats again. Over 10,000 barges serve the trade of the port of London.

The Port of London Authority.—In our discussion of the port of New York, reference was made to its Port Authority as having been patterned after the Port of London Authority. The latter commission has been so successful in its administration and development of the port that a résumé of its organization and functions is worth recording.

The Authority has twenty-eight members, eighteen of whom are elected by "payers of dues" and ten appointed from government bureaus and certain public organizations. The members serve without pay. Its function when established in 1908 was "to unify, reorganize, and to secure the development of the tidal portion of the River Thames, formerly under the jurisdiction of the Thames conservancy. Its permanent function is to preserve and administer the Port."

The Authority not only performs the functions noted but also engages in the warehousing of merchandise, in sorting goods, and otherwise performing important services for private interests as well as providing for the most effective handling of imports and exports. It even provides for the display of goods to prospective buyers and handles the transactions if so desired. A nominal charge is made for these services, but the Authority does not operate for profit. In addition to this revenue, the Authority receives tonnage dues from vessels using the port and certain dues on goods involved in the import and export trade. Its interests focus both upon the trade of the port and the physical development of the harbor.

In the establishment of the Port Authority, London recognizes the growing competition of Bristol, Southampton, and other ports. These centers, particularly Southampton, are more easily reached by ocean traffic than is London. The improved rail connections with London make possible a saving in time for mail and express goods. For example, a ship coming from the west, may enter the roomy Southampton deep water harbor and deliver its cargo to fast trains which reach London in four to six hours, saving a day's sail through the channel, the Straits of Dover, and into the dangerous Thames estuary. The coördination of the parts of the London port and improvement of its facilities through the Port Authority is doing much in the face of keen competition toward maintaining the prestige of London.

London's Stability.—London's hinterland extends to the limits of the British Empire. Hence, the local region within England and Wales constitutes only a small fraction of the total. In contrast with that of most other ports, London's hinterland is largely detached from her, and in consequence the port's stability is always threatened. So long as the world is at peace, this hinterland is secured to her, but in the event of war it may be disturbed partially or entirely. Having a hinterland spread over the earth, producing almost every manner of raw material and finished goods in every season, London enjoys in peace times a degree of stability given to few ports. Her fate, however, is always highly sensitive to the fate of England and the Empire. In order to assure herself of permanent economic independence she has always fostered the policy of British supremacy upon the seas.

To-day, however, aerial navigation has introduced a new element which not only threatens this supremacy but probably has definitely made it no longer possible of complete realization. London is nearer the continent to-day than ever, due to the airplane, and nearer in an uncomfortable sense. Defense against aerial invasion cannot be assured to the degree that defense was possible against a naval attack. Consequently, London merchants must favor continuous peace as never before if they wish to maintain the high commercial rank which their port has heretofore held.

Hamburg—A Free Port

The port of Hamburg, sixty-three miles up from the Elbe River mouth, serves Germany and Czechoslovakia much as London serves England, but its mode of operation differs strikingly from the latter. Hamburg carries the traditions of independence, dating from the rise of the Hanseatic League. Whereas the League began a rapid decline when Columbus' voyage to America turned European eyes westward, Hamburg was destined to acquire further prestige as a commercial center.

FIG. 39. LONDON—A BARGE PORT

One of the most remarkable aspects of the rise of London as a port lies in the fact that its natural handicaps are severe. Its high tidal range has led to the development of special types of barges (12,000 or more) to handle most of the freight in the loading and unloading process. When the tide goes out these barges rest upon the river bed and readily refloat when the tide comes in. (Courtesy of Port of London Authority.)

FIG. 40. THE FREE PORT OF HAMBURG

This free port (in the background) which set the example for all other free ports of to-day, is a heritage of the time when Hamburg was a principal actor in the trade drama of the Hanseatic League. The directors of the port have steadfastly clung to the idea, that the more convenient trade facilities are made for the shipper, the more trade will a port attract. The truth of their philosophy has been upheld by the rise of numerous other free ports, especially in the post-war period. (Courtesy of German Railroads information office, New York.)

The final disintegration of the League near the end of the sixteenth century left a triad of Free Cities—Hamburg, Bremen, and Lübeck—whose history reveals a thrilling and fascinating trade romance. Hamburg's advantageous location and a far-sighted citizenry at once gave her a dominant influence in northwestern Germany and in the general commerce of northwestern Europe.

When the German Zollverein (customs union) was organized, involving free trade among German states, Hamburg and its sister free cities refused to join. Even with the establishment of the Empire in 1871 at the close of the Franco-Prussian War, Hamburg remained outside the customs union, although it became a part of the new monarchy. Later, however, having enjoyed the privileges of the Empire and greatly benefited by its rapidly growing prosperity, she consented to join the Zollverein (1882) on condition that she be allowed to maintain a free port. Although the present tendency is to consider Hamburg as having a *free zone* because all of the port is not free, we are not yielding to that new appellation since the port has been known too many years as a *free port*. A free zone differs from a free port in that the former is a relatively small area set aside to function as a free port, whereas the latter includes the entire port.

Nature of the Port.—Since about seven-eighths of the port is devoted to free-port purposes, a description of the port as a whole has equal application to the free port. It is relatively free from tidal difficulties, the tide having a range of but six and one half feet. It has a depth of twenty-six feet at low tide. While silting is continual, the river depth is maintained without great difficulty. Strong winds and fogs are infrequent and ice rarely causes trouble. The mechanical equipment ranks among the finest in the world. The distance up the river from the sea necessitates several hours of careful navigation. In order to save time for incoming passengers and mail, ships dock at Cuxhaven at the river mouth, an outer port for Hamburg. Last-minute outbound mail is taken on board at Cuxhaven.

Free Port Principle.—When introduced at Hamburg the free port principle was entirely new. The free port permits carriers to unload their wares upon the docks of a fenced-off portion of the port, there to be sorted, converted into different forms, or warehoused without the payment of duty. Sales may be effected, and any goods remaining over may be reloaded and carried to some other port. A tariff is assessed only when the goods pass from the free port into the city. While the free port principle involves a form of free trade, it differs from the latter in that the freedom of its trade concerns a trade center rather than a country and, furthermore, does not mean that goods may enter the country or even the trade center free of duty.

The success of the free port of Hamburg has been so marked and has exerted so large an influence upon the establishment of a similar institution in nearly every European port of consequence and in some non-European ports that it seems worth while to note why the free port was successful at Hamburg and what its advantages are.

Free Port Development.—The vast hinterland of Hamburg extending up the Elbe Valley well into Czechoslovakia and tapping even Austria and Hungary, a territory marked by diversity of habits, customs, and tastes, offers the port of Hamburg an opportunity to serve as a sort of liaison between it and the over-seas world. The network of canals connecting the Elbe and its tributaries with other important waterways such as the Weser, the Oder, and the Wisla (Vistula) Rivers brings the greater portion of central Europe to Hamburg's door.

These waterways, subsequently augmented by the railways, have brought the port into connection with the vast potash resources of the Halle Region and the sugar beet fields in the Magdeburg-Leipzig and Silesian areas. The coal deposits of southeastern Germany attract iron ore and at the same time furnish the basis for a variety of industries in southern and central Germany. Many of these industries afford goods for export which balance the importation of foodstuffs for the ever-growing population. Hamburg has served not only Germany and an important part of pre-war Austria-Hungary but also has acted as a trans-shipment center for the Baltic region. Ports like Lübeck, Stettin, Danzig, Riga, Tallinn, Helsinki, and others have become in a sense outposts for Hamburg and contributors to Hamburg's commerce. In these circumstances a free port at Hamburg was destined to meet with success.

Cargoes come to Hamburg for sale to its hinterland. Prospective buyers go to the port to inspect the goods, unhampered by any port ceremonials involving tariffs which are not paid until the goods reach the country of their destination. Should a German buyer decide to make a purchase he pays the tariff when the goods enter Germany. On the other hand, the buyer may come from Riga. Should he make a purchase, he may have the goods loaded upon a ship scheduled for his port without having paid duty even though they had landed on a German dock. Bonding is unnecessary in a free port. Port dues are levied on ships but these are small. The free port under these conditions clearly is of advantage to both buyer and seller and the owners of the port benefit accordingly.

Since Czechoslovakia has been extended the privilege to lease a portion of the port of Hamburg in consequence of the internationalization of the Elbe River, the Germans in Hamburg may lose some of the free port benefits. Czech trade, no doubt, will be handled by Czechs in the leased section of the port.

Application to the United States.—The growth of Hamburg's free port and the establishment of many others in Europe led a number of persons and organizations in the United States to argue for a similar port or free zone upon our Atlantic seaboard. In 1934 our Congress passed a bill legalizing the establishment of "foreign-trade zones" or free ports. Certain outstanding differences between the conditions favoring free ports in Europe, especially those at Hamburg, and the conditions to be found in the United States demand careful consideration in this connection. We note them only briefly here.

The Hamburg hinterland includes a heterogeneous population and a number of international boundary lines. Only two international boundaries are associated with the United States and they bound countries which are well served by their own ports whose positions on the world trade routes are satisfactory. The international boundaries back of Hamburg are at right angles to the general flow of traffic in its immediate hinterland. The port is one of a number of ports located in several foreign countries and all within short distances of each other. It is not the terminus of an ocean route. Ships have the opportunity to put into ports of different nations fronting on the waters off northwestern Europe where demand and production differ. They may carry goods from one port to another nearby but in a different country without violating national or international shipping laws. Along the Atlantic coast of North America the ports of the United States represent termini with respect to trade routes. Foreign ships may not carry American goods in our coastwise trade. Again, the demands of the people in the hinterlands of the American ports do not show such variety or contrasts as characterize those in European regions. The free port or free zone advantages accruing to European ports could hardly accrue to American ports if similar zones were established here.

The new law provides no financial support from the United States Treasury, but merely permits trade centers or private organizations to build free zones. Statistical data indicates that even in our most prosperous years the available trans-shipment traffic totaled just a few hundred million dollars. If all of it could be concentrated in one free port that port might show a modest profit. But if many free zones were established along our coasts it is doubtful whether any could profit, even with an increase in total in-transit trade, owing to the fact that it would be thinly distributed among all these ports. The development of the first free zone in the port of New York will be keenly watched.

BERLIN—AN INLAND "SEAPORT"

A trade center located at a point remote from the sea and upon a waterway navigable only by barges ordinarily would not be construed as a seaport. Yet Berlin, characterized by just these conditions, considers itself as the equivalent of an ocean port. It records imports and exports just as any port upon the coast does. In this respect, it is unusual among the world's major trade centers.

Location.—The port of Berlin flanks the diminutive Spree River and the canal waters tributary to the Spree. The Spree flows into the Havel which drains through a cleared channel to the Elbe. By this somewhat tortuous route a barge may move from Berlin to the Elbe and down to Hamburg where it transfers cargo to ocean-going freighters. By the same route, but in the reverse direction, transoceanic goods reach Berlin.

The new Mittelland Canal connects Berlin via the Spree and Havel rivers with the Ruhr and Rhine rivers. This same canal establishes contact with the Weser and so gives to Berlin sea connections at Rotterdam on the Rhine mouth and Bremen on the Weser mouth.

Berlin has access to the Baltic Sea via the Spree or the Havel Rivers and several canals connecting with the Oder River. In fact, so important is the route for Berlin freight as interpreted by the city of Stettin that it sometimes announces itself as the "port for Berlin." Berlin, however, acknowledges no such service, preferring to consider itself an ocean port. It is not only on a water route to the North Sea and the Baltic but its carriers may reach Czechoslovakia via the Elbe River or the coal fields of upper Silesia in southeastern Germany via the Oder.

In addition to the water routes, the port has a central location with respect to Europe's rail network. Eleven through railroads, with their branches, place it in easy access to all parts of the continent. The coördination of these lines with the waterways makes Berlin a primary trade center. No other inland city of Europe is better located for the exchange of commodities.

Berlin's central location is evidenced by its water distances from cer-

FIG. 41. THE WEST HARBOR OF BERLIN

Although Berlin is an inland trade center, it has developed its waterways connecting with the Elbe and Oder Rivers. The West Harbor, whose major business is with Hamburg via Havel See and the Elbe, assumes all the aspects of an ocean port if we except the absence of ocean liners. Berlin considers itself an ocean port.

tain other important centers; from Breslau it is 252 miles, from Hamburg 222 miles, and from Duisburg-Ruhrort via the Mittelland Canal it is 366 miles. These waterways accommodate barges with a capacity ranging from 600 to 1,000 tons except for a few short stretches here and there which as yet allow only of boats up to 250 tons.

Port Equipment.—If one viewed the docks only in Berlin and could ignore the absence of ocean-going vessels alongside one could easily imagine himself in a typical coastal port. Warehouses, traveling cranes, railroad tracks along the docks, grain elevators, coal docks—in short, all of the elements present in a port upon the sea characterize this port. Many of the world's ports fall far short of the facilities which Berlin affords its shippers. The mere fact that its waters are remote from the sea seems in no way to have affected the "sea-mindedness" of these inland people. In spite of the eleven railways radiating from Berlin, the freight handled by waterways recently has at times exceeded that by rail. Upon inquiry as to the profitableness of the canals in these post-war days of increased labor costs the response comes in the revelation of further plans for the improvement and extension of the canal system.

Commerce.—On the 300 acres of port area distributed among eleven units, 6,866,000 tons of freight were handled in 1925 (a prosperous post-war year), 20 per cent of which represented exports and the balance imports. While the products represented a large variety, bulky goods predominated. Coal, grains, heavy hardware, petroleum, tobacco, wines in barrels are among the major commodities. It has long been the practice in Germany to assign to the waterways bulky freight and to the railways, package goods. This policy may be considered as the one applied to the traffic of Berlin.

Growth of Berlin.—A contributing factor to the growth of the port of Berlin has been the growth of the trade center itself. Some maintain that Berlin has experienced a more rapid growth than any other trade center. It witnessed a notable population increase during the past quarter century, rising from 1,888,848 in 1900 to 4,346,437 in 1929, a gain of 130 per cent. This was due in large measure to the acquisition of suburban areas, particularly Charlottenburg, Wilmersdorf, and Spandau. Berlin to-day is an agglomeration of small communities each of which has had a steady growth.

Naturally, its increase in population to almost 7 per cent of the national total has stimulated the demand for goods and has attracted a wide assortment. A trade center of Berlin's dimensions, even though located in the interior, inclines toward the utilization of every means which will facilitate the movement of goods both in and out. Consequently, the waterway as an inexpensive auxiliary to rail has been favored and the port of Berlin has developed.

CHAPTER X

FAIRS

Fairs[1] rank among the oldest as well as the most fascinating of trading institutions. The exact date of their origin can not be recorded for they represent one of those human activities which slowly evolves without receiving special notice until it attains a more or less institutional character.

One may ask why fairs are classified under the caption "Trade Centers" since they are merely institutions within urban or rural centers and are not a single independent unit. Our justification for inclusion here lies in the fact that major fairs have served as stimuli to trade upon which in many instances the economic welfare of an entire community depends. At the time of occurrence of these fairs it is customary for nearly the whole local citizenry to concentrate its attention and its energies upon fair activities to the end that the institution meet with success. Success spells satisfying returns for the whole trade center. For the period of its existence, then, the fair is essentially synonymous with the trade center and accordingly may be placed in the category of trade centers.

History.—Fairs may be traced to the bazaar and to the caravan trade of a period dating several centuries B.C. When currency as a medium of exchange was unknown and when credit in business transactions had yet to be born, people appointed a particular time and place for meeting so that they could bring their wares together for exchange purposes. A caravan might stop at any settlement along its way and strike bargains with the local people or it might even engage in exchanges with other caravans en route. The bazaar, too, carried with it the suggestion of a center for exchange where a variety of goods was gathered from which prospective buyers could select wares in exchange for their own surpluses. To be sure, the bazaar was purely local in character, but, nevertheless, in principle it did not differ radically from many of the modern fairs. We may definitely assign the birth of the fair to the

---

[1] The word "fair" is probably related to two Latin words, "feria" meaning holiday and "festus" meaning feast.

commercial world of Central Asia, India, and the Eastern Mediterranean.

Fairs assumed prominence in Medieval times when the people looked upon them not only as occasions for the transaction of business but as opportunities for social exchanges. Sometimes they marked festival periods or religious celebrations. The church festival, bringing together large crowds, offered an excellent market in which tradesmen could sell their wares. Other times, they were merely market periods established by feudal lords who found considerable profit in the returns from the granting of special trading privileges to certain merchants.

The oldest of these fairs is said to be that of St. Denis, near Paris, founded in the early part of the seventeenth century. While it endured for several centuries, others rose in succession, particularly in the Paris basin and along the main highways across the western Alps and down the Saône-Rhône Valley. By the late twelfth century, Troyes, Provins, Bar-sur-Aube ranked high among these early centers. A few, less important in size, established in Flanders and some at points en route to Italy served to stimulate the activities of the primary fairs. Traders representing northeast Africa, Syria, Asia Minor, or other parts of that active world met those from Italy, Germany, Spain, Holland, and even a few from England. The most noted of the English fairs at this time was that of St. Bartholomew in Smithfield. Business at these fairs was so brisk that the rise of fairs elsewhere became merely a matter of time and opportunity. Geneva and Lyons, both on the main arteries traveled by the traders to the northern fairs, established markets of their own by the end of the fifteenth century. With their rise at points more accessible than the Paris-basin fairs, the latter declined. Many English fairs degenerated into mere pleasure resorts.

While fairs in France enjoyed conspicuous positions in the international trade of their time, fairs of local significance had risen at Mainz (Mayence) and Köln (Cologne) on the Rhine in the tenth century and at Leipzig in 1268. Fairs were held at numerous other centers in Germany, as at Frankfort on the Main, Frankfort on the Oder, Brunswick, and elsewhere. These eventually took on an international aspect although none of them attained the importance of the French centers except Leipzig which to-day still supports the world's outstanding commercial fair. For a time after the middle of the 19th century, Leipzig experienced a decline, but was revived just as the century closed.

During the rise of the western European fairs the people of old Russia exchanged wares with Asiatics. Caravans from the Orient entering territory which we shall note here for convenience as Russian reached the Volga River and followed it up stream to the great bend and beyond. They met the Slavic inhabitants in the vicinity of Kazan and western Europeans at Novgorod just south of Leningrad when Novgorod was the easternmost outpost of the Hanseatic League. Later a permanent exchange center was established at Nijni Novgorod, now Gorki, not far from Kazan near the confluence of the Oka and Volga Rivers. This fair, although recently discontinued, ranked along with that at Leipzig as one of the most important in Europe. It long represented a primary point of contact between Orientals and Occidentals. Up to 1913 furs and skins stood foremost among the products bringing fame to this fair.

Other fairs of pre-war note not already mentioned are those at Budapest, Hungary, Senigallia and Teramo in Italy; Batavia in Java; Kiakhta in Siberia; Hurdwar in India; and Mecca in Arabia. The fair at Mecca is associated with the annual Mohammedan pilgrimage. Reports have it that as many as 100,000 persons attend this fair.

Classification.—Fairs may be classified according to (1) their primary function, (2) the nature of their products, or (3) their scope of influence. If function be selected as a basis we may classify fairs as (a) trade and (b) educational. The trade type, such as that of Leipzig, is established primarily for the sale of goods by the manufacturer direct to the dealer and to an incidental degree to the consumer. The fair functioning educationally involves an assemblage of commodities which shows the progress made by a people during a selected period. The latter type of fair is well illustrated by state fairs in the United States or World's Fairs such as those held at Paris, Chicago, and St. Louis. Fairs classified according to the nature of their products may be designated as (a) specialty, in which a single commodity dominates, such as the fur fair at Leipzig, the silk fair of Lyons, or the wine fair of Dijon, or in which a group of closely associated products are displayed as in agricultural or horticultural fairs; (b) the industrial fair, as illustrated by the Great Engineering and Building Fair at Leipzig; (c) miscellaneous fairs at which all manner of products are exhibited. Most fairs fall under this last broad heading.

Under the third classification, namely, scope of influence, we may list (a) local, (b) continental, and (c) intercontinental fairs. As in the case of the miscellaneous class, most fairs qualify under the heading local. Many local fairs naturally entertain an ambition to become continental or intercontinental or both. By continental we mean a fair at which exhibitors from several countries on the same continent take part, while intercontinental includes exhibitors from more than one continent. The Leipzig fair is now truly intercontinental, although until the post-war period it was strictly continental. If one considers buyers or visitors not interested in purchases, then many of these fairs would be classified as intercontinental. In fact, the fair management at Leipzig has for years characterized itself as international, as have the fairs at Wien (Vienna), Praha, and Poznan (Posen) because, in addition to some purchasers from abroad, thousands of tourists from many parts of the world have been numbered among the interested observers.

The Sample vs. The Commodity Fair.—We have already suggested that fairs may have grown out of early bazaar or caravan trade. Obviously, this business in which the direct exchange of commodities prevailed was pure barter. As life became more complex, society better organized, transportation relatively safe, and an international currency exchange created confidence among traders. Barter proved cumbersome to say the least, and purchases based upon samples proved infinitely more convenient. Merchants learned to trust each other, particularly as organized society afforded some protection to those involved in business transactions. One could actually select his needs from samples, perhaps, make a partial payment, and feel confident that upon a promised date he would receive his merchandise. On the other hand, the seller became equally satisfied that after delivery of his products the buyer would reimburse him with the balance payment due. The *sample* fair accordingly is distinguished from its forerunner the *commodity* fair. The latter still occurs in the less accessible parts of the world and in some regions where the level of European civilization has not yet been attained.

In the several classifications cited fairs were not indicated as sample or commodity because in advanced countries virtually all those of the commercial type which exert a wide influence are sample fairs. They conform in all their major aspects to the generally accepted modes of operation in modern business.

The Leipzig Sample Fair.—For the best illustration of a great sample fair we must turn to Leipzig. This fair is unique, although it has been the pattern for many others.

The Leipzig fair dates from medieval times, possibly as early as the twelfth century, when Leipzig, located at the cross-roads of north-south and east-west routes within Saxony, was favored as a center for the exchange of the products of the local region. Three small

FIG. 42. STREET SCENE AT THE LEIPZIG FAIR

Although many of these people are sight-seers, many are actual buyers from various parts of the earth. Display rooms in these buildings often rent for an amount during the ten days to three weeks period of the fair equal to that which would be paid if they were occupied all year. (Courtesy, Leipzig Trade Fair, Inc.)

streams, the Pleisse, Elster, and Parthe, have their confluence here and, although diminutive in size, furnished better avenues of transportation in early times than did country roads. Emperor Maximilian I gave official status to the fair in 1507, and under his patronage, which included arbitrary restrictions in favor of Leipzig, the growth of the fair was, for a time at least, assured. In those days the fair was not of the sample type, but of the commodity class. Up to the beginning of the nineteenth century the fair was still retail in character. Groceries, cotton, and raw wool passed out of the trade by the middle of the century, leaving furs, leather, and drygoods as the principal commodities exchanged. While certain items were dropped, others were gradually introduced, such as china and glassware, hardware, novelties, machinery, musical instruments, and a host of other goods, until to-day the kinds of products run into the thousands. Paralleling the shift in types of products handled, there came about a change from the retailing of wares to wholesaling. To-day the rules of the wholesale trade are rigidly enforced and the fair is sometimes officially designated The Leipzig Wholesale Fair.

In Leipzig three fairs are held in a single year, two of major size and one minor, although the latter is not unimportant with respect to the trade involved. Of the major fairs, one is held in the spring formerly known as the Easter Fair and one occurs in the autumn, beginning usually the last week of August or the first week of September. The Easter Fair lasts a week or ten days and that of autumn for two to three weeks. The third fair, equaled by none other of its kind, is the fur fair held in January after the New Year celebration and operated independently of the Leipzig Trade Fairs. Leipzig furriers had acquired such skill in the curing and dyeing processes that in pre-war days they enjoyed a world monopoly. Most of the world's raw furs are shipped to Leipzig to be finished and for this reason the fur fair assumes an intercontinental as well as an international importance.

Although exhibitors in the earlier years of the Leipzig fairs were almost entirely from the state of Saxony, to-day they come from all parts of Germany, and from neighboring countries, chiefly Czechoslovakia and Austria, and from overseas. Exhibitors total annually about 10,000, while foreign buyers reach figures running into the thirty thousands and German buyers about 180,000. Some state fairs in the United States attract as many visitors in a single day, but they are mostly sight-seers. A fair which can bring to its doors as many as

200,000 actual buyers representing wholesalers and dealers from all quarters of the globe merits high regard.

Space for exhibitors is available in thirty-one permanent buildings erected for the merchandise fair in the inner city and eighteen large exhibition halls at the exposition grounds on the city outskirts. Recent growth of the fairs has necessitated the erection of temporary structures on some of the public squares. The buildings within the business district house the General Sample Fair. The Technical Group occupies the halls of the exposition grounds.

The fair is managed by a corporation apart from the civic administration but in close harmony with it. The Chamber of Commerce, travel bureaus, hotels, and all interested parties lend such assistance as they can to further the success of the event. All responsibility for the conduct of the fair is assumed, however, by the fair administration (Messamt) which has its own building and staff for governing the entire proceedings. While this independence of jurisdiction exists, the entire city seems to acquire the fair spirit and all lines of business naturally attempt to capitalize the opportunity afforded by the presence of thousands of visitors. Much unique advertising is displayed either in the form of placards and other types of literature or through the medium of the show window. Humorous advertisements by way of clowns and grotesque figures parading the exhibit streets arouse the interest of the spectator and attract attention of the passing potential buyer. The narrow streets of medieval origin with banners and signs in abundant variety displayed from thousands of windows lend color and a carnival aspect to the scene.

Formerly, temporary stalls for retail vendors were allowed in the heart of the city. These are now for the most part relegated to the outlying districts. Their resemblance to the bazaars of a street in India or China or Netherland India presents a distinct oriental atmosphere. Perhaps they are a true souvenir of the eastern trading world from which the modern fairs seem, in part at least, to have evolved.

Location of Fairs.—The location of fairs sometimes has been due to geographic advantages and again, to arbitrary selection or happenstance. The success over a period of years of any one of these fairs can be attributed to its favorable location. The decline of one-time thriving fairs has often been ascribed to a shift in relative position. Fairs held in towns along the caravan routes eastward from the Caspian Sea into Central Asia lost patronage with the establishment of an all-sea route to the Orient at the end of the sixteenth and beginning

FIG. 43. THE ENGINEERING AND BUILDING DIVISION OF THE LEIPZIG FAIR

These exhibition halls represent a recent expansion of the fair. They are permanent structures located away from the original downtown fair area. (Courtesy, Leipzig Trade Fair, Inc.)

of the seventeenth centuries. We have already noted the decline of fairs in the Paris Basin when those at Lyons and Geneva rose in influence. At Bruges, a busy seaport in medieval times, the fair went out as the city itself was relegated to a secondary position.

Just as trade centers which rise at the cross-roads of important routes attain a healthy growth, so fairs in similar locations enjoy a substantial development. Both Lyons and Leipzig have such locations, although the cross-roads qualities of the latter city in recent times have not been conspicuous. A region of considerable industrial production is favorable to a fair either at its center or at any easily accessible point.

When a fair arises as a direct consequence of the productivity of a region and serves as a center of trade in the local products, it is likely to develop an export trade if it lies upon through-routes readily accessible to merchants at considerable distances. So it is that Leipzig's fair has evolved into one of intercontinental proportions.

The Public Market.—No European trade center seems too small to have a public market in progress either daily, on alternate days, or at other intervals. South American centers, too, and many of those on other continents give emphasis to the market. Many centers in the United States have public markets, but in this country they play a secondary rôle in the general trade structure.

The markets in Europe find equal expression in village and metropolis. They differ from the great fairs only in size, in their frequency of occurrence, and their personnel. These markets rarely include manufacturer or wholesaler, but rather the dealer who sells to the consuming public. Farmers, truck gardeners, horticulturists, and other small producers also set up stands on the market place from which they dispense their products direct to the consumer. In a few instances a portion of a public food market may be set aside for wholesalers as, for example, at the fruit and vegetable market along the Elbe water-front at Hamburg or at the great fish market at Rotterdam. These markets may be legitimately included within the classification of fairs for they exhibit all the characteristics of the "standard" fair.

In the United States we usually look upon the public market as a center in which foodstuffs only are sold. This is by no means the case in foreign countries. Markets show diversity. There is the flower market, the dry goods market, the small household-goods market, and the boot and shoe market. These may be held entirely independently of the food market or they may share some space with the latter. In this respect the public market again resembles the fair, that is, it may show specialization or it may be miscellaneous in character. These markets are held either in buildings erected for the purpose or upon an open square in the midst of the trade center or in both places. Usually some space in the immediate vicinity of market buildings is allotted to open-air stalls or sales spaces.

The public market, like the great sample fair, furnishes an excellent cross-section of the life of a region. The life is much more local in character than that of the sample fair, but it may not be any the less interesting. Markets bring together all classes of people, rich and poor, bank president and office boy, preacher and laborer, housewife and maid, energetic wide-awake seller or crippled decrepit beggar. The public market verily is the heart of a locality where one may observe, within small compass, the pulsating life of the masses.

The Convention.—The convention, which is recognized in business circles as a gathering of manufacturers, wholesalers, or retailers who discuss problems of mutual interest and sometimes display samples of their products, may be included within the classification of fairs. Although conventions generally are either local or national in character, occasionally they are intercontinental. Among such conventions are the National Automobile Show, the National Hardware Dealers Conventions, the Annual Toy Exhibition, and many others devoted to single fields of commodities.

Future of Fairs.—The persistence of the fair as a trading institution for 2,500 years or more serves as good evidence of its likely continuance. Its form has changed somewhat and may change further, but its effectiveness in trade promotion has been established beyond a doubt.

One change in the United States is illustrated by the furniture industry. For years fairs were held twice yearly, in winter and in summer. Now the industry operates through a permanent exhibition located in Chicago. In what is claimed to be the largest commercial building constructed for manufacturers' furniture may be viewed at any time by jobber or dealer. Although seasonal markets are still maintained, more than 50 per cent of the buyers register in the inter-market periods as well.

In the Bush Terminal Sales Building in New York City are displayed samples of over two hundred manufacturers and importers of art wares. While not a true fair, nevertheless, this organization service involves some of its principles and is in line with the tendency of manufacturers to exhibit their products throughout the year at a commercial center visited by large numbers of buyers.

FIG. 44. THE MARKET PLACE

This flower, fruit, and vegetable market on the square in Hildesheim, Germany, typifies the market institution so common throughout Europe. The market place brings together peoples in all stations of life and presents a cross-section of the kinds of commodities in use. Markets are often specialized and widely scattered over the city.

The bulb growers of Holland have held annual fairs for many years, but not always at a fixed center. Now they have established at Haarlem permanent display gardens and a building for indoor exhibits. Tulips, hyacinths, narcissi, and other flowers are seasonal in character and buyers attempt to visit bulb headquarters at blossom time. Yet, the concentration of the interests of all the growers in this single center carries with it continuity rather than periodicity in plant exhibits.

The opportunities for trade expansion via the exhibit method at centers with excellent transportation facilities seem to be limited only in proportion to the aggressiveness of those upon whom the responsibility for these fairs rests.

TABLE 8

A FEW OF THE MORE IMPORTANT FAIRS [2]

ARGENTINA—La Plata
  International Sample Fair (annual)
AUSTRIA—Wien (Vienna)
  International Sample and Technical Fair (semi-annual)
BELGIUM—Bruxelles (Brussels)
  Official International Commercial Fair (annual)
BULGARIA—Gorna Orehovitsa
  International Sample Fair (semi-annual)
CANADA—Toronto
  Canadian Commercial and Agricultural Exhibition (annual)
CUBA—Habana (Havana)
  International Sample Fair (annual)
CZECHOSLOVAKIA—Praha (Prague)
  International Sample Fair (semi-annual)
DANZIG—Free City of Danzig
  International Sample Fair (semi-annual)
DOMINICAN REPUBLIC—Santiago Fair
ECUADOR—Guayaquil
  Sample Fair
ESTONIA—Tallinn (Reval)
  Commercial and Industrial Exhibition and Fair (annual)
FRANCE—*Lille*
  Lille Commercial Fair (annual)
  Lyon (Lyons)
  International Sample Fair (annual)
  Marseille
  International Sample Fair (annual)

[2] Commerce Reports, Feb. 8, 1932 (Dept. of Commerce, Washington, D. C.) and other sources.

Nice
Exhibition and Fair (annual)
Paris
Sample Fair (annual)
GERMANY—*Frankfurt on the Main*
International Sample and Technical Fair (semi-annual)
Leipzig
International Sample Fair (semi-annual)
GREECE—Saloniki (Salonica)
International Fair of Saloniki (annual)
HUNGARY—Budapest
International Sample Fair (annual)
ITALY—Milano (Milan)
Milano Sample Fair (annual)
JAVA—Soerabaja (Surabaya)
International Sample Fair (annual)
LATVIA—Riga
International Agricultural and Industrial Fair (annual)
LITHUANIA—Klaipeda (Memel)
Lithuanian Agricultural and Industrial Exhibition (annual)
NETHERLANDS—Utrecht
The Dutch International Industries Fair (semi-annual)
NEW ZEALAND—Auckland
International Industrial Exhibition and Winter Show (annual)
PALESTINE—Tel Aviv
International Sample Fair (annual)
PHILIPPINES—
Philippine Commercial and Industrial Fair (annual)
POLAND—*Posen* (*Poznan*)
International Sample Fair (annual)
Lwow (*Lemberg*)
Eastern International Fair (annual)
SALVADOR—San Salvador
International Sample Fair (annual)
SPAIN—Seville
Ibero-American Exposition
SWEDEN—Göteborg (Gothenburg)
Official Industries Fair (annual)
UNION OF SOUTH AFRICA—Johannesburg
Witwatersrand Agricultural Show (annual)
YUGOSLAVIA—Zagreb
International Sample Fair (annual)

PART II

TRADE ROUTES

INTRODUCTION TO PART II

Having discussed trade centers with respect to their interrelations, their structures, functions, and their future, we now turn to a consideration of trade routes, not in the usual sense, but with reference to their relation to trade centers. We shall not be interested in what commodities are carried along the world's trade channels, but rather in the rôle of routes with respect to trade centers and in the effect of trade centers upon routes.

We shall approach the subject in an all inclusive sense as we did trade centers; that is, instead of confining our interest to the generally accepted conception of a trade route, we shall interpret trade routes to include all forms of communication and as each phase of communication which ordinarily is not construed as a trade route is discussed we shall attempt to justify its inclusion here.

CHAPTER XI

TRADE ROUTES AND TRADE CENTERS

Since the objective in trade is the exchange of goods, services, or ideas, the trade route is, of necessity, intimately associated with the place of residence of the people engaged in trade, that is, with trade centers. The close relationship between trade routes and trade centers becomes especially impressive when one raises the question, which precedes the other, the trade center or the trade route? Logic dictates that trade routes and trade centers be discussed at the same time because of their interdependence. This, however, can not always be done without confusion; hence, the systematic method of discussing them in succession, yet with some correlation, has been followed in this book.

The close correlation of the trade center and trade route is well-emphasized by Hoyt in his discussion of Chicago where he states:

... already paramount as a railroad center even before the Civil War, the extension of the railway net westward [after the Civil War] from the Mississippi River added the rapidly growing West to its hinterland and absorbed portions of the tributary territory of its rivals. . . . The completion of the Union Pacific and the Central Pacific across the continent in 1869 brought Chicago in contact with the Pacific Coast and the trade of the Orient. Such was the wider market gained for Chicago by the extension of the mileage of its railroads from 4,912 in 1860 to 7,019 in 1869, while the profits to the railroads themselves were shown by an increase in their earnings from $17,609,314 to $48,886,305.[1]

He says further:

The Chicago wholesale houses took full advantage of the opportunity created by the railroads. Not waiting for business to come to them through the new channels, they sent out "drummers" to the western States to solicit orders—a business policy unknown before the war.[2]

Trade, as popularly understood, involves a change in ownership of goods and usually implies the movement of goods from the place of

[1] Homer Hoyt, *One Hundred Years of Land Values in Chicago* (The University of Chicago Press, 1933) p. 83.
[2] *Ibid.*, pp. 519.

151

sale to the place wanted. Trade, of course, is a two-way transaction which may call for an exchange of products, an exchange of money for material things, an exchange of services alone or of services for goods or ideas, and still other kinds of exchange. The route along which the goods, services, or ideas move may be designated technically as a trade route. Yet, if an exchange of commodities occurs in a given direction only once, the shipping world hesitates to describe that avenue of movement as a trade route. Steamship operators prefer to denote a trade route as a route either frequently used by ships or a charted path recognized as the best route which a ship can follow between two selected ports. At best, a trade route is an intangible affair, albeit, shippers discussing trade routes use the expression without danger of misunderstanding.

While trade routes as ordinarily interpreted are pathways along which goods move, modern trade requires services and ideas as integral parts of the transactions which set the goods in motion. Quite often ideas are exchanged via telegraph, cable, wireless, or telephone before a sale is completed. Likewise, ideas are exchanged without relation to sales but for their own sake or in association with activities other than business. In these circumstances it seems proper to interpret the *means* of communicating ideas as trade routes. Thus, conceiving the trade route in its widest sense, we shall consider, besides the means of communication just mentioned, the mail, the motion picture, and the public press.

TRADE STIMULI

Trade arises (1) from the unequal distribution of the earth's resources, (2) from differences in economic development of peoples, and (3) from differences in stage of civilization.

Unequal Distribution of Resources.—From the days when primitive men dominated the earth down to modern times, the earth's available resources have been subject to movement. The surpluses have been traded. This activity has brought together peoples of the highlands and the lowlands, of the coasts and the interiors, of the regions of contrasting climates, of areas of dense and scant populations. The unequal distribution of our resources has tended, through numerous exchanges, to bring peoples of diverse portions of the earth into contact, has afforded an exchange of ideas, and has advanced the respective stages of civilization.

In the Mediterranean world of 1000 B.C. the Phœnicians profited as carriers of tin deposits from England to the peoples of the eastern Mediterranean who combined tin with copper to make their bronze ornaments and utensils. For the silver of Spain they traded highly prized oriental raw products. Venetian tradesmen enjoyed their greatest prosperity when they served as intermediaries between the people of Asia and of central and northern Europe.

One of the stimuli to our industrial development lay in the effort to get resources which are abundant in one region to regions where they are scarce. To accomplish this end, man's ingenuity has often been challenged. Perishable products of the soil in the southern hemisphere could not be moved to densely populated areas north of the equator until ships equipped with mechanical refrigeration became a reality. Heavy and bulky commodities, such as coal, limestone, marble, petroleum, could not be economically transferred from their sources to distant centers until effective loading and unloading machinery was devised. We sometimes lament the fact that the world's economic materials are so unevenly distributed, but perhaps we would not enjoy them as much as we do had we not been required to invent many devices to make them available.

This scattering of the earth's useful products, as already suggested, having effected an irregular distribution of trade centers, has, in turn, greatly influenced the direction of movement of commodities. While exchanges in trade are between individuals or institutions, in a wider interpretation they are exchanges between individuals and organizations as parts of trade centers and, accordingly, their movements may be interpreted in terms of the trade centers.

Differences in Economic Development.—Probably the largest current influence in the establishment of trade lies in differences in economic development. These differences often are due to contrasts in the natural endowments of a region, but frequently arise from temperamental contrasts.

The rise of Germany to one of the world's foremost commercial nations, within a period of forty-two years from 1871 to the beginning of the World War, represented quite as much a temperamental reaction as one of resources. The country certainly was not the possessor of rich agricultural lands. True, it was endowed with vast potash deposits, but without the intelligence to experiment with them it is doubtful if the people would have succeeded in producing enough food to care for two-thirds of the population. Germany acquired vast iron deposits in consequence of the Franco-Prussian War, but without her systematic turn of mind she could never have developed that perfection in many phases of the steel industry which gained the world's admiration. Incidentally, it remains to be seen whether France as a consequence of the return of Lorraine will show a similar development in steel manufactures. Germany's economic development stimulated a tremendous trade between herself and other countries. It meant growth of a dense population with high standards which, in turn, demanded a high production of goods in order to pay for consumption demands. Industrialization called for numerous agglomerations of people, that is, for the establishment or growth of trade centers. Industrial Germany has developed a distinctly urban cast.

Differences in Stage of Civilization, Habits, and Customs.—To-day trade is influenced less than ever by differences in stage of civilization. People's demands become increasingly alike as the power of the white man dominates the earth. Yet, striking differences still occur as, for example, that between the advanced European type and the native of the Congo River Valley, the Mohammedan of central Asia, the Indian of the high Andes, or the head hunter of northern Australia. As long as these differences exist, an exchange of goods will be effected, although the latter groups of peoples are as yet so primitive that their needs remain simple and exchanges continue to be unimportant.

Differences in habits and customs among peoples of similar levels of civilization often give rise to trade. For example, among European types, a style in women's clothing may originate in France or Germany, and soon its arrival in the United States and other parts of the world creates a demand. The American shoe is shown in Europe, and shortly Europeans demand it as a part of their apparel. The English habit of five o'clock tea strikes the fancy of Europeans only to be followed by an increased importation of tea. The Czech woman wears glass beads, made from native sand deposits, as a part of her national or provincial costume, and soon Czechoslovakia is called upon to supply beads to women in other lands.

Territorial Conquest.—Trade tends to reduce the apparent size of the earth by making possible the realization of our respective desires for each other's goods. Trade is the great leveler among the nations and may serve for the betterment of mankind provided we can submerge jealousy and envy, reactions too often revealed when we survey the world's resources and find some peoples the fortunate possessors of more than others. All too often in the world's history this latter attitude has served as a stimulus to the acquisition of territory on the part of aspiring peoples. The expansion of the Roman Empire, no doubt, grew partly out of a desire for the control of the then known resources in Europe; the growth of the British Empire may be ascribed in large part to a quest for ownership of materials essential to the subsistence and the development of the United Kingdom; German commercial aggression sought as one of its ends the possession of territory upon which it could draw for materials and goods to nourish and maintain its ambitious peoples. Even the United States of America, long a non-acquisitive country with regard to foreign territory, has changed its attitude since the days of the Spanish-American War. We have hesitated to relinquish the Philippine Islands because tropical products have attained a new significance in modern industry and we are lacking in the ownership of extensive tropical lands.

As trade centers grow in size they find their economic positions becoming more sensitive, owing to increased dependence of the populace upon sources of supply of raw materials beyond their national boundaries. Hence, the conquest of additional lands may often reflect the instability of trade centers.

Strategic Routes.—Nations, to retain detached lands, usually require a merchant marine and a navy as a reminder to the colonists of their subservience and for defense against possible aggressors. Oftentimes railroads are constructed within these territories not primarily for commercial purposes, but either to make remote districts accessible to the power of the governing center or for the psychological effect which transportation facilities may have in harmonizing the parts of a country. The Cape to Cairo route in Africa, the Canadian National Railways, the Union Pacific in the United States, some of the steamship lines between England and her colonies or in pre-war days between Germany and her outlying possessions represent strategic connections which were followed by trade. Often trade routes are developed with reference to the strategic position of trade centers or because governments deliberately focus their energies upon trade centers in order to give them importance. For example, Berlin, originally declared by decree to be the home of the Hapsburg family, was arbitrarily made readily accessible to all parts of Germany by rail and canal. When Leningrad served as the capital of pre-war Russia, the trade center, then known as St. Petersburg, was connected by rail with Moskva by royal decree.

Especially well developed are the military railroads between Berlin and the French and Polish frontiers. Most capital cities, and port cities too, are shown transportation preferences, the more so when their activities in international trade or political relations reach considerable proportions. Study of a map showing the distribution of trade centers brings to light a concentration of roads upon the outstanding ones.

The question may arise as to whether or not trade centers attract transportation routes or whether the junction of routes creates the trade center or encourages the growth of those already in existence. Cases representative of all these situations can be found. Certainly trade centers established in pre-railroad days, such as most of our outstanding eastern seaboard centers which now possess excellent railroad facilities, are the attraction for the roads. The physical improvement of ports has drawn ships to them. Cherbourg and Southampton are excellent examples of ports which have grown because of their improved facilities. On the other hand, in a new country the location of trade centers is likely to be determined by river routes, mountain passes, or open country, all involving the element of ease of access. We return to the thesis that trade routes exert a large influence upon trade centers and that the relation of the two is reciprocal.

TYPES OF TRADE ROUTES AND THEIR ESTABLISHMENT

The world's trade routes may be classified into three general types, (1) land, (2) water, (3) air. While the land route usually suggests rail and country roads, it may well include canal, river, and lake, inasmuch as these routes of travel are completely enveloped by land. We can restrict the water type to ocean highways and great seas such as the Baltic or the Mediterranean which in many respects are comparable with the oceans.

Although we attempt to classify trade routes, we may recognize their integral relation. In modern trade many routes such as the transcontinental and transoceanic may be considered as continuations of each other, the coastline constituting merely a point of change in mode of transportation. Inland the intimate relation of water and land routes is effectively revealed in the standard expression "lake and rail" as often applied to freight rates. We present the classification in this discussion largely for purposes of convenience and clarity.

Land Routes.—Since man seems to have been first a "landlubber" and subsequently a seaman reference is made first to land routes. Our slowness to leave the land for the seas is well illustrated in English history. Many persons carry the impression that the English were always expert seamen, acquiring this idea no doubt from the power of their navy and the high degree of skill exhibited by their navigators. Yet, centuries elapsed before the British took to the seas despite the island character of their abode.

Land routes possess two fundamental characteristics, namely, direction and site. Direction is affected by climate or by the relative location of the objectives of the route, such as regions of raw materials versus centers in which they are to be used or location of manufacturing centers versus place of consumption of finished goods. Site may be influenced by topography, likely financial returns which the service of a route may render or military exigencies. The location of iron ore deposits in northeastern Minnesota and coal and limestone in the northern part of Illinois and eastern portions of Pennsylvania assured a trade route in a general northwest-southeasterly direction. On the other hand, the presence of the Great Lakes in close proximity to both deposits determined the site of the route. The greater economy in shipping ore to the coal and limestone, instead of the latter two commodities to the ore, combined with the location of the primary markets in the eastern United States made certain that the raw materials would move toward the east.

The mountain pass has played a part in the direction and site of routes from time immemorial. Classical examples are found among the magnificent heights of the imposing Alpine highland where the Brenner, the St. Gotthard, the Simplon, the Furka, the Semmering, and still other depressions have served man's routes in that territory. To some degree we have modified the passes through the medium of tunnels underneath them, but the passes account for man's choice of location of the tunnels. In the United States, transcontinental rail routes have focused upon the passes in the western mountains. In the eastern half of the country the Mohawk-Hudson pass is noteworthy. In South America the Mendoza-Uspallata pass between Argentina and Chile invited the first transcontinental rail route of that continent. If the Khyber Pass at the western end of the Himalayas could speak the story of the early intercourse between India and China it would no doubt tell wondrous tales of man's most ancient history. Even to-day it has lost little of its earlier trade significance, although its military rôle has been greatly enhanced.

Political conditions play their part in route directions where several countries must be crossed in order to link two seaboards or to connect a port with a capital city located beyond an international boundary. The pre-war route from Hamburg to Wien (Vienna) crossed but one international boundary. To-day it must cross two if the same route is followed. To cross Czechoslovakia, en route to Wien, means carrying the goods in bond through the country of the Czechs. This arrangement does not commend itself to the Austrians and, accordingly, other routes are encouraged. Numerous changes have been made or are in

FIG. 45. A PASS PROVIDES THE STIMULUS TO THE RISE OF TRADE CENTERS

The Mohawk Pass, route of the New York State Barge Canal, is impressive for its succession of vigorous trade centers. This galaxy is surpassed probably by only one other group, namely in the Ruhr-Rhine Valley. The effect of geographic conditions upon the localization of population is suggested here.

process of being made as a consequence of the post-war realignment of boundaries in Europe.

Land Routes—Past and Present.—The character of land routes has changed more rapidly during the nineteenth century than within all time up to the recent period. Travel on foot, by pack animal, by horse, by oxen and wagon, or by river and canal have marked the standard of travel for all the earth until the introduction of the portable steam engine made possible the railroad. These primitive means of travel, however, are by no means confined to the past. China, Peru, India, and many other countries still depend upon them for carrying freight and people. Even the most advanced countries are not without some remnants of the early modes of travel, but they occur for the most part in the less accessible portions of the countries and in those parts which are only thinly populated. Explorers seeking a way into new regions select rivers and lakes, when they can, as the media of easiest transportation. To the extent upon which these ways must be used depends the course of trade routes, and not infrequently these courses remain the determinants for subsequent permanent routes, being used either by modern ship, or paralleled by automobile road, railroads, and airplane or airship. The caravan route to China in the thirteenth century, which was followed by Marco Polo, is to-day slowly but surely being replaced by rails which link the Caspian Sea with Merv, Bukhara, Samarkand, Kokand, and Andijan. Some day the locomotive will come puffing (if not of the electric type) out of the vast Asiatic interior into the station at Shanghai, marking the complete replacement of the ancient romantic route. The mighty Volga, still navigated as it was a thousand years ago, is paralleled along its lower course by the modern railroad. Upon the river surface the steamship shares freight with hand-powered boats of old. The trail blazed through the great Northwest by Lewis and Clark and their successors is replaced in the main to-day by the Northern Pacific transcontinental railroad.

These are but a few illustrations which reveal the hand of nature in fixing our trade routes no matter what the means of locomotion. Even the airplane, freest of all carriers, seeks the river, the railroads, the coast lines, the valleys, and the mountain passes as its guides. Down through the ages we have learned ways of coping with nature, but we still must confess our subservience to her.

Rivers and Canals.—The course of a river trade route lacks the flexibility of an overland route. The river itself predetermines direction if it is to be used at all. Its meanders may be cut through to straighten a course, but the general direction can not be altered. Largely because of this fixed character of rivers the United States, which was to a large extent settled during the railroad and motor vehicle era, has not used them as much for trade purposes as other countries have. Rivers as carriers of freight seem to represent three stages in a country's economic development, namely, (1) the period of settlement when the rivers constitute main highways in the absence of overland routes,

(2) the transitional era when a nation is shifting from a primary agricultural life to a manufacturing one—a time when overland rapid transit is being developed and is preferred to slow river traffic, and (3) the manufactural stage when a dense population demands the utilization of every possible route which may give the respective trade centers access to each other. Exceptions to this assertion may be claimed as, for example, in Soviet Russia (a country not usually construed as new) where agriculture is dominant and the rivers are still used as important routes of trade. In places the population is dense, yet the country is in an early developmental stage as measured by the standards of northwestern Europe and the United States. China or India might be cited as exceptions because, whereas the rivers are important highways, these countries can not be classified as manufactural, yet they have reached a stage of dense population. Their religions, illiteracy and superstitions have retarded them from attaining a high degree of industrialism and have encouraged an excessive density of population. The people, however, reveal evidences of their ability to measure up to occidental standards whenever they choose to throw off that yoke of retardation just recorded. Applied to the most progressive countries such as our own, England, Germany, France and others, this three-stage theory finds support.

Canals are located largely according to the bodies of water which they connect or by topographic circumstances or by both, usually with respect to the desirability of making accessible given trade centers. They present somewhat greater flexibility than rivers because man may predetermine their courses within the limitation of the conditions noted. Like rivers they possess in some instances an ancient history. Their practicability to-day has been strongly challenged by keen students of transportation problems. Some assert that the cost of upkeep and of carrying goods on them is too high to permit a fair profit, and others assert they can only be operated under government subsidies which, of course, means that in addition to the direct payment of a freight rate the public pays an additional charge indirectly through taxation. On the other hand, where canals parallel railways, as in the case of the New York State Barge Canal, their mere presence serves to maintain rail rates at a lower level than if they did not exist, and consequently in this manner they return a profit to the public.

Apparently canals can not return profits on long hauls; they are distinctly short-haul trade media and, therefore, best suited to regions of dense population. The recent activity in the United States associated with the proposed Great Lakes-St. Lawrence Waterway, the Lakes to the Gulf movement, the Lake Erie-Ohio River Canal revival and other projects point unmistakably to the influence of the increasing density of population upon the revival of canal enthusiasm.

Ocean and Sea Routes.—We have referred to man's innate attachment to the land and have cited the initial reluctance of the present-day-world's greatest maritime power to take to the sea. It is worth noting that a sufficiency of foodstuffs and other necessities of life at various periods in man's history have detained him upon the land, while fear of the unknown seas and ignorance of the sphericity of the earth played influential parts in further retarding his maritime activities. The ancient continental Asiatics rarely ventured upon the open ocean, although some of them may have skirted their coasts in diminutive junks, always remaining within sight of land. As for the island peoples of the Pacific, the Malays and Polynesians, we can not be so certain. It seems that some tribes may have ventured with their outrigger boats considerable distances between islands, but in all probability not upon sailing schedules.

Probably the first people who ventured out of sight of land to conduct a regular sea trade were the Phœnicians, although even they may have hugged the coast of the Atlantic when they dared to pass the Straits of Gibraltar in quest of England's tin. The Phœnicians, as is well known, occupied a coastal strip unfavorable to an easy life yet favorable to marine activities. The Norsemen, likewise, took to the sea probably because of a hinterland adverse to food production. The abundance of edible fish in the coastal waters invited them to the sea. The presence of tall straight timber in close proximity to the water's edge facilitated boat construction. Gradually all the waters about the European continent became familiar to the peoples of the time, and when Columbus prepared to find a water route to the Indies navigation of enclosed seas or coastal waters was no longer looked upon as offering unusual obstacles. Even so, from the trading days of the Phœnicians in the sixteenth century B.C. to Columbus' first crossing of the Atlantic nearly thirty-two centuries elapsed or six times as long as the period since this critical event. Within 150 years after the establishment of a mid-trans-Atlantic route the entire Atlantic, the Indian Ocean, and the mid-Pacific were navigated and in recent times routes sought around the continents, such as the northwest passage and the northeast passage, brought an acquaintance with Arctic waters.

In the latter part of the sixteenth century Queen Elizabeth offered a bounty to those who would engage in the fishing industry because she had recognized the value of the fisheries as a training ground for seamen and because the British defeat of the Spanish Armada in 1588 demonstrated the necessity for a navy and merchant marine to assure Great Britain's independence. Sir Walter Raleigh at this time is reputed to have said, "Whosoever commands the sea, commands the trade of the world; whosoever commands the trade commands the riches of the world and consequently the world itself."

Freedom of the Seas.—The new regions lying overseas required that the conquering country provide itself with a merchant marine or navy or both to maintain its connections and to derive the benefits of the added resources. Here was the basis for new trade and for subsequent study of the seas and of oceanic navigation in order to make the conduct of that trade easy and secure. The best routes for sailing vessels were gradually determined from experience and from surveys which revealed the wind systems of the earth, particularly stormy localities, and the topography of the ocean floor. When steam-powered ships became a reality and when the first trans-Atlantic crossing by a steamship, the *Great Western,* was effected in 1838, without refueling or assistance of sails, the establishment of trade routes largely independent of the elements became a possibility.

Questions involving the "freedom of the seas" became more acute as the number of ships rapidly increased and as the nations sought to dominate the world's trade.[3] The right to navigate the open ocean in recent times has not been challenged, but navigating these waters accomplishes no purpose unless a ship may have as an objective a port (trade center) and has business to transact. Nations have been inclined to restrict terminal areas through reserving to their own jurisdiction that part of the ocean within three miles of their coasts and also by prohibiting foreign vessels from engaging in coastwise trade. These restrictions and others involving port dues, operations within ports, and the carriage of goods in vessels of non-nationals or with foreign crews are still occasionally a subject of controversy.

Aerial Routes.—Aerial routes are in their infancy. We have already noted that their altitude and direction are greatly affected by topo-

[3] As this publication goes to press the United States Congress has surrendered its right to the principle of the "Freedom of the Seas" in time of war as a means of attempting to insure our neutrality in the event of a European conflict.

graphical circumstances as well as by the distribution of the trade centers which are their objectives.

One of the severest handicaps to the establishment of routes for airplanes and airships is the weather. Much success has been attained in the present system of forecasting the weather and reporting actual conditions along any aerial route, although many refinements need yet to be worked out. If, however, we can develop aerial navigating machines to withstand all weather conditions and can perfect blind flying, then the weather forecast may be relegated to secondary importance. Flying at great altitudes may, likewise, subordinate the importance of the forecast.

That the airplane and the airship are destined to play a large part in our future transportation problems is not to be doubted. Their rapid development to date insures the realization of uses which but a few years ago would have been held by most persons as fantastic. Aviation certainly has moved all the world's trade centers closer together in point of time. In many instances, too numerous to detail, it has reduced the time from days or weeks to a mere matter of hours. Few would gainsay the argument that such revolutionary realignment of our trade centers must eventually have a profound effect upon international trade, not to say upon our whole economic and perhaps in some instances political system.

CHAPTER XII

TRADE ROUTES OF NORTH AMERICA

The diversity of climate and of soils of North America permits of extensive agriculture in a vast variety of products. The great store of mineral deposits is readily accessible. The broad lowlands of the Eastern two-thirds of the continent afford a convenient surface for the construction of overland routes permitting distribution of the products at low cost, and natural waterways offer effective supplementary avenues for trade. The Western third of North America presents some obstacles to transportation, but not insurmountable barriers. Parts of the Arctic region in Canada and 'Alaska, and the rainy tropics of Central America as yet are not easily reached, but give no indication that they may not be readily penetrated when the necessity arises.

These circumstances have encouraged the rise of trade centers throughout an extensive area, and the centers, in turn, have stimulated the development of routes along which the products of the continent are distributed for consumption or processing for further distribution.

Trade Routes of the United States and Canada.—The development of the trade routes of the United States and Canada has occurred simultaneously and in much the same manner. The differences in political jurisdiction over the two countries have probably had little effect upon the evolution of their respective trade routes. Underlying their establishment, resources have dominated. Little has it mattered what the nationality of the pioneers, English, French, Dutch, or others, they all sought the riches of the lands and a way to get them from their place of occurrence to a place of utilization.

Distribution of the Routes.—A map of North America showing the density of population reveals an uneven distribution. The major population centers are concentrated in the Eastern areas, thinning out toward the central lowlands until in the vicinity of the cold prairies of the far North or the desert plains and plateaus of the South the density of population falls to less than one per square mile. On the Pacific slope the density increases, but except in a few localities does not attain the figures of the Atlantic side of the continent. This distribution, com-

164

bined with an equally irregular distribution of our natural resources, has given rise to surpluses of products sufficiently different from each other to serve as the basis for exchanges.

Grains from the Northwest are in demand along the Eastern Seaboard; fruits and cotton from the South flow toward the North; iron ore from the Lake Superior district finds its way to the Ohio Valley, and coal from the latter is returned to the Upper Lakes. Petroleum pumped from beneath the surface of Texas and Oklahoma is piped to Illinois, Indiana, and to the Eastern States for which these districts exchange farm implements, rubber goods, and motor vehicles. California ships walnuts, borax, oranges, and lemons to the eastern half of the continent and receives in return manufactured goods essential to her well-being. Eastern Canada sends asbestos and pulpwood southward into the United States in exchange for sub-tropical fruits and finished manufactured products. Mexico and Central America send sisal, petroleum, and bananas northward and import ammunition, machinery, and general merchandise.

Observe that population is held accountable not only for the production of the commodities but for their exchange. Since most of our population consists of scattered aggregations ranging from so-called villages to cities, the shuttling of the exchanges among them helps to define the routes which have been finally established.

Classification of Routes.—The directions of trade routes are modified not only by the distribution of people, but by the economy of transportation in relation to the relative demands of the trade centers. These routes may be classified in general terms as major and minor, the major confined largely to east-west directions and the minor, north-south. North American trade routes can in the main be reduced to nine major ones, namely (1) the North Atlantic Coast to the Great Lakes and the Mississippi River, (2) the North Atlantic Coast to the Gulf of Mexico, (3) the Great Lakes to the Gulf, (4) the Great Lakes or Mississippi River to the Pacific Southwest, (5) to the Pacific Middle West, (6) to the Pacific Northwest, (7) the Canadian Transcontinental, (8) the Gulf of Mexico to the Pacific Southwest, (9) the Rio Grande to Central Mexico. No attempt will be made to describe the evolution of each of these routes. We shall merely point to a few of the factors which influence the establishment of certain of them as illustrative of the kinds of elements which may affect any route.

North Atlantic Coast to the Great Lakes and the Mississippi River.— With the early settlement of the Atlantic coastal strip from Chesapeake

Bay northward, the major business activities of the country were focussed upon this territory. Pioneers who dared to invade the wilds across the Appalachian highland sent back stories of the wealth of the "West," and stimulated the Easterners to devise improved means of communication with the back country. Although dirt roads presented a possibility, they were hardly practicable because of the difficulty of upkeep, especially in a sparsely populated country. They became muddy after rains and were broken up during the freezing and thawing spells of early spring. Again, the freight to be handled was for the most part bulky or heavy, including among other things, salt, hides, livestock, some grains, whisky, and tobacco.

Sufficient pressure was brought to bear upon Congress to cause that body to authorize (1806) the construction of a road from Cumberland, Maryland, westward to the Ohio River and subsequently to the Mississippi. The contract for the actual construction of the first ten miles of the road was let in 1811 and by 1818 the entire road to the Ohio was completed. By 1833 it was extended to Columbus, Ohio, stimulating the growth of this trade center and stamping it henceforth as one of importance. This road, known as the National or Cumberland Road, may have been more important for its strategic than for its commercial value, although the latter was by no means unimportant. "The building of the National Road was undoubtedly one of the influences which secured the west to the Union, and the population which at once poured into the Ohio Valley undoubtedly saved the western states in embryo from greater perils, even, than those they had known." [4] When, through the years of its construction, Congress raised some doubts as to the advisability of appropriating more money for the continuance of the road, the military argument proved to be one of the strongest in convincing doubters that the work should be completed. The subsequent inflow of population, however, contributed to urban as well as rural development along the route and eventually gave it greater economic than military significance.

The New York State Barge Canal.—A flood of immigrants from Europe, having freshly in mind canals and rivers as the most natural avenues for transportation, helped to direct public thought to canal building and river improvement. While many fantastic suggestions for canals across the Appalachian barrier in Pennsylvania, Maryland, and West Virginia were actually tried, they were doomed to failure by the combined height and steep slopes of the mountains. The urge, however,

---

[1] A. B. Hulbert, *The Old National Road* (Columbus, Ohio, 1901) p. 14.

for a means of transportation much more efficient than the overland wagon kept the canal idea before the public, particularly since the steam locomotive was still in the experimental stage and only a few persons could appreciate a future for it. Among the saner suggestions for a canal route from tide-water to the interior was that which proposed a connection between the Hudson River and Lake Erie via the Mohawk Valley. This was realized when the Erie Canal, as previously indicated, was opened for use in 1825. Some idea of the immediate effect of this route upon trade may be derived from a report issued in 1826 which cites the passage at a given point of 15,000 boats and rafts in a single day. Temporarily, the Erie Canal detracted public interest from all overland routes and concentrated attention upon canal possibilities.

At the same time some men were interested in railroad transportation and were carrying on investigations of England's successful railroads. The differences of opinion, however, between the advocates of the two modes of transportation were of less significance than the fact that the Mohawk Pass route proved a boon to the entire country. It not only facilitated trade but also the migrations of peoples which, in turn, augmented trade. The greater the number of settlers in the Great Lakes region, the more goods became available for exchange, since the raw materials which they secured were shipped to the East and to Europe, in exchange for manufactured products. To-day the galaxy of trade centers along this route bears testimony to its influence upon both the movement of people and the growth of trade. (Fig. 44.)

Railroad Flexibility.—It was not long until the railroad followed the canal routes and established competition with them. While at first the cost of rail transportation was higher than canal, railroad flexibility was destined to triumph over canals. Many trade centers could not be reached by canals nor could the latter be extended to them, but railways could be built practically anywhere. In spite of the continuation of the waterway era and a rapid development of steamships on the Great Lakes, the Ohio, Mississippi, and other rivers, railroads slowly but surely penetrated the mountains, the forests, and the plains. In the decade 1830-1840 railroads made notable progress, a total of 2,264 miles having been completed. Although water transportation held its own fairly well until as late as 1850, its fate was sealed. Practically all of the interior water routes charged tolls until the advent of railroad competition when the latter forced the canals to eliminate tolls. This was the forerunner of canal decline, for virtually their entire upkeep was shifted to the taxpayer who resented and resisted an increase in taxation. As railroads improved their facilities, speeded up their schedules, and offered good service throughout the winter season as well as the summer, shippers lost interest in canals and gave their support to the railroads.

The Great Lakes versus the East-West Routes.—No doubt an important urge to the building of the Erie Canal was the prospect of a connection with the Great Lakes and hence an all-water route from the Atlantic to the very heart of the continent. Four of the Great Lakes could not be reached direct from the sea via the St. Lawrence because of Niagara Falls and the one accessible at all, Lake Ontario, could be reached only during the months from mid-April to early December. The lake region could not be approached via the southerly-flowing navigable Mississippi and its tributaries until steamboats became a reality because early river boats could make little headway up stream.

The first steamboats on the Great Lakes were launched in 1816 and the first one to put in to Chicago arrived as a war vessel, the *Thompson,* in July, 1832, carrying troops and supplies for the prosecution of the Black Hawk War. Regular schedules were subsequently adopted between the West and East for the carriage of freight and passengers. The first Sault Ste. Marie twelve-foot Canal, between Lake Superior and the Lower Lakes, opened in 1855, encouraged trade, but not until its deepening to sixteen feet in 1881, followed by the construction of the first steel freighter at Detroit in 1882, did lake traffic begin to attain sizable proportions. Commerce on Lake Superior increased in the next fifteen years from 1,567,000 tons to 16,239,000 tons.[2] Improvements in shipping facilities went on apace, and successive discoveries of iron ore in upper Michigan, northern Wisconsin, and northeastern Minnesota contributed to increased manufacturing in the East. Wheat farming development in the Red River Valley of the North during the 1880's furnished further cargo for the lakes, and in return for the wheat and ore the carriers brought coal into the Northwest. But, while the Great Lakes have been significant as a highway for the handling of bulk cargoes, including primarily iron ore, grain, coal, lumber, and copper, they have played an even greater part in our economic development through their effect upon rail routes, rates, and the growth of urban centers.

Rail Competition.—The Great Lakes, having afforded so easy a highway for ships of large capacity and having attracted bulky raw materials

---

[2] George J. Miller, "Some Geographic Influences of the Lake Superior Iron Ores," *The Bulletin of the American Geographic Society* (Dec., 1917) Vol. XLVI.

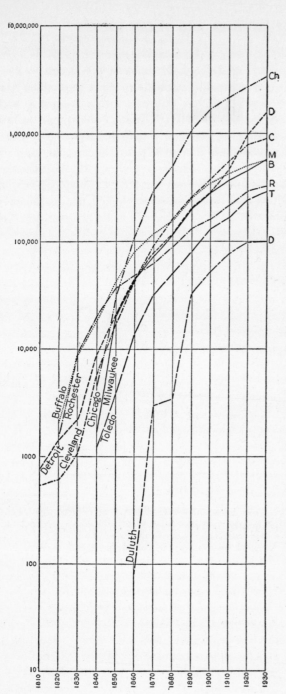

FIG. 46. THE GREAT LAKES STIMULATE TRADE CENTER GROWTH*

This group of Great Lakes ports reveals an unusually rapid rate of growth. While some of their growth may be attributed to the general development of the upper Mississippi Valley, the services rendered by the lakes as a transportation highway and source of water supply have undoubtedly played a major part in their activity. (This graph should be held in a vertical position when read.)

* Curves are drawn upon a logarithmic base.

such as those just mentioned, materials which railroads could not economically carry long distances from the regions of production to those of consumption, attracted short-line railroads to their ports. The map reveals the radial arrangement of our railroads with reference to such ports as Duluth-Superior, Chicago-South Chicago, Toledo, and Buffalo.

Railroad rates on certain products show a remarkable parallelism with lake rates. While some economists doubt the lake influence, the graph of

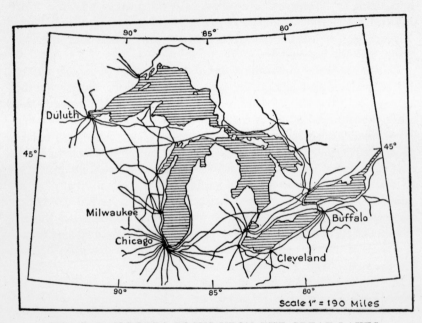

FIG. 47. RAILROADS FOCUS UPON THE GREAT LAKES

The attraction of a navigable waterway for railroads is strikingly illustrated by the above map. The roads converge in particular at critical points where bulk is broken as at Duluth or where there is a change in direction of traffic as at Chicago or where cities constitute nodal centers for the collection, manufacture, and distribution of commodities as at Cleveland or Milwaukee.

comparative rates over the years seems incontrovertible. Lake rates themselves have not always been as low as they might because for years the railroads operated lake vessels and determined water rates. Nevertheless, since carrying costs on the lakes have been notably less than on land, the former rates have reflected some of this cost difference, particularly in bulky and non-perishable goods, and, therefore, the rail differentials on commodities sought by both carriers have undoubtedly been lower than they otherwise would have been. As long as the United States Government subsidizes shipping on the lakes through defrayment of the costs of upkeep of harbors, channel improvements, lighthouses, and other right-of-way elements, the cost of transportation on these waters must remain low for ship owners as compared with the costs by rail to the rail owners who receive no government assistance. Lake carriers, freed from a right-of-way overhead and from interest upon such an investment, are relieved of a tremendous burden which railroad corporations can not escape when determining their charges. Nevertheless, railroad corporations have to make concessions in competition with the waterway.

In spite of water competition, railroads succeeded in rapidly extending their lines throughout the lake territory, always having the advantage of being able to offer an all-year service to the rising centers while the lakes could only serve about eight months. They paralleled the lakes where freight became available and supplied feeders to the lakes to supplement lake shipping. In consequence of the development of the vast agricultural lands and extraction of non-agricultural products such as coal, clay, salt, and other raw stuffs and the concentration of population in trade centers, manufacturing industries developed which contributed further to the creation of freight. The railroads cut through the Appalachian barrier wherever necessary, crossing it almost at will in quest of rapidly growing business. The lines connecting Chicago or St. Louis with the Atlantic Seaboard attained great importance. The Baltimore and Ohio Railroad, the Pennsylvania System, the New York Central, the Erie, and still others developed a dense rail network.

As the efficiency of the railroads increased, virtually all of the waterways except the Great Lakes came into disuse. Only recently have the New York State Barge Canal, the Ohio River, and the Mississippi shown a revival of trade service.

Had the railroad as an effective carrier of goods come into use about the time of the War of Independence or a little earlier, canal routes probably would not have been constructed. In fact, it is more than likely that not even the Ohio and Mississippi Rivers would have acquired prominence as freight carriers. That the Great Lakes would have served, there can be no doubt, because of the vast quantities of raw materials bordering them which could not have been so economically carried by rail to the consumers of the East. Early immigrants came from a region where the waterway as a carrier of freight was a standard device. Centuries of waterway experience had been accumulated. The railroad was unknown until the early nineteenth century and experience with it had yet to be acquired.

The Transcontinental Routes.—The term "transcontinental" in its literal sense is a misnomer as applied to railroads in the United States. We have no through rail routes from coast to coast, except one from the Gulf of Mexico to the Pacific Coast. However, since this expression has become a part of our trade route language and since its application to those roads which traverse the continent from the Mississippi River or from Chicago to the Pacific Coast is clearly understood, presumably, we are justified in using it. Only Canada, Mexico, Guatemala, Costa Rica, and Panama have transcontinental railroads in the real sense of the term.

Perhaps the most striking feature of a map showing our western routes, whether they be rail or country road, is their paucity, their parallelism, and the large gaps between them. This is in conspicuous contrast to the number and distribution of the routes east of the Mississippi. We need not wonder long about this contrast if we compare the route maps with topographic and climatic maps. The high Cordilleran chain concentrates the routes west of the one-hundredth meridian at trade centers represented by the passes. These routes lead to the minerals, the timber, the agricultural crops, and the centers of population along the Pacific slope. These passes, however, do not account for the sudden reduction in number of routes west of the Missouri River and their subsequent expansion in the Pacific States. The rainfall map tells that story. Wherever precipitation falls below twenty inches and the rate of evaporation is high agriculture without irrigation is impossible, or, at best, hazardous. The natural vegetation contributes no important economic products; the native animal life supplies neither food nor furs of consequence and minerals exert little influence. In the absence of foodstuffs sufficient to support a thriving population, trade is reduced to minor proportions and trade routes diminish in number.

The contrast between West and East illustrates the influence of the distribution and accessibility of resources upon the establishment of trade routes. The expansion of routes in California, Oregon, and Washington, a region of abundance, is easy to explain in the light of the conditions farther east. Agricultural and mineral products in abundance along a coast bordering a great navigable ocean contributed to the development of trade centers and these, in turn, gave added momentum to activities along the routes of exchange.

Canadian Transcontinental Trade Routes.—We have asserted that the development of the Canadian trade routes paralleled that of the American and that fundamentally the influences upon all of these routes were much the same. However, one striking difference exists with respect to the continuity of the several transcontinental railroads. Both the Canadian National Railways and the Canadian Pacific Railway extend from coast to coast. They are truly transcontinental.

The regions which these roads penetrate are neither productive throughout nor densely populated; yet in their eastern portions the major part of the Canadian population, concentrated in numerous trade centers, produces some manufactured goods as well as agricultural commodities, while the western areas just east of the Cordilleran ranges provide sufficient wheat tonnage to keep the roads busy to capacity in the late summer and autumn seasons. But a great gap in productive area, except for a few mines, lies south of Hudson Bay where the surface consists largely of barren igneous rock masses and scattered glacial lakes—as yet, a sort of no man's land.

The Canadian Pacific Railway supplements its internal freight deficiency through the operation of ocean steamships. It has survived without many difficulties, but the Canadian National Railways have been saved only through government control. The latter, for the present, must be looked upon as a military railroad shortening the distance from sea to sea, because of its high latitude,[3] and reducing the length of a link in the all-British round the world communications. No doubt, the day will arrive when the northern lands through which it passes will offer enough freight, particularly in the western wheat provinces of Canada, to make it self-supporting, but until that time it must be looked upon, not as a route developed out of the exigencies of production and demand, but rather for military and political reasons.

One other railroad route of especial interest in Canada is that extending from Pas in the wheat regions of Saskatchewan to Port Churchill on Hudson Bay. The significance of this route lies in the possibility of carrying wheat from Canada to Liverpool by the shortest of all routes. The distance from Port Churchill to Liverpool is 2,970 nautical miles, as compared with 2,785 from Montreal and 3,107 from New York. The difference of 185 miles between the Hudson Bay and the Montreal

[3] Just as a great circle sailing on the seas involves the reduction of distances the farther north or south of the equator that meridians are crossed, so the same principle holds for routes on the land. On the North American Continent the higher the latitude between given meridians the shorter is the distance in miles between them.

sea routes is more than offset by the rail haul to Port Churchill which is considerably less than the combination rail and lake haul from western Canada to Montreal. Its handicap lies in the short navigation season on Hudson Bay from about mid-July to the first of November. The effect of this new route upon the rate of growth of Churchill will be worth observing. Its immediate hinterland seems to offer little of natural resources and slight prospect of agricultural development owing to poor soils and an unfavorable climate.

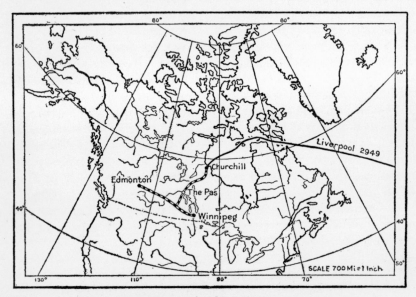

FIG. 48. CANADA'S SHORT ROUTE TO EUROPE

The new route via Churchill to northern Europe, developed to allow of direct wheat exports, means not only a saving in distance and time but also encourages the northward extension of settlement in the Hudson Bay Region in spite of many physical handicaps in terms of climate, drainage, and soils.

Transcontinental Routes in Mexico and Central America.—The mountainous character of the western part of Mexico has been a severe obstacle to transcontinental railroad construction. Engineers finally succeeded, however, in spanning the country in the approximate latitude of Mexico City and the middle states. The route splits at Guadalajara, one division approaching the coast and paralleling it northward to Guaymas and the other division running southward to Manzanillo. While neither one of these lines is heavily traveled either by passengers or freight, they have the strategic value of knitting the west coast districts with the interior and the national capital.

Farther south another transcontinental route follows through a low pass across the Isthmus of Tehuantepec. Puerto Mexico, on the Atlantic side and more specifically on the Gulf of Mexico, is connected with Salina Cruz on the Pacific Ocean. This is a north-south transcontinental route because here the continental land mass swings sharply eastward as one travels southward and the break in the mountains occurs where the highland axis assumes an east-west direction. The route is not difficult to maintain and as a short-cut in this vicinity from one side of the continent to the other renders effective service.

Although railroad routes in Mexico are not numerous, they seem to offer adequate facilities to the population which can afford to use them. Overland trails still play an important rôle, while automobile highways are slowly but consistently penetrating both mountain areas and plains. Semi-arid conditions in the north and wet tropical situations in the south present difficult problems in road building and maintenance, but the Mexican government has in recent years exhibited a determined attitude to provide, even at great cost, the kind of transportation accommodations with which a progressive nation greatly desires to be identified.

In Central America as in Mexico both topographic and climatic elements challenge man's engineering ingenuity and also require the expenditure of vast sums of money for railroad and highway construction wherever they are attempted. Lacking abundant capital, improved routes are few. The route map of this part of the continent is impressive because of the paucity of roads. Tegucigalpa, the capital of Honduras, has yet to experience the convenience of a railroad outlet.

The west coasts of these countries are better supplied with railroads than the east coasts, probably because most of the population inhabits the highlands near this coast where the climate is more favorable to man than that on the wet tropical lowlands draining toward Caribbean waters. The number of important trade centers on the west coast is greatly in excess of those on the east coast.

In the entire length of Central America there are but three transcontinental railroad routes. One of these crosses Guatemala, connecting Puerto Barrios on the Gulf of Honduras with San José and other points on the Pacific. A division penetrates El Salvador to the southward terminating at La Union, thus providing a transcontinental connection for El Salvador, albeit through a foreign country. Another road traverses Costa Rica between Limon and Puntarenas and the third parallels the Panama Canal in the Canal Zone.

A longitudinal line from Mexico City penetrates the western coastal plain of Guatemala and has been projected southward to join eventually with other links now in existence as far as the Canal Zone and even Colombia in South America. Reference to this intercontinental route will be made again in association with South American trade routes.

Throughout Central America trail and pack animal are still common modes of transportation. Small boats on short shallow streams are utilized where possible and coast-wise steamers either supplement land routes between ports or, in the absence of such communication, represent the only means of transportation. Numerous trade routes are not essential in this region, owing to the small population and to its rather low level of civilization. White people are in the minority, and the native Indians under the influence of a warm tropical environment are not aggressive.

The Panama Canal as an important transcontinental route will be discussed as an ocean trade route owing to the fact that its primary purpose is to connect the Atlantic and Pacific Oceans by a route which eliminates the long "round the Horn" distance. Hence, it is interpreted here as an ocean route as well as a transcontinental route.

Aerial Routes.—The accompanying map (Fig. 49) reveals clearer than words, the network of aerial routes already recognized as standard and some of those proposed. We have previously noted various elements affecting the routes. One not yet mentioned is the terminal itself. Those who have observed the tremendous progress made in the field of commercial aviation must, it seems, see this form of transportation in terms of a permanent integral part of our commercial means of communication and consequently must favor the establishment of thoroughly modern terminals. In 1937, 2,355 [4] airports and landing fields of varying grade were available in the United States. While this number appears considerable, it is in fact quite small when compared with the vast area of the country and the total number of trade centers. Only 740 of the airports were municipal. The progressive community will either defray the entire cost of a landing field or share such cost with private corporations desirous of including that center upon its trade route. Landing fields may exert two types of influence, namely, (1) attract airplanes

[4] U. S. Department of Commerce, typed report, March 1, 1937.

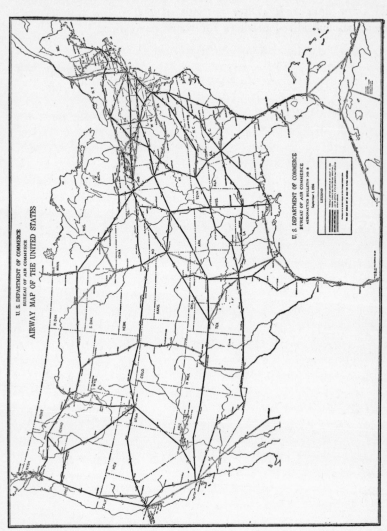

FIG. 49. MAJOR AERIAL ROUTES OF THE UNITED STATES

The airway map is a map of trade center distribution too. This map shows only major lines. If all services were shown the network would be so dense as to obliterate much of the map surface. As the services increase in number and in efficiency the trade centers are drawn closer and closer together.

that have not heretofore stopped and (2) encourage those that have called occasionally to continue calling. In addition to trade center support, the national government has already come forward with markers and guides for inter-trade center portions of the routes, just as the government has subsidized markers for water navigation.

CHAPTER XIII

EUROPEAN TRADE ROUTES

If we compare the railway maps of North America and Europe, assuming that the railways represent the primary land routes, we note a striking contrast in their respective patterns. The network in North America forms a rectangular pattern whereas that of Europe is largely radial. These arrangements suggest a profound difference in the reason for their evolution.

Whereas in North America the development of railroad routes occurred to a large extent simultaneously with the economic occupance of the country, the settlement of Europe was already well under way at the beginning of the railroad era. Such trade centers as London, Paris, Berlin, München (Munich), and many others had already become stabilized centers and seats of considerable influence, politically, economically, and culturally. When railroads were first recognized as important transportation media they were built with reference to major trade centers, and hence their geographic distribution was definitely shaped by the distribution of these centers. In other words, railroads in Europe followed very largely the rise of trade centers rather than preceded them as was frequently the case in North America.

As the political divisions of Europe evolved into numerous independent countries the element of national defense became of vital importance. Every effort was made to link the capital cities with international boundaries in order to facilitate the movement of armies and munitions from the heart of the respective countries to the field of possible conflict. Before the World War Germany boasted of the fact that it could send from Berlin to the French border within twenty-four hours a fully equipped army which would be capable not only of defending the country from any threatened encroachment by France but could, if necessary, assume an aggressive attitude. Practically the entire railroad system reaching from Berlin to the Ruhr Valley had been built with respect to the problems of national defense. Wherever we follow the distribution of railroads over the continent of Europe their radial arrangement stands out in contrast with the rectangular non-

179

military pattern in North America. Commercial considerations in their building have been largely secondary. Many trade centers at their termini are located quite as much for their military strategic value as for their trade value.

Land Routes.—The topographic characteristics of Europe as a whole are highly favorable to the development of trade routes. Not only has the construction of railroads been relatively easy but throughout the historical development of Europe convenient natural avenues for both overland and water traffic have been at hand. Furthermore, the deeply indented coast line brings most trade centers into relatively close proximity either to the ocean or to a waterway connecting directly with the ocean. Although southern Europe and portions of the central area are interrupted by mountains rising here and there to considerable altitudes, the mountain passes are sufficiently low to invite relatively easy passage across them. For example, between the western end of the Transylvanian Alps and the North Central Balkans, the "Iron Gate," occupied by the mighty Danube, affords an easy pass between central and southeastern Europe. The Rhône River Valley provides a convenient north-south passage between the high Pyrenees and the rugged Alps. Through the heart of the Alps themselves such passes as the Simplon, the St. Gotthard, the Furka, the Brenner, and Semmering have moderated the barrier characteristics of this majestic mountain mass.[1] And the approach to each of these passes is marked by trade centers which have stood "guard" over them since shortly after they first came into use.

Owing to the fact that the continent is split into numerous political entities, transcontinental trade routes are not of quite the same quality as those in North America where the transcontinental railroads and highways lie wholly within a single national unit. However, in peace times the transcontinental railroads function satisfactorily. The major routes are the Paris-Berlin-Moskva route, the Paris-Milano-Brindisi route, and the Berlin-Wien-Istanbul route. All these routes can be considered as including London, provided we recognize the fact that a break occurs at the English Channel and the North Sea. These waters are not generally crossed by railroad ferry, but passengers and freight must be transshipped from rail to water and water to rail.[2] The Paris-Milano-

[1] Because of space limitations and also the availability of excellent maps of the continents, no attempt is made to detail the topographic characteristics of the terrain along the trade routes.

[2] The first experimental rail ferry between Dover and Calais was established late in 1936.

Brindisi route, a distance of 1,169 miles, makes possible a considerable saving in time in connection with mail and express shipments from northwestern Europe to the Orient. Items may be dispatched from London or Paris several days after ships for the Orient depart from channel ports and meet them at Brindisi for further movement to the Orient. The Paris-Berlin-Moskva route is linked with the Trans-siberian Railroad. However, until traffic on the latter route grows in significance and until the Siberian territory becomes economically more active, this transcontinental way for freight and passengers can not be regarded as of great consequence. On the other hand, for traffic between Paris, Berlin, Warszawa (Warsaw), and intermediate points it provides an effective service of first rank. The Berlin-Istanbul route is a portion of that famed pre-war "Berlin to Baghdad Route." This latter route is one which splits Europe into two parts and has not only large commercial value but critical military value. Among the ambitions of Germany prior to the war was the control of the Berlin to Baghdad route, which would have made Germany supreme in central and eastern Europe and in southwestern Asia. Whoever controls this avenue of trade splits Europe into two interdependent areas and, hence, is in a position to shape the international economic progress of the respective areas.

These routes afford not only connections with London but with the northern countries of Europe. The Baltic waters are essentially enclosed. The Scandinavian countries which border this sea have developed close cultural relationships with Germany. Efficient means of communication in this region are developed among which is a railroad ferry service. There are ferries between Denmark and Germany and between western Sweden and Germany. The ferry link with Denmark operates between Warnemünde and Gjedser and that with Sweden between Sassnitz and Trälleborg. There are railroad ferries between Denmark and Sweden, particularly between Kobenhavn (Copenhagen) and Malmö and between Helsingör and Halsingborg. These railroad ferries, operating on regular schedules throughout the entire year provide continuous rail routes between central and northern Europe. Although the transportation surface changes in character, bulk is not broken.

Rivers, Canals, and Lakes.—The use of waterways in Europe to-day represents an inheritance from past centuries. The arrangement of the rivers has favored their use by untold numbers of people who have roamed over the continent. When it is recalled that the early migrants into Europe, who played a major part in the development of its civilization, entered from the southeast, then the southeast-northwest parallelism of the major river axes becomes all the more significant.

Those peoples who trekked along the north or the south shores of the Black Sea and came upon the Danube found an easy route through the heart of central Europe. Some of them left the Danube in the vicinity of Wien and after a short overland portage found themselves

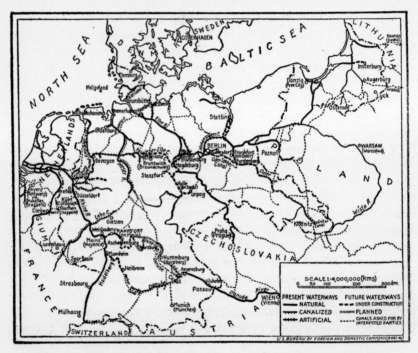

FIG. 50. THE WATERWAYS OF NORTH CENTRAL EUROPE

This network of waterways not only consolidates the nations but brings the trade centers into closer economic proximity to each other. It makes many of the inland centers "ocean" ports and helps provide the citizens with a world outlook through world contacts. (Courtesy of *Commerce Reports*.)

at the Vltava (Moldau) River, a tributary of the Elbe which carried them into north Germany. The source of the Danube River approaches close to the waters of the Rhine which furnishes another easy highway down to the North Sea. At one time there was a very lively trade, especially in amber, between the Baltic and the Mediterranean Seas via the waters of the Bug and the Wisla (Vistula) Rivers; likewise the Dnieper and the Niemen furnished an essentially continuous highway.

In western Europe the close approach of the Rhône-Saône River system to the Seine River provides a convenient north-south highway. The great network of rivers in European Soviet Russia have furnished from time immemorial some of the best and most convenient trade routes across that vast plain. In the winter season the frozen rivers make excellent roadways.

In more recent times these and many other rivers of Europe such as the Weser, Scheldt, and the Oder have played a significant part in the carriage of freight. Many of them have been deepened, canalized in some cases, and, in general, improved for modern transportation purposes. In some respects they are as important links in the conduct of trade as the railroads or auto highways.

Waterways in Europe as avenues of communication were fairly well-developed before the era of railroads. Until about the middle of the nineteenth century when railroads were generally accepted as the future transportation medium the inland waterway was standard. The value of the waterway having been so deeply impressed upon the European mind, its survival in the face of railroad development is readily understood.

Since both the railways and waterways of the mainland of Europe were under government ownership until the World War, there was no freight competition between water and rail as in the United States. In fact, in most countries, but particularly in Germany, heavy freight was generally allocated to the waterways, whereas light or package freight was assigned to the rails. In some instances even package freight went by canal and river in order that enough business might be handled by the waterway to make it "pay for itself."

Obviously there has been some question as to whether these waterways really paid for themselves. If the subsidies given by the respective governments be taken into consideration the probabilities are that these waterways have not paid as commercial ventures. On the other hand, they have functioned effectively as carriers of munitions in times of war. Therefore, if considered from a military standpoint they have no doubt "earned" their way.

In consequence of the large use to which these waterways have been put there have been developed special types of barges which carry upwards of 4,000 to 6,000 tons of freight. Many inland trade centers located upon these waterways have evolved efficient ports to which reference has already been made in Chapter IX. That these trade centers have profited from the waterway improvements is not to be denied. One need only note the galaxy of port cities along the Rhine River.

Northern Europe and the Alpine region have numerous navigable lakes. Small trim vessels ply their waters upon regular schedules as long as the lakes are ice free. In some parts of Finland and on a few Alpine lakes diminutive trade centers have developed upon the lake shores without supplementary railroad communication. When the lakes are frozen, they are utilized as "paved" highways. Naturally, in the transition seasons from autumn to winter and winter to spring the settlements experience temporary inconvenience having neither frozen highways nor ship service. We emphasize the fact that, although some of these lakes have a small area and are shallow as compared with the Great Lakes in the United States, accommodating boats in certain instances of not over six feet draft and twenty to forty feet length, they are no less important in the eyes of the local inhabitants than are the lakes of world renown.

Coastal Routes.—In addition to the inland waterways, the coastal waters have played an important part in European transportation. As already suggested, the coast line is exceedingly irregular and arms of the sea penetrate far into the continent. In fact, this penetration is so deep that it has brought most of the people of Europe within less than seven hundred miles of the sea, and most of the people west of the twentieth meridian within less than four hundred miles from the sea. The majority of the trade centers of western Europe are either within fifty to one hundred miles of the sea or of a navigable river connecting with the sea. Thus, there has developed a type of sea-mindedness among Europeans which has fostered the improvement of both coastal and inland waterways.

Coastwise traffic was stimulated, particularly in medieval days when the Hanseatic League was active and when a lively commerce was established between the League centers on or near the Baltic Sea and the Mediterranean centers. Baltic herring were in great demand among the Catholic countries of the Mediterranean and this brought into North Sea waters traders from the Mediterranean and the Baltic. Bruges, in Belgium, was a major meeting place. Even to-day these coastal waters support an extensive traffic.

In consequence of the development of good ports and the ease of communication by water, we have seen the establishment of numerous free ports patterned after that at Hamburg. Through the free port each country has hoped to attract ships of other nations plying in these waters. They expected thereby to relieve themselves from the expense of supporting a merchant marine of their own for which they might have difficulty in supplying sufficient freight. At the same time they have been able to take advantage of diversified cargoes which the ships of the larger nations bring from various parts of the world, but only a small part of which any one of them can afford to purchase. The experiment has proved successful.

One of the most interesting of the coastal routes skirts the west side of the Scandinavian peninsula to the Arctic Ocean, follows the coastline past Finnish waters, terminating at the practically ice-free port of Alexandrovsk. An attempt was made during the latter part of the World War to develop this port by improving it at tremendous cost and establishing a railroad connection with Leningrad. Although this work was of an emergency character at the time, the immediate objective being to bring support to the rapidly disintegrating Russian army, there was hope that Alexandrovsk might be developed into a first class port commanding considerable trade. Failure of the Russians to realize that ambition is readily appreciated by a glance at the map which reveals the remoteness of this trade center from not only major routes but also from most secondary routes. Even the Soviet régime with all its ambitions for trade has been unable to induce traders into those far northern waters.

Aerial Routes.—Although the airplane was invented in the United States, European nations were pioneers in the development of commercial aviation. Showing an appreciation of the value of aviation in military maneuvers, many of the countries subsidized commercial aviation with a view toward offering to large numbers of men an opportunity for training. Again, some of the smaller countries having limited transportation connections with larger centers have seized the opportunity to support commercial aviation thereby bringing themselves in point of time much closer to the critical commercial hubs than was possible by rail or steamship.

Western Europe developed a dense network of aerial routes, a network unsurpassed by any other equivalent area. Until quite recently both the service and the efficiency of European airways has been the best in the world. The people of the United States finally awoke to the possibilities of this form of transportation and now have developed an aerial system comparable to that in Europe.

Not only has Europe pioneered in the use of the airplane for commercial purposes but it has contributed the airship. Germany has blazed a trail in this branch of aviation and has established a regular commercial service with the east coast of South America. Plans are in the making for expanding the service with North America.

The U. S. S. R. has found aerial navigation peculiarly suited to its needs, owing not only to the vastness of its domain, but to the pioneer state of so many of its trade centers. Rail communication and improved highways among these centers are either totally absent or wholly inadequate. The inability of former régimes to control the country because of poor transportation means is almost wholly offset by the presence of the airplane. Now officials from the central government at Moskva can reach any center quickly and comfortably whenever they find that the enforcement of their dictates requires their presence.

The development of commercial aviation in Europe has been the more remarkable because of the many small countries, the numerous international boundary lines that must be crossed, and the sensitivity of each nation to the matter of keeping secret their respective military defenses. The nations have agreements with each other with regard to the points at which boundary lines may be crossed. Sometimes mistakes in flight have been made due to bad weather conditions. These errors have been interpreted occasionally as "intentional" accidents and have caused considerable international friction. On the whole, however, such difficulties have been avoided and the business men of Europe have been provided with a highly effective service practically to all parts of the continent, irrespective of topographic and climatic conditions.

CHAPTER XIV

OTHER LAND TRADE ROUTES OF THE WORLD

ASIA

The surface conditions of Asia present many obstacles to settlement and to the movements of peoples and products. The heart of the continent rises to an extensive plateau over 10,000 feet in altitude and is interrupted by deserts which are severely cold in winter and intensely hot in summer. The main axes of the mountain ranges interrupt the surface in both longitudinal and latitudinal directions. The major rivers of the northern portion of the continent flow down to a sea frozen most of the year and in the eastern and southern areas many of the rivers such as the Hwang-Ho, Yangtze, and Ganges annually flood their valleys wreaking havoc in trade centers and on cultivated lands. Temperatures in the northern part of the continent are the lowest recorded upon the earth's surface, while those occurring in the southern parts, particularly in northeastern India and Indo-China are among the highest of sensible temperatures.

Under these topographic and climatic conditions the maintenance of trade routes must be ascribed to the courage and endurance of the natives. Chinese and other peoples of eastern and southern Asia early utilized the rivers but seemingly did not venture along the coasts in their little junks until perhaps medieval times. Communication between India and China prior to the use of the seas was via the difficult Khyber Pass and forbidding overland caravan routes across the high plateaus already mentioned. Naturally, under these conditions there could be no regularity in transportation service. Many peoples had to be economically self-sufficient, and it is conceivable that the rise of numerous small centers in very early times was partly a response to the difficulties of communication.

Northern and Western Asia.—To-day the northern part of the continent is crossed by the Trans-Siberian Railway which has helped to some extent to knit the highly scattered population of that region and to give to the pre-war régime, as well as the present Soviet government, the means for increasing its political influence in Asiatic territory. However, this railroad line, only partially double tracked, is one not easily maintained in the best of condition. Consequently, it has not yet developed into a route of large commercial influence. Recently the Soviet government has completed an important link from Novo-Sibirsk southward into Turkestan, connecting there with the once renowned caravan route across Turkestan to the Caspian Sea. This old route, which was a part of the transcontinental caravan highway from Europe to China, marked by such famous towns as Tashkent, Bukhara, and Merv, is now replaced by a railroad which is connected with the branch line from Novo-Sibirsk. In this portion of the U. S. S. R. these railroads are serving to revive old trade centers and to open up agricultural and mineral possibilities of a vast area which undoubtedly will contribute considerable wealth to the Soviet peoples.

The extreme southwestern portion of Asia is impressive more for the absence of railroads than for their presence. The southern end of the Berlin to Baghdad route is represented by a railroad connecting Baghdad with the head of the Persian Gulf. A short line runs from Jerusalem to Medina and extends northward to Alep (Aleppo) and the Berlin to Baghdad route. A few short railways are scattered in Asia Minor. Vast areas yet remain to be penetrated by the railway.

India.—India reveals the densest railroad network among Asiatic countries, thanks to the activities of the British. It is unlikely that India, left to its own destinies, would have developed so effective and complete a railway network. No consequential part of the country is beyond the reach of a railway.

Except for the waterways of the Ganges Valley, the rivers are of relatively slight importance as avenues of communication. The distributaries of the Ganges delta are important locally for the dense population gathered there and not only supplement the rail routes but in some instances supersede them. The Brahmaputra serves also as a useful route penetrating the northeastern portions of the country.

The topography and irregular seasonal rainfall in many regions present engineering difficulties for both rail and river improvement. In the Deccan, for example, flood waters or steep gradients prevent river navigation, and high relief of the terrain, particularly along the Western Ghats range, has called forth the best skill of British railroad engineers to negotiate the connections between such trade centers as Bombay and Calicut on the west coast and Madras on the east coast and interior centers like Hyderabad, Bangalore, and intermediate points. In fact, the urge, as it were, of the trade centers for rapid and convenient communication with each other and the military exigencies have been paramount factors in the determination of the courses of these trade routes and influential in the first instance in the decisions which effected their construction.

The dense railway network in the upper Ganges and Indus River valleys represents a response to the need for relieving famine conditions, which occur in this region when the monsoon fails, and in part to provide military routes between the Khyber Pass and the interior. Then, too, that impressive lineal sequence of trade centers in the Ganges basin, Delhi, Lucknow, Cawnpore, Benares and others, is provided with a convenient means for exchanging commodities. Famine areas, too, on the Deccan have been partially responsible for railroad building.

As in other parts of the world where railroads have enjoyed a healthy development, so here they find themselves confronted with motor competition. The automobile, auto-truck, and bus are making their impression upon the mass of struggling humanity in India.

China.—The Chinese as a whole have been slow to see the advantages of railroads. Those rulers who have shown an interest in their construction have been unable to make their desires effective owing to the lack of sufficient capital. Still, railroad building is in progress but not at an impressive rate. There is no railroad line extending the full length of the country from north to south nor from east to west. In vast areas "travel is on foot, by sedan chair, on muleback, in two-wheeled carts or by boat. Twenty miles a day is a good average." [1] Throughout centuries efforts have been made by provincial officials to keep their capital cities in touch with the national capital and with each other, but the difficulties of maintaining the crude highways have been at times impossible to surmount. The term "trail" would be more appropriate than highway in many instances. The back of man is still a primary carrier of freight. In the light of these conditions the three great rivers, the Hwang-Ho, Yangtze, and Si, and the canals must serve as major carriers of overland trade. Coastal waters supplement these routes as the most effective connection among the seaport centers. Inasmuch as land conveyances are insufficient and inadequate, large trade centers in the interior are fewer than we might expect in view of the enormous population for the country as a whole. Cressey says, "China does not have an urban civilization. The real China is rural. ... Three-fourths of the people live on farms and nearly all of the

[1] G. B. Cressey, *China's Geographic Foundations* (McGraw-Hill Book Company, Inc., 1934) p. 25.

area of China lies outside city walls." [2] Yet some centers are very busy at certain times of the year, when camel caravans gather either in the spring or fall to begin a long trek across the interior deserts. Such a center is Pootowchen [3] at the end of the railroad in the Suiyuan Province from which caravans of foods and miscellaneous merchandise supplementing the railroad head into the "wastes" of Mongolia and Sinkiang (Eastern Turkestan).

That part of China where the railroad has evidenced a critical influence in the affairs of the nation is in Manchukuo (Manchuria). But here its military value has accounted more largely for the conspicuous notice it has received than its commercial service. The Chinese Eastern Railway, linking the important cities of Harbin, Moukden, and Port Arthur and penetrating Chosen, practically bisects Manchukuo. Whoever controls that line is master of the entire province, hence, the recent Japanese efforts to absorb it as a part of the campaign to establish itself commercially and politically in this section in China. Having gained control of the route Japanese supremacy in Manchukuo has been attained.

The wheelbarrow with its accompanying sail, an exceedingly ancient institution whose invention is attributed to China, has long served the Chinese as a convenient vehicle for the transportation of goods across densely settled plains. In some areas wind-blown soils (loess) have been worn hundreds of feet below the original level upon which the routes were first established.

Japan.—In Japan the need for railroads as highways of transportation is not so great as in China because of the close proximity of all parts of the interior to the sea. The major part of the population lives near the sea and the sea waters afford avenues of communication among the numerous coastal and nearby trade centers. Nevertheless, that progressive country has introduced an effective network of railroads which together with the coastal waters provides ample carrying service for the conduct of their local trade. Practically all of the trade centers of consequence are connected by rail with other parts of the country, ferries, of course, serving where narrow straits interrupt the continuity of the land. The trend toward urbanization in Japan is marked, due probably to that nation's adoption of occidental ways of life and especially to its effort toward industrialization. "At the present time...the commonest unit of settlement is the agri-

[2] *Ibid.*
[3] *Commerce Reports* (January 10, 1927) p. 78.

cultural town of 2,000 to 10,000 dwellers, 57 per cent of the population residing in such agglomerations." [4] The same writer indicates that 28 per cent of the nation in 1925 lived in 217 cities containing over 20,000 each. If we recognize centers of 2,500 or over as urban, as we do in the United States, then the urbanization of Japan becomes the more striking even though large numbers of those in the small agglomerations are engaged in agricultural pursuits.

The Automobile, the Airplane and Wireless Communication in Asia. —In all areas of Asia, except some of the major trade centers, the automobile has penetrated very slowly and still remains an implement of trade that is rare. The airplane, too, is a device of the future so far as commercial activities are concerned. Eventually it will move the trade centers closer together and bring about frequent and economical changes. One can not study this vast continent with its dense population of relatively backward peoples of exceedingly low purchasing power without coming to the conclusion that both the automobile and airplane may play in the future a larger part than the railroad. Both of these means of transportation involve a lesser expenditure of money and fewer difficult engineering problems than the railroad in a region whose topography and climate present almost insurmountable obstacles to inexpensive railroad building and maintenance.

Construction of telegraph lines is almost as difficult as railroad building with respect to both engineering problems and capital investment. Far cheaper and easier is the building of wireless sending stations for commercial telephony, telegraphy, and entertainment broadcasting. This device can do much to aid in overcoming the physical disunity of the continent. Its potential effectiveness in inter- and intra-country communication is impressive. Obviously, remote centers now isolated can be revitalized to the end that eventually the physical means of contact between them and major trade centers will be hastened, leading to mutual gains for all of them.

AFRICA

Although Africa has long been known as the "dark continent," the sunshine of a new day is rapidly spreading throughout the land as new trade routes of various kinds are being established. Routes already in service are being improved. The desert caravan route in the north is giving way to the motor vehicle; the sail boat on the Nile is being

---

[4] Glenn Trewartha, "Japanese Cities," *The Geographical Review* (July, 1934), Vol. XXIV, No. 3, pp. 404-417.

replaced by the steamship and the motor launch; and the trails of the southern portions of the continent are giving way to the modern railroad. And all of these types of overland communication are being supplemented by aerial navigation and the wireless.

Trade routes in Africa have been relatively few in consequence of negligible immigration. This lag of occupance by peoples from other parts of the world has been due not alone to the absence of good first class ports and few navigable rivers but also to the climatic handicap of a vast, hot desert in the north and a hot, rainy, tropical lowland in the west central portions.

With the opening of the Suez Canal in 1869 the limited amount of traffic up to this time around the Cape of Good Hope between Europe and the Orient was further reduced, making the continent in some respects economically more remote from Europe than ever before. Again, the political struggle among the nations of Europe for possession of parts of Africa served to break up, in a sense, the physical continuity of the region. Numerous international boundary lines became established because of these different international proprietorships, and as a result the establishment of trade relations among these units was delayed. As the European powers became interested in exploiting their possessions in Africa, trade between themselves and their respective colonies became more active than between any two possessions. Furthermore, with the exception of the extreme southern part of Africa and the northern rim, the population has been essentially of the non-productive type and of a kind which has not lent itself readily to education in modern modes of life or to the development of the natural resources of the area which it occupies. Even village life among these peoples has been negligible.

The Cape to Cairo Route.—The most notable trade route of the continent is that which has been known for some time as the Cape to Cairo route. This route has been facilitated in large part by the building of railroads and by the introduction of modern navigation facilities upon the Nile River and on some of the lakes in central Africa. The creation of this route as an all rail route was the dream of Cecil Rhodes, the far-seeing colonial statesman of England. The map indicates those portions which have been completed and those which remain to be replaced by the railroad. The section of the route in middle Africa has not been completed owing to the fact that until the Great War the Germans occupied German East Africa, now known as Tanganyika, and Belgium controlled the Belgian Congo. This situation has been relieved by the mandate over German East Africa assigned to Great Britain during the war. If this territory becomes permanently British, as is likely to be the case, the rail route may be completed as far as the Nile River. Whether it will ever be completed the entire distance between the Cape and Cairo is problematical owing to the airplane, which has been shown to be feasible as a carrier of passengers and of such freight or express as is likely to demand movement over this route in the immediate future. The growth of trade centers between the two extremities of the route will in all probability be slow unless a considerable influx of population foreign to Africa sets in, a movement not expected in the immediate future.

Eastern Africa.—Along the east side of the continent short lines extend from the seacoast toward the interior, generally connecting with the north-south route. These short laterals, no doubt, will serve effectively as links between interior regions and the coastal trade. Thus the north-south route loses its significance as a commercial transcontinental line. However, it serves as a political and military link for British interests in Africa.

Western Africa.—The French have established a trans-Sahara automobile route from Algiers to Gao on the Niger River. It was opened in March, 1930. This has been accomplished through the construction of a special six-wheeled type of vehicle for loose sandy surfaces, although part of the way is over firm surface. The time required to negotiate the route, which is 1,600 miles in length, is three days. Perhaps in the not distant future tourists with ordinary automobiles will find it possible to make this run. Most of the travel is limited to the months of September to May. Although pioneer routes often are the fore-runners to the birth and healthy growth of trade centers, the climatic limitations along this right of way probably preclude such possibilities.

Other Routes.—The development of other routes in Africa awaits two important economic activities, namely, (1) a denser settlement of the territory and (2) the extraction of mineral resources and development of agricultural lands. How soon this will come about, of course, can not be predicted. Continued expansion makes it evident that many portions of the continent are not as objectionable to settlement as was thought some years ago, and, accordingly, these areas offer satisfactory physical conditions for occupance by the overflow population from the more densely peopled countries of the earth. Improved oceanic steamship services between Africa and other con-

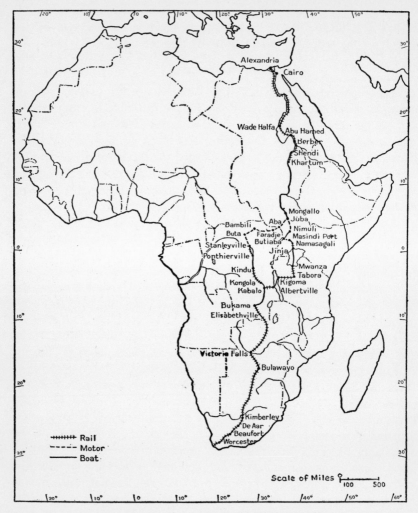

FIG. 51. THE CAPE TO CAIRO ROUTE

The dream of Cecil Rhodes is approaching reality. The commercial significance of the route has declined somewhat as aviation has developed, but the military value still obtains. Even commercially the route will be important for heavy cargo and for local or short run traffic. Now that England virtually owns Tanganyika (formerly German East Africa) the route may be straightened out in its middle course to be confined so far as possible to all British terrain.

tinents is evidence of the increasing appreciation of the rest of the world for the economic potentialities of this continent.

SOUTH AMERICA

Topographic conditions in South America present certain striking contrasts which on the one hand are highly favorable to trade routes, and on the other hand present great obstacles. The massive and high Andes, fringing virtually the entire west coast of the continent and having no low passes, have long challenged the ingenuity of the world's engineers. Even after it was found possible to throw railroads or highways across these mountains, the cost of construction proved greater than most of the countries involved could afford. Consequently, until quite recently there was but one railroad (opened in 1910) which crossed the Andes highland. This road crossed via the Uspallata pass, connecting Valparaiso on the Pacific Ocean with Buenos Aires on the Atlantic. During the past few years this transcontinental railroad has been augmented by two crossings to the northward, one connecting the capital city of La Paz, Bolivia, with the west coast and the other connecting Uyuni with Antofagasta on the Pacific. Uyuni, in turn, is linked with Sucre and La Paz to the northward and with Salta, Tucuman, and many other centers in Argentina to the southward. Buenos Aires may be reached from both Bolivian centers.

On the lower western slopes of the Andes highland, a longitudinal railroad from southern Chile to Peru is connected by numerous short laterals to the sea. The design of this railroad network is very much like that of a vertebrate column and is the consequence largely of the desirability of connecting the coastal trade centers with the highland interior centers across a desert and semi-arid, practically uninhabited lowland. From southern Peru northward the longitudinal railroads are frequently interrupted and laterals are much less common than in the southern territory.

Much remains to be done by way of improving overland travel facilities in this high mountainous portion of South America. As in the case of many other areas of the world which are still relatively scanty in population and consequently lacking in funds for the construction of adequate transportation media, the airplane is coming to the rescue. In fact, the airplane is serving so effectively that it undoubtedly will postpone for many years the consummation of many projected railroads and automobile highways if it does not entirely preclude the building of a number of them.

The Intercontinental Railway and Highway.—An intercontinental railway has been proposed to provide continuous service from New York City through Mexico City, the west coast centers of Central America, along the western slope of the Andes highland, gradually ascending that slope until a crossing is effected in Bolivia, thence into northern Argentina, and on to Rosario and Buenos Aires. A map of the route showing sections now completed reveals relatively few breaks in it. However, the missing links would be exceedingly costly to introduce. It is doubtful that such a route could pay for itself, but its psychological effect upon the people of the trade centers along the way might make a worthy contribution toward cementing among the countries involved a spirit of good will, with commercial development incidental thereto.

More recently an intercontinental motor highway has been suggested and, in fact, is partly under construction. This, if eventually realized, would probably interfere with any further attempts to complete an intercontinental rail route. On the other hand, the airplane has established itself as a connecting transportation medium between North America and South America with the effect of discounting both the railroad and the motor highway.

The Prospect.—A favorable element for railroad construction in South America is found in extensive level river basins. But, since most of the rivers of South America flood their banks, the building of railroads is hampered over a considerable portion of the lowland area. Still, there are such well drained plains as the region of the Pampas and the Gran Chaco and the hill country of southeastern Brazil where a railroad network of considerable density has been developed. No serious obstacles occur to railroad extensions in these regions.

The wide distribution of rivers and the close approach of their head waters to each other via relatively low divides has suggested to many persons that there might some day be developed an all-water route from the Atlantic on the north to the Rio de la Plata on the south. This route would follow, in general, up the Orinoco and its tributary, the Rio Cassiquiari, thence down the Rio Negro, a major tributary of the Amazon, down the Amazon to the Rio Tapajoz, up this river to some one of its several tributaries whose headwaters approach closely to the Paraguay River and down the Paraguay to the Parana and the Rio de la Plata. The divides between these rivers are so very narrow and low that the construction of canals to connect them would be a relatively simple matter. However, this conception of an all-water route represents perhaps more of a fancy than a practicality because, again, the airplane can function so much more efficiently than these waterways and the scarcity of trade centers along the way means that most of the freight would have to classify as long haul. Experience has shown that this could hardly be profitable.

The east coast of South America is well provided with good ports. Consequently, transoceanic communication with other parts of the world for this portion of the continent is excellent. The ports on the west coast are not so good but they are slowly being improved, thanks to the Panama Canal which has stimulated oceanic commerce between Europe, North America, and the west coast of South America and has made the approach to the west coast of South America much more convenient, much safer, and less costly than it was in the days when it was necessary to sail through dangerous waters around Cape Horn or through the Straits of Magellanes.

With few exceptions, the important trade centers of South America are located close to the coast. Many of them are in the highlands, where the climate is more favorable for life than on the nearby lowlands. Most important centers in the lowlands, removed some distance from the sea, are on rivers. Thus, the urge for railroads, wagon, or motor highways has been perhaps less pressing on this continent than in North America or Europe. Again, the low standard of living and the simplicity of life among great masses of the natives has made them more or less self-sufficient. Therefore, a need for quick and efficient transportation has not been felt. As the continent becomes more densely populated by a people with high standards of living, trade routes will grow in quality and also numbers.

AUSTRALIA

Since the major economic activities of Australia are carried on close to the coast, where the trade centers are concentrated, the principal trade routes are located in the coastal areas. The railroad network is densest in the southeastern corner of the continent. A secondary center occurs in the extreme southwestern region. A single transcontinental line connects the southeastern and southwestern networks. Population is distributed along the periphery of this vast island land mass, but most of it has developed in the southeast.

We can account for the peripheral distribution of population by comparing it with a rainfall map. The heart of Australia is a desert and only the edges of the continent have sufficient rainfall to permit of agriculture without irrigation. Even portions of the coastal areas, particularly the western coasts, have insufficient precipitation for agriculture. The railroad line which connects the southeastern and southwestern sections penetrates the southern boundary of the desert region and, hence, may be viewed as merely a link between east and west. A railroad line branches to the northward from this east-west route,

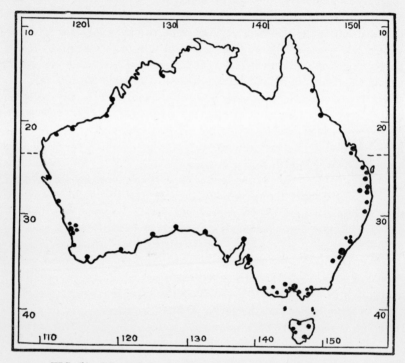

FIG. 52. TRADE CENTERS UPON THE PERIPHERY

The peripheral location and distribution of most of the important trade centers of Australia reflect the physical conditions, more particularly climatic, which "shove" the centers out to the edges of the continent. Since the trade centers occupy the fringe, we expect this area to be the region of major population.

connecting the port center of Adelaide with Stewart (Alice Springs) in central Australia. Plans call for the eventual continuation of this railroad to the short spur which now runs southward from Darwin to Daly Waters. A telegraph line already spans the continent, paralleling the completed sections of the railroad and continuing to Port Darwin. An unfortunate circumstance in the railroad system is the presence of three different gauges. Steps are being taken to remedy this inconvenience.

The railroads of the continent seem to serve present purposes adequately. Future building in all probability will be slow, as further settlement of the continent no doubt will progress at a moderate rate. The growth of new, large trade centers is unlikely.

Water Routes.—As one might anticipate from a study of the precipitation distribution, waterways are relatively few. Many in the southeast are intermittent in flow. While some of the rivers are navigable for shallow draught vessels, none are navigable for ocean going vessels. Such navigation as is attempted must figure on an uncertain water flow and interference from sand-bar formation. The population as now distributed, a distribution likely to be permanent, does not have need for inland navigable waterways. Important trade centers on the coast are easily reached by coastwise steamers and they, in turn, are connected by rail with their respective hinterlands, which are limited in area and close at hand.

The northern portion of the east coast is handicapped by the presence of the Great Barrier reef. This reef prevents the free and easy navigation of these northern coastal waters and, hence, for some time to come will obstruct the development of trade centers located on the mainland opposite the reef.

Other Highways.—Motor highways are restricted to the more densely populated sections of Australia. Their extension is not likely to be effected upon any large scale owing to the scant population of the country as a whole.

As in other regions of the earth, so here the airplane makes its contribution. It may prove even more valuable to Australia than to regions that are favored with a climate that permits of dense settlement. The airplane serves as an economical form of transportation across those areas that can never hope to support even a small population. It will also bring Australia into closer touch with the mainland of Asia and with Europe than has been the case heretofore. The airplane "race" from London to Melbourne in 1934, when the distance of approximately 11,325 miles was covered in less than three days, made a profound impression upon the people of Australia as well as the rest of the world. Once again, the world's great centers were literally moved closer together.

CHAPTER XV

TRANSOCEANIC ROUTES IN RELATION TO TRADE CENTER DISTRIBUTION

Until recently the oceans have been looked upon as separating the continents. However, as man has succeeded in reducing the time required to cross the oceans, these bodies have become less forbidding, and now we are thinking of them as *connecting* rather than separating the continents. As aerial navigation develops upon a more extensive scale and becomes a convenient medium for crossing the oceans, we shall probably consider the waters of the earth still less as handicaps.

The routes upon the seas and oceans should, therefore, be interpreted largely as linking the world's trade centers, more especially since steam has become the primary motive power. Transoceanic navigation becomes less a matter of prevailing winds and more a matter of the location of the immediate destination of the ship.

Water Routes versus Land Routes.—The seaway presents a higher degree of flexibility than the land way. There is no fixed track over which ships must operate. A steamer may start with a cargo of wheat for a given port, for example, Hamburg, but en route the captain may receive instructions to put into Naples. The route is changed without the captain asking permission of any one to use the new right of way or in any sense establishing an obligation to another company. He is not operating over a route belonging to another corporation.

Unless unusual circumstances exist in a port, such as war, or disease, or the fact that the owners of his ship are specifically prohibited from using the port for any one of many reasons, the captain knows that he may enter the port without advance permission and that, by paying harbor dues, dock dues, or other small local charges, he may utilize the port facilities. Even where the ports can not be entered, owing to shallow water, uncertain channels, absence of lights or other markers, cargo may be unloaded by anchoring off shore and lightering it. This is quite in contrast with the possibility of any railroad at will using the terminals of another road in countries where railroads are privately owned and operated.

Beyond the three mile limit off the coast of various countries of the world the seas are free to all who wish to navigate them. Regulation is non-existent except as international agreements have been made for the safety of navigators. Ships are peculiarly autonomous, their captains enjoying an atmosphere of absolutism that surrounds few other persons and certainly can not be found among the powers of the engineer of a train. On the other hand, government regulation of terminal waters is not infrequently reflected in the extent to which given ports are used and in the intensity of activity along the trade routes which focus upon them.

As indicated in Chapter X an ocean trade route is an avenue over which a ship carries goods or renders a service between any two given centers. One trip defines a route quite as well as a hundred trips. The various nations, however, have plotted steamship routes on maps, not because they represent paths which have been followed a particular number of times by trading ships, but because they present what may be considered the best routes between given trade centers in terms of sailing distances, winds, ocean currents, ice, fog, fueling stations, and other elements which navigators must take into consideration. Since there are so many different routes which are possible, we shall make no attempt to describe them. The accompanying map tells the story in many respects more satisfactorily than words could portray. However, in order to emphasize their relation to trade centers, a relationship not clearly revealed by the map, attention is directed briefly to the following routes: the North Atlantic, the Mediterranean-Asiatic, the Panama route, and the North Pacific route.

The North Atlantic Routes.—So much of the traffic on the North Atlantic Ocean moves between North Atlantic ports of the United States and Canada on the one hand and the ports of northwestern Europe on the other that reference to the North Atlantic trade routes usually suggests a single highway. That most of the passengers and freight traffic should shuttle between the ports of the continents just noted is not surprising because freight originates where people are located. Since the population of northeastern North America and northwestern Europe includes in all probability the most numerous and greatest producers of surpluses of goods and since these goods involve a wide diversity, it seems reasonable to expect the most frequent exchanges to take place between the two groups.

The actual route taken by steamships is one which is influenced not only by the relative locations of the respective port centers on the

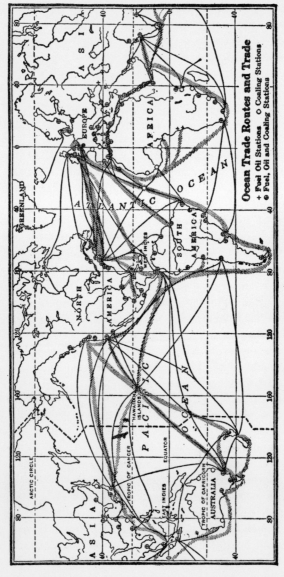

FIG. 53. MAJOR TRADE ROUTES

The width of the shading is proportional to the amount of trade. Note the correspondence between fueling stations of various types and the route terminals, also the concentration of routes in the northern hemisphere and their relation to the distribution of major trade centers. (Courtesy of Allyn and Bacon, Boston.)

two continents but also by the curvature of the earth. Obviously, ships will attempt to take the shortest course possible in order to save in the cost of transportation. Consequently, they seek to follow the great circle sailing route. Since the irregularity of the land masses prohibits the establishment of all courses upon great circle routes and since in the far Northern Atlantic the elements of ice and fog are dangerous to shipping, the path followed deviates from the true great circle route.

Furthermore, a summer and a winter route are recognized, the winter route being the more northerly and approaching the great circle more closely than the southern route. It is followed in general during the months of late September to mid-April or possibly a little later depending upon the character of the particular winter period. The determining factor in the shift from one route to another depends upon the period during which icebergs are likely to float into the ship lanes. Some measure of safety has been introduced since the sinking of the *Titanic* in 1912. Through the ice patrol which operates in the early fall and late spring every iceberg is located and its course plotted. Ships are warned of the presence of any such bergs in the regular lanes. At all times during the patrol season captains of the ships may communicate by wireless with the iceberg patrol and learn the exact location of those bergs which might threaten them along a particular course. The expense of this patrol internationally supported is justified owing to the large number of ships using these lanes and the frequency of use.

One might well express surprise that ships will run the risks involved in the North Atlantic route. The reason for the risk is well illustrated in the case of the Canada-Europe route. Quebec and Montreal are the two principal objectives on the Canadian side of the ocean during the summer season. Ships operating between these centers and Europe not only risk the hazards already mentioned but hazards greatly increased at the mouth of the St. Lawrence River. In consequence, insurance rates on this route are considerably higher than on the Liverpool-New York route. Nevertheless, Montreal continues to maintain its front rank as the largest shipper of grain on the continent, and both ports retain their strong attraction as trans-Atlantic route terminals. To paraphrase a well-known literary expression, we may say that in the determination of oceanic trade routes, *the port is the thing.*

Routes and trade centers, as we have already suggested, have reciprocal relationships. Not only have the routes been largely determined by the distribution of trade centers but the latter have in turn been affected by the routes. Ports on the east coast of North America and those on the west coast of Europe which have engaged in exchanges for the past century have constantly had to meet the competition of new rivals eager to share in trans-Atlantic traffic. Whereas the ports of New York City and London monopolized much of the trade in the early years of the nineteenth century, to-day the proportions of all the trade handled is less, although their own total has continued to grow. Boston, Philadelphia, Baltimore, Charleston, Jacksonville, and other ports must be reckoned with by New York City, as London must compete with Southampton, Bristol, Hamburg, Antwerp, Rotterdam, and a host of other European ports. So the trade routes have been

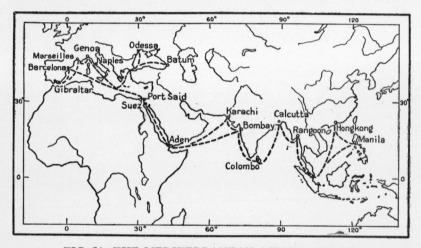

FIG. 54. THE MEDITERRANEAN-ASIATIC ROUTE

This map shows how trade centers determine the links in trade routes, and in turn the rôle of the route in connecting the trade centers. The reciprocal relation of routes and trade centers is always significant in world trade relations.

responsible for trade-center growth, just as the trade center has increased the route activity.

The Mediterranean-Asiatic Route.—This route, as the name implies, follows the Mediterranean Sea and connecting waters, the Red Sea and Indian Ocean, to the waters of eastern Asia. Its importance dates from 1869 when the Suez Canal was opened. As previously indicated, the opening of this canal, which permitted an all-water route from Europe to Asia via northern coastal Africa, greatly reduced the activities along the trade route around South Africa. On the other hand, the business on this same route was offered serious competition dating from 1914 when the Panama Canal was made available for traffic.

The Mediterranean-Asiatic route not only links Europe and Asiatic ports but brings into the picture the ports of Australia. The route, on the whole, has certain distinct advantages over the Panama Canal route in that the frequency of fueling stations is high, thereby freeing space for cargo that would otherwise be necessary for carrying fuel. Furthermore, the frequency of ports provides opportunity for trade which might in a sense be regarded as short-haul when compared with the Panama route which spans the waters far removed from settlement. Consequently, there is no probability that the Panama Canal route will render less useful the Mediterranean-Asiatic route or materially reduce the traffic on that route except in so far as the traffic may be intended for an exceptionally long haul, as for example, between western Europe and eastern 'Asiatic ports or even Australian ports.

Once again, we are reminded that trade routes imply people. The yield and demand of goods among people determines the objectives of the carriers. As long as this remains true the route just considered will be little disturbed by other routes, for along its way are many trade centers close together, growing steadily and inviting increasing exchanges with each other as well as with thousands of other widely distributed trade centers.

The Panama Route.—The Panama Canal route has contributed to the convenience of world trading in three particular directions, namely, (1) between the east and west coasts of the United States, (2) between western Europe, eastern Europe, and the west coast of South America, and (3) between eastern United States and western Asia and Australia.

No doubt its greatest contribution has been to the movement of trade between the east and west coasts of the United States on the one hand and the trade between western South America and the North Atlantic Region on the other. It not only has eliminated the long haul around Cape Horn but also the danger of navigating the waters in the vicinity of the Cape.

This route has also had a marked influence upon transcontinental freight rates in the United States. It has been said that "The operation of the Panama Canal and the realignment of rates since the war have resulted in moving Chicago away from the Pacific Coast on the average about $3.36 per ton of staple goods, while moving New York City

$2.24 nearer." [1] In fact, when the canal was first proposed, manufacturers in the upper Mississippi Valley opposed it because they recognized that the ocean ports on the two coasts of the United States would be given a distinct advantage in trade through a lowering of the freight rates. However, after the canal was brought into use and the transcontinental railroads were confronted with competition offered by lower water rates, they in turn lowered their rates on many commodities. This adjustment, plus a reformation in methods of distribution, which was forced upon the manufacturers located in the Mississippi Valley, have largely offset the initial damage to the latter shippers.

Doubtless the total advantage accruing to the coastal trade centers has been greater than to the interior centers. In fact, the urge among Mississippi Valley centers for the improvement of inland waterways connecting with the seas reflects largely their desire to remove still further any handicap which they may yet suffer from inter-oceanic competition. The Panama route, seemingly, has been particularly beneficial to the Pacific Coast trade centers. We qualify this statement because it is one difficult to demonstrate. There is a coincidence in the growth of our coastal centers with the post-Panama Canal opening period, but this period also corresponds with that of the World War and the subsequent boom, as well as with the era of tremendous advances in aviation, improvements in steamship transportation, lowered costs for passenger travel, motor highway construction, and increased popularity of the automobile and autobus.

After a longer period of time elapses, allowing for a certain amount of stabilization of traffic under these new improvements, we shall be better able to determine the direct effect of this route upon trade center growth. Apparently, new trade routes can be as effective in our present complex civilization in modifying the rate and intensity of development of trade centers as was the discovery of a route to India around Cape of Good Hope or the establishment of the Mediterranean-Asiatic route with the advent of the cutting of the Suez Canal.

Viewed from a military standpoint, the canal has reduced the need for a double navy, that is, one for the Atlantic and one for the Pacific and thereby has also made possible the protection of our trade at a cost far below that which would have been necessary had the canal not been constructed.

North Pacific Trade Routes.—A comparison of the North Pacific

[1] *Encyclopedia of the Social Sciences,* Vol. IX, pp. 585-593.

trade routes with those of the North Atlantic presents similarities throughout with, however, a few striking differences worthy of mention. In the first place, the amount of traffic following the shortest route across the North Pacific is far less than that along the corresponding

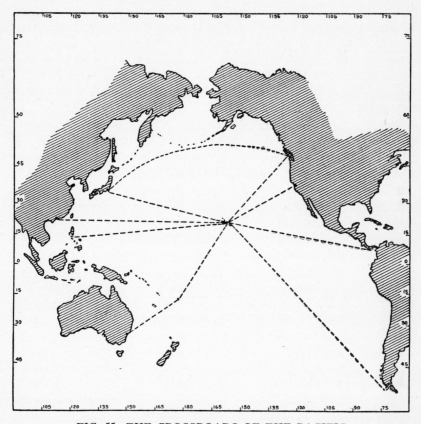

FIG. 55. THE CROSSROADS OF THE PACIFIC

The "magnetic" attraction of the Hawaiian Islands for the ships of the Pacific Area is impressively shown in the design of the steamship routes. Many of the steamers in the east-west traffic would not route themselves via these islands were it not for the business available at Honolulu and other centers there.

route in the North Atlantic. Again, in the North Pacific, we find a focal point by way of the Hawaiian Islands which attracts a fair amount of trade from both continental coasts. This group of islands sometimes called the "cross-roads of the Pacific" is the meeting point for a number of routes such as those between the Pacific coast of the

United States and Australia and New Zealand, and those from the Panama Canal region to eastern Asia.

Certain routes as, for example, some of those between San Francisco, Seattle, or other west coast ports and Japanese ports would not be deflected by the attraction of the Hawaiian Islands were it not for the trade opportunities available at Honolulu. If the trade with that port were not profitable few ships would be likely to stop there except perhaps for fuel, and certainly those plying the trade routes between United States and Japanese ports would not go by way of these islands in preference to the much shorter Great-Circle route farther to the north. Once more, the trade center is the magnet which determines the route.

The short Great-Circle sailing route across the North Pacific is not modified, as in the case of the Atlantic, by iceberg threats because the configuration of the land masses in this region is such as to prevent icebergs from drifting into the steamship paths. On the other hand, the route is beset by considerable fog and differs from the North Atlantic in its much greater length.

The amount of trade following this northerly route is relatively small because it connects a region of low population density in the United States and western Canada with regions in which the population demands for foreign goods are small. No such aggregation of trade centers fronts Pacific waters as we find along the coasts of the Atlantic. In spite of the high density of population in China and Japan the purchasing power of the people is low and their needs simple. Therefore, their importations from Canada and the United States are restricted. Their lack of industrialization means few surplus goods for export.

Aerial Routes.—If we look ahead some years we might anticipate the time when much of the trade to be carried between the continents will move in airships and airplanes. Whether such movements will largely eliminate steamship traffic or whether they will merely supplement steamship traffic is impossible definitely to say. Much experimentation remains to be done to bring about that element of safety and certainty in aerial navigation which will establish public confidence in this mode of transoceanic operation. That success will be attained can hardly be doubted.

In the event of common intercontinental aerial freight and passenger routes, speculation justifiably arises as to the effect upon the courses of the present routes. Aerial sea traffic enjoys a distinct advantage over steam or sailing craft. Physical obstacles such as the configuration of the land and the iceberg menace do not exist for the aviator as we can imagine him in future years. Will he be able to take short cuts, take advantage of the Great-Circle route and ignore the distribution of the trade centers? Consider the following case.

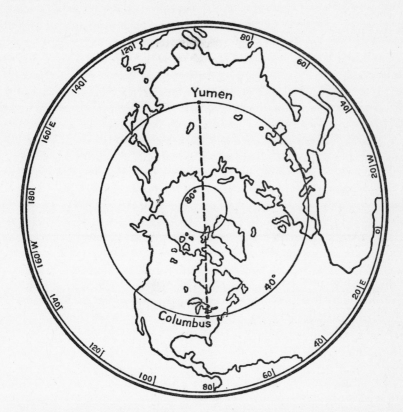

FIG. 56. THE GREAT CIRCLE VS. THE SMALL CIRCLE ROUTE

The saving in distance via the Great Circle Route over that via the Small Circle Route is well illustrated by the extreme case shown here in which the first route lies across the pole and the longer route along the 40th parallel. The day may not be far distant when the aerial route over the pole, seemingly fantastic now, will become a commonplace. The small circle distance is 9,551 miles while the Great Circle distance is only 6,870 miles.

If we compare the distance half way around the earth between two trade centers on the fortieth parallel with the distance between the same two points measured along the Great Circle via the North Pole, we shall find that the Great Circle route is roughly 2,000 miles shorter than the small circle route which follows along the parallel. Seemingly fantastic now, the route across the pole may be real in the future.

The question naturally follows, will aerial craft be able to afford a short route of this nature at the sacrifice of ignoring intermediate trade centers on the small circle route? There are several possible answers. In all probability both the old and new routes, the long and short routes, will be maintained, the newer one, however, only when the pay load is rich. On the other hand, the new short aerial route may give rise to the creation of new centers and the increased growth of old centers, both at the expense of intermediate centers on the longer aerial route.

There will be great savings in distance across both the North Atlantic and North Pacific Oceans as compared with the distances now covered by steamships. For example, the route from New York City to Cherbourg will follow over eastern Massachusetts, Maine, St. Johns, and Newfoundland instead of the water route which must divert its course eastward first and then northeastward to avoid the continental land obstruction. Greenland and Iceland may be included in the itinerary either for trade purposes or for fuel and rest stops or for all of these reasons. Clearly, the objective in all this communication is to connect trade centers quickly but still at a profit. Obviously, when reducing distances and time to a minimum, a whole new adjustment among the world's trade centers may have to take place. Such uncertainties as these must be given careful consideration by those responsible for planning the future of trade centers.

CHAPTER XVI

TRANSPORTATION SERVICE—THE RAILROAD AND MERCHANT MARINE

We have described the railroad networks of the continents and the steamship routes of the seas, but we have not considered them in the light of their services to the trade centers of the respective countries. It is one thing to report upon the general characteristics of transportation routes and the factors influencing their establishment, but it is quite as significant to know how far these routes fulfill the economic requirements of the trade centers.

RAILROADS

Total Mileage of Nations Compared.—Ranking the nations by total railroad mileage we find that the United States, with nearly 250,000 miles, has an overwhelming lead, Soviet Russia playing a poor second (see appendix). The large mileage in our country is not due alone to the area, but rather to the fact that this nation witnessed its major development during the railroad era and that settlements far apart demanded the convenience of transportation with each other. There were vast natural resources yet to be exploited during the era beginning with railroad expansion. Railroad investors sought to serve the pioneers and to profit from the prospective freight.

Density in Terms of Population.—It is not sufficient to view the railroad service of the nations in terms only of their areas, for in the last analysis people rather than land are served. Let us consider, then, the number of persons who must be served by each mile of railroad.

Densely populated Belgium heads the list with 1,240 persons per mile of railroad. The country is highly industrialized, and trade centers are numerous and close together. In the United States the number is 488. The respective areas of Belgium and the United States are, however, so strikingly different that a comparison ignoring the contrast is unfair. If we select portions of the United States whose density of population is comparable with that of Belgium the picture changes. Grouping the states of Massachusetts, Connecticut, Rhode Island, New

211

York, Pennsylvania, New Jersey, Delaware, and Maryland, we find the number of people per mile of railroad to be 1,259. In other words, in the United States where the population density is comparable with that of western Europe our railroad system shows no distinct superiority in terms of the ratio between the number of miles of line and the population served.

The Network in Terms of Accessibility.—Mark Jefferson[1] has portrayed in striking graphic manner what we have just shown statistically. Instead of drawing railroad network maps of the continents in the standard fashion, tracing the routes with a series of black lines, he has drawn the routes by means of an interpretative method.

Jefferson decided that a railroad line serves all the population within ten miles of either side of the line, this representing the distance to which a farmer might drive a horse and wagon to the railroad and home again within a day. Since great numbers of farmers the world over are still without motorized equipment, this seems to be a fair assumption. By using white lines equal to twenty miles in width to represent the railroad routes, the resultant maps depict areas of white interrupted by black.

The maps of North America and Europe show correspondence in that the northeastern portions of the former and northwestern areas of the latter regions both adjacent to the Atlantic, are covered with continuous white. On the assumption that trains operate in the white areas on a standard service basis, the people of these regions possess complete railroad facilities for carrying on trade.

The lines thin out rapidly as we follow the maps into their more remote parts. In a sense, we might interpret these maps to mean that wherever white areas appear there is either a dense population or a progressive one, or both, or the exercise of control by a government which is convinced of the value of railroads to trade stimulation.

We might very properly ask here whether natural resources, agricultural production, goods originating in trade centers, or people constitute the underlying cause of this density? For Europe we may add to the query, the influence of military exigencies. The answer upon a statistical basis is probably impossible to arrive at, owing to lack of data or to different interpretations which different persons would place upon such data as are available. Nevertheless, we are safe in asserting that, while all of these elements are influential, probably none are quite so significant as the trade centers themselves which the railroads con-

[1] State Normal College, Ypsilanti, Michigan.

nect. These centers are the major foci for both the consumption of raw materials and the production of manufactured goods, much of the latter for redistribution among many other centers as well as among rural peoples. Again, we should recall the black line railroad map of Europe which reveals the radial arrangement of the roads with respect to its trade centers and the rectangular system of the United States with respect to the common lineal arrangement of our trade centers.

Passengers and Freight Carried.—The total number of passengers carried by the railroads of the United States has shown a decrease since 1913, whereas that for the earth as a whole shows an increase. Our decline of 30 per cent stands out in contrast with Europe's remarkable increase of 60 per cent. Several reasons underlie this situation, but perhaps most important is the far more rapid expansion in the use of the motor vehicle in the United States than in other countries. This period represents the automotive era. Mass production of the motor vehicle, the rapid rise in purchasing power of the people in the United States, and concentration of population in urban centers marked the certain decline of the railroad as a medium for transporting the population. On the other hand, in Europe and most other regions purchasing power showed no such growth and, furthermore, government ownership of railroads secured to the public low rates of fare, thus encouraging the continued use of this means of transportation.[2] Again, many peoples have acquired greater autonomy in the post-war years than they had enjoyed before, permitting of their building of more railroads and of improving their services. The new countries of Europe such as the New Baltic States, Finland, and Poland have greatly facilitated rail travel within their own areas.

The story of freight changes has paralleled in some regions that of changes in passenger traffic. The world's tonnage has increased 20 per cent over that of 1913, whereas on the railroads in the United States the gain has been 10 per cent. We have held our own in this instance because the development of long haul freight by motor truck has moved much more slowly than the growth of ownership of passenger automobiles and the increase in use of motor busses. However, with the more recent acceleration of the motor truck in long haul service, we shall probably find in the near future considerable inroads upon railroad tonnage, perhaps even to the extent of causing the latter to decline. Europe has shown an increase in tonnage, consistent with the improvement in railroad facilities stimulated largely by the War.

[2] See also Chapter 17 on the Motor Vehicle.

If we compare the ton mileage of our railroads with that of Europe we find that ours is nearly double that of our transatlantic neighbors. This may be accounted for on the basis of extensive water routes in Europe, coastwise, canal, and river which share with the railroads in freight transportation. The highly indented coastline of Europe bordered by relatively protected waters allows of their intensive use by small craft. Were the data available for the total movement of intra-continental water-borne freight, we would probably find that it approaches closely the total ton-mile rail freight. In some countries, as previously stated, heavy, non-perishable freight is definitely allocated to the waterways, thus diverting tonnage which would normally, as in the United States, go to the railroads.

Railroad Future.—In all probability the peak of aggressive railroad building has been passed except for the construction of major lines in newly developed lands or in revived regions. Short lines are a thing of the past even in undeveloped parts of the world because, generally speaking, highways for the operation of automotive vehicles can be constructed and maintained more cheaply. Furthermore, individual ownership of automobiles provides a means for individuals or small groups to transport themselves to points within short distances of their trade centers and to do so at their own convenience, thus eliminating the demand for short-haul rail service. The War taught many countries the economy of motor vehicles, and in consequence numerous plans for railroad expansion have been cancelled in favor of this new movement.

We have demonstrated in the United States that greater efficiency in railroad operations makes possible a more satisfactory use of the equipment now on hand. We are moving more freight than ever before over a somewhat reduced trackage and at a higher rate of speed. Passenger-train speeds have, likewise, been increased. Although the increases have not been uniform in all directions and proportional between all trade centers, reductions have taken place (during the past decade) in time range amounting from a few minutes for short runs to upwards of twelve hours on transcontinental trips. Every such reduction in time brings trade centers that much closer together, intensifies competition for the trade of the intervening territory, and tends to stabilize the general economic situation viewed areally. This theoretical moving of centers into closer proximity to each other is the equivalent of increasing the density of settlement of the region in which they are located and probably slows down the rate of growth of population in the larger centers. In order to secure evidence we must await the lapse of more years.

We may look forward to a consolidation of ground, as it were, in the realm of railroading rather than an expansion of routes. Of course, in new territories we may expect railroads to follow settlement, although not as rapidly as they did in earlier years, confining themselves largely to routes that are transcontinental in nature or to mountain terrain where more power may be required to haul loads than can be supplied by the auto truck. At the moment, engineers consider the field of long-haul, heavy freight still safely within the domain of the railroad carrier. Whether super-motor highways between major trade centers will eventually displace the railroads is a question which can not be definitely answered at present. Railroad expansion is likely to be checked too by the further development of aviation.

THE MERCHANT MARINE

Just as the sea route may be interpreted as a continuation of the land route, so the merchant marine may be viewed as complementary to the railroad. The major part of international trade is transported by a combination of sea and rail carriers.

Ship Service.—Ships carrying oversea freight are classified into two major types—line and tramp. Line steamers operate upon regular time schedules between stipulated ports. Generally they carry mixed cargo and passengers. The cargo usually consists of small-bulk, high unit-price freight. There are times when such ships carry bulky freight like wool, rubber, even cotton occasionally, and other commodities which are clean to handle, are in wide demand, and withstand a fairly high freight rate.

Liners differ in the nature of their service, depending upon the most profitable trade upon a given route or the objective for which a particular ship has been constructed. Some liners operate in a manner corresponding to certain express railroad trains. Speed and regularity at almost any cost are basic. They sail from port regardless of the load available. Other liners specialize in freight and carry passengers largely as an accommodation.

The tramp steamer, as its classification suggests, goes wherever business is available and is unrestricted by time schedules. Sometimes these ships are called charter ships because they frequently are leased to large corporations either for single shipments or for a season when grains, coal, lumber, or other products are sent into oversea trade channels. These ships in some respects are far more "romantic" than their line relatives because their movements are so uncertain; their speed, generally, is very slow, perhaps nine to ten knots an hour; their size small; their sometimes ungraceful forms dirty in appearance and yet showing earnings oftentimes greater than those of any other type of vessel. Tramps may put out from New York City to-day for Argentina with agricultural implements, carry flax from Buenos Aires to Bremen, load there with sugar for Helsinki, secure a cargo of timber from nearby Kotka for some Mediterranean port and so continue as a carrier from one port to another not returning to New York City for a year or several years.

Both the liner and the tramp have their particular function in the movement of international freight. We can think of the liner as serving a larger number of shippers than the tramp because its cargo is made up of many small packages consigned to numerous individuals. On the other hand, we can look upon the tramp as serving more consumers since its bulky cargoes are distributed more widely by the time they perform their ultimate service. For example, many manufacturers offer their respective products for shipment to a single liner, but one tramp carrying wheat may be serving thousands of persons who eventually will receive the flour or bread made from that wheat.

Interest in ships' tonnage is decidedly greater in port centers in the United States than in inland centers. In western Europe this is not so true, for, as previously cited, so large a part of that continent is relatively close to the sea coast or to navigable waters connecting with the sea. Nevertheless, oceanic transportation should attract national attention because international exchanges affect all the people, albeit the incomes of those in the trade centers which have the particular job involving the physical handling of this freight necessarily are more visibly affected.

The data illustrating the tonnage flying the United States flag in the years since the beginning of the nineteenth century reveal a striking anomaly when compared with the curve for our exports and imports during the corresponding period. Our trade has grown almost continuously, whereas the size of the merchant marine shows marked fluctuations. In the half century from 1860 to 1910 our foreign trade tripled, whereas our merchant marine tonnage declined to one-third of its former size.

During the first half of the eighteenth century the United States was an important ship builder. We had excellent timber resources near the Atlantic Seaboard and had developed considerable skill in building and operating ships both before and after colonial days. The American flag was frequently seen in the world's principal ports, and our sailors were looked upon as second to none. But in 1855 England contributed to the world the Bessemer process which had a revolutionary effect not only upon the iron and steel industry but particularly upon the ship building industry. The scene of ship construction was shifted from the United States to European waters. The new process of steel manufacture which reduced the time of manufacture of a unit quantity from hours to minutes made possible not only cheap production but also the building of larger ships than were possible from timber. Since we, in the United States, were unaware of the vast deposits of iron ore in the Lake Superior District, we were a country without iron ore for all practical purposes, and, hence, we were in no position to compete with the British in the iron and steel industry.

Shortly after the introduction of the Bessemer process the Civil War broke forth and contributed further to turning our attention away from the business of carrying the world's oversea trade. From 1861 to 1865, while the nation's thought was concentrated upon prosecuting the war, opportunity was given England to build ships and to engage in ocean transportation upon a more extensive scale than before, largely at our expense.

After the war the Reconstruction Era turned the eyes of the public toward the development of new lands in the upper Mississippi Valley and the new West. Railroads extended their lines farther into the interior and facilities for reaching remote points were greatly improved. "Mushroom trade centers" came into being all along the new frontier. The completion of the first transcontinental railroad in 1869 removed threats of secession by California and opened up a whole new potentially wealthy empire. Thus, the sea mindedness which had largely dominated our early economic activities was completely overshadowed and virtually abandoned in favor of an economic provincialism. The coastal ports had to look toward the interior, for much of their income came from being service centers in the absorption of the newly uncovered resources. They shipped to Europe the raw materials and imported her manufactured wares for the use of the "western" pioneers and they let Europeans carry these goods. Many of the centers founded in this era, especially in the Great Lakes Region, were destined to become permanent economic foci and others to pass into oblivion after a short but sometimes vigorous life. The curve of population growth for practically all the larger centers which have persisted to the present reflect the post Civil War westward migration.

When the World War broke out the markets of Latin America, Canada, South Africa, and the Far East turned to us to supply them with commodities which they had heretofore purchased from Europe. The entrepôt trade of such centers as London, Liverpool, Hamburg, and others was now dealt a severe blow. We began ship-building upon an unprecedented scale and established direct steamship service to many ports in these markets which we had heretofore not reached directly. Our Merchant Marine grew at an unheard-of rate. In the period 1915 to 1920 we launched 518 ships of over 100 tons with a capacity of 1,877,000 tons, as compared with only 162 ships between 1910-1914 with a total capacity of 253,000 tons. Our percentage of the world's tonnage rose from 10 per cent in 1915 to 17 per cent in 1920 while the tonnage in ships engaged only in foreign trade increased 500 per cent.

The national government has encouraged a continuation of merchant ship construction through liberal loans at low-interest rates (the Jones-White Act of 1928) and by granting profitable mail contracts. Our public policy has been one of opposition to outright ship-subsidies, but through these indirect methods we accomplish the same purpose.

The change in the position of the merchant marine with respect to our trade relations during the past century has been notable. During the first half of the period the fleet was large, owing not only to the natural conditions which favored ship construction but also to our extensive raw materials which Europe and other places desired in exchange for their finished goods. To-day, our merchant fleet is growing because we have finished goods which we wish to supply to foreign nations in return for which we can use their raw materials. Thus, the direction of movement of finished goods and raw materials has reversed itself, while our merchant marine has passed through a cycle ranging from growth through decline to growth again. In the last stage we have overcome to some extent national indifference to transoceanic shipping and have encouraged local capital to invest in our own ships instead of foreign services. Moreover, owners of branch plants abroad are showing a greater inclination to employ American cargo ships in preference to the ships of the countries in which their plants are located.

During the recent depression a nationalistic sentiment once again asserted itself. However, it was not long before government and business leaders became aware of the impracticability of isolation and of the dependence of the nation upon international trade. Port centers naturally were among the first to appreciate the seriousness of an indifferent or negative attitude toward foreign trade. The adverse effect was felt in a direct way. Employment of persons associated with the handling of exports and imports was reduced. Those same centers and others engaged in manufacturing found that the domestic market could not absorb all of their surpluses. Furthermore, they discovered that when we discouraged purchases from foreign lands the peoples in those lands could not or would not buy from us. Consequently, our industries suffered, and those losses were reflected in the "hard times" in our industrial trade centers.

This consideration of the vicissitudes of our merchant marine and its effect upon our trade centers recalls the fifteenth point listed in an earlier chapter as one of the points trade centers should observe, namely, a world outlook. Every trade center, no matter how far removed from the sea, should be interested in the welfare of our merchant marine because in proportion to its efficiency the people in all centers either lose or gain.

CHAPTER XVII

SERVICE OF THE MOTOR VEHICLE

Greater speed has long been one of man's ambitions. Had it not been so we should not to-day be witnessing the phenomenon of crossing the United States from New York City to Los Angeles in less than twelve hours' time. The accelerated pace of most phases of life in trade centers everywhere, even in the crossroads village, has become the normal mode, and nothing has contributed more to this swiftly moving pageant of life than the motor vehicle in all its different forms.

WHEELED CONVEYANCES

The Automobile.—In 1930 the people of the United States owned 88.4 per cent of all automobiles then in operation throughout the world. The U. S. Department of Commerce estimated one automobile for every 55 persons in the world and a ratio of one for every 4.5 persons in the United States. The ratio of cars to population outside the United States is one for every 216 persons.

Those countries ranking next to the United States, measured upon a per capita basis, are Canada, New Zealand, and Australia. The newer countries, in the sense of their recency of settlement and development, have shown a decided inclination toward the use of the motor vehicle. With the exception of New Zealand they are countries of large areas, extensive lowlands, and populations with a relatively high purchasing power. Much of their population is concentrated in the larger trade centers where roads are good. These are countries where distances are considerable and where few or no traditions exist to check enthusiasm for quick action. In fact, the new lands were peopled largely by those desirous of freeing themselves from the bondage of the past. The motor vehicle fits well into their new environment.

Purchasing Power.—Purchasing power of the people is of paramount consideration in analyzing the employment of the automobile for transportation. No matter how low the price of motor vehicles, people whose incomes may be as low, for example, as fifty or one hundred dollars annually are not in a position to make purchases. The peasantry of

Europe, millions of Chinese, other millions of Mohammedans, Brahmans, tribal groups in Central and Southern Africa, and Indians scattered throughout Latin America classify among the low-income groups. Hence, we need not be surprised to find few automobiles in the trade centers of old regions.

Manufacturers of automobiles in the United States argued at one time that saturation of the market was impossible. They attempted to show that not only could the people of the United States own more than one automobile per person but that a vast foreign market was available which could not be fully supplied for many years to come. After some investigation of the theory of saturation, followed by the beginning of the depression in 1929, they recognized that a market consists not alone of people, but of people with incomes sufficiently large to provide the capacity for making purchases beyond a mere subsistence level and, therefore, the foreign markets were not as alluring as they at first seemed.

Density of Population.—Another reason for the difference in extent of ownership of automobiles between newer and older countries is found in the density of population in the trade centers. The areas of European centers, as already suggested, are generally smaller than in the United States. This means that distances between given points within the communities are relatively shorter than here. The mass of people are generally closer to market, to each other, and to places of recreation than are the people in the trade centers of the United States. In going from place to place, less time is spent either on foot, by street car, or by auto-bus. Consequently, the urge for saving time is not great and the desire for the ownership of an automobile correspondingly less.

Furthermore, these compact trade centers, with their dominant apartment life and concentrated buildings, can not make easy and economical provision for garage space. Therefore, the convenience of a garage upon the premises, so common in the United States, is not generally available, while the cost of storage in a public garage adds considerably to the expense of maintaining an automobile.

The Taxicab and Cost of Fuel.—During the era of development and popularization of the automobile, the taxicab became a far more important institution in foreign trade centers than in our country. In the first place, the "droschke" or horse-drawn cab had already attained widespread use, and the charges were so nominal as to be easily within the purchasing power of the mass of citizens. The powered cab became merely a new form of mechanism with the old low-priced fare. In contrast, both horse-drawn cabs and taxicabs were for many years practically in the luxury class in the United States and catered to a limited clientele. With cheap facilities afforded in European centers, the utilization of public conveyances was far more economical than private ownership. Again, these facilities have been available not alone in the heart of the trade centers but in the outlying neighborhoods, and since these neighborhoods were not far distant from the central business district the cost of transportation for a round trip was nominal.

Another major reason for the slow growth in individual ownership of automobiles abroad is associated with the cost of fuel and perhaps the lack of convenient service stations. Fuel, in general, has ranged from two to four times as costly as in the United States. This enormous price has, of course, made the cost of private operation so high, as compared with the cost of using a public taxicab or bus, that only persons of some affluence find it possible to enjoy the privilege of operating a car for themselves. In recent years the cost of fuel has fallen somewhat, and engines have been developed which provide an increasing mileage in proportion to the fuel consumed. These adjustments have aided materially in the enlargement of the market.

Naturally enough, all of these adverse elements in foreign centers where they are effective have militated somewhat against the amount of business transacted and have influenced the methods of conducting trade both within and between centers. Whether for "good or evil" presumably is a matter of opinion rather than principle, and that can only be determined by personal observation and experience. Even so, the widespread use of the motorcycle furnishes a partial answer to this problem.

The Motorcycle.—A glance at motorcycle statistics reveals a situation in striking contrast with that for automobiles. The newer countries give way to the older. Here, the United Kingdom, Germany, and France head the list while the United States, Canada, and other countries drop to secondary or inconsequential positions.

The reason for this reversal of rank is found first in the element of purchasing power. In Europe a motorcycle is cheaper than the cheapest automobile corresponding to our low-priced models. This means that the motorcycle falls within reach of the purchasing power of more persons than does the automobile. The second important influence is the fuel cost. The motorcycle can be driven nearly twice as far as the automobile per gallon of fuel, and where fuel may cost forty cents a gallon or over the vehicle securing the greater mileage is likely to gain the greater favor.

Another factor, which may seem less convincing but undoubtedly contributes to the popularity of the motorcycle, is the narrow street in the older parts of foreign trade centers, so narrow that at certain times of day when pedestrian traffic is heavy vehicles are either prohibited or allowed to proceed only in one direction. Short distances within the trade centers, once more, are effective in making the motorcycle satisfactory for deliveries, and that same element of density of population, expressed largely in terms of apartment houses built closely together, makes storage of the motorcycle more economical than that of the automobile. In many parts of the countryside paved roads are lacking but foot-paths or bicycle paths in some cases can be used by the motorcyclist, especially if his machine has no side-car attached.

The Motor-Bus and Motor-Truck.—The growing use the world over of the motor-bus and truck has been noticed by none more than by the owners and operators of railroads. The bus has made serious inroads into passenger receipts, and the truck has deprived the railroads in the United States of from 5 to 15 per cent of their former freight loadings. Busses and automobiles together, it is estimated, have cut railroad passenger receipts close to 50 per cent since 1929. Although in no country has the growth in number of busses and trucks been comparable to the total attained in the United States, yet their local economic value has probably been none-the-less significant.

The War brought home an appreciation to most nations that the bus and truck are highly economical devices. It appeared at once that the cost of rolling-stock and right-of-way maintenance were far less for bus and truck than for the railroad and, besides, a greater flexibility in usage could be attained. Hence, for many countries such as Finland, the New Baltic States, and Poland, which acquired new life after the War but had little capital, the high level of efficiency of the bus and truck proved a tremendous boon. Whereas they could not afford extensive railway expansion, they could provide themselves with improved highways and auto-busses and trucks at a relatively small cost. In the period between 1927 and 1931 the percentage increase in trucks in Finland was 140 and in Poland 135, whereas that in the United States was only 24 per cent. This activity has resulted in a rapid growth of good roads which has helped to knit the parts of these countries as never before and to remove to a large extent the isolation of many trade centers which had heretofore led a primitive existence owing to lack of effective means of communication. In most of these rejuvenated areas trade centers in pre-war days were either conspicuous or inconspicuous; there were few in an intermediate stage. To-day great numbers of the inconspicuous centers have taken on new vigor and economic importance because the auto-bus and truck have made them more accessible.

A By-Product.—As a by-product of the increased use of the motor vehicle, good roads have developed. In some respects this spectacle presents a strange phenomenon.

The value of a paved road versus one not paved has long been appreciated, but the expense of construction has been a handicap to the paving of many roads outside of the political limits of trade centers. Europe had shown the way to the rest of the world from the time of the building of famous Roman roads to the inauguration of the automobile era. As recently as the beginning of this century, we in the United States frequently pointed to the good roads of Europe as examples worthy of emulation, but little was done about it.

When the pleasure value of the automobile became evident to the urban citizen and its price fell within his purchasing power, he demanded paved roads. He found his radius of operation limited to the political boundaries and therein further restricted to just a few smooth avenues. There was no pleasure in riding on rough roads, and, besides, here was a vehicle meant for speed as compared with the horse and carriage, although early speed laws set a limit of only eight miles an hour.

Undoubtedly, the manufacturers of automobiles played a hand in influencing sentiment in favor of good roads, for their products without roads could hardly be marketed. The public was unquestionably receptive to such arguments as quickly as they recognized the potentialities of the new mode of transportation.

While the peoples of the trade centers wanted the convenience and pleasure of a smooth highway, the farmer in his traditional conservatism opposed a rapid extension because that meant a heavy increase in taxation. He did not seem to sense the advantage to himself in taking to the railroad his produce at reduced costs, or, if close enough to large trade center markets, taking his product direct. He failed to appreciate the saving in wear and tear upon his equipment and the saving in his time. Hence, we witnessed the strange phenomenon of good road expansion responding at first largely to the pleasure and comfort-seeking urban man and forcing the rural man to accept an accommodation which has in many respects given him more real economic advantages than proportionately received by his urban brother.

AERIAL CONVEYANCES

The Airplane.—The rapid evolution of the airplane since December 17, 1903, when Orville Wright made the first flight at Kitty Hawk, North Carolina, is so recent that its detailed review here does not seem necessary. It's worth noting that this experience of Wright's did not assure future success; it was merely encouraging. But by 1909 flights of relatively long duration were being made which left no doubt as to the probable development of the airplane as a practical vehicle. In this year Bleriot, the French flier, crossed the English Channel from Calais to Dover in thirty-seven minutes and Wilbur Wright flew around the Statue of Liberty. Shortly after 1910 Glenn Curtiss made the first extended flight, covering a distance of 135.4 miles from Albany to Governors Island in two hours and thirty-two minutes.

The World War gave further impetus to aviation. Costly as it was in human carnage and monetary expenditures, the War undoubtedly served to hasten by many years the solution of perplexing problems in aerial navigation. These problems have not all been solved as yet, of course, but we no longer hesitate to say that the airplane is not only a practical means of transportation but has become an indispensable part of our commercial system.

Air Mail.—Although commercial aviation for the carriage of passengers and miscellaneous light weight articles has evolved slowly and steadily since practically the beginning of the era of sustained flights, probably the greatest impetus to the extension of the service has been contributed by the postal departments of the nations. The subsidies to private companies for carrying mail has enabled them to survive the introductory period during which it has been necessary to educate the public to utilize the airplane both for the transportation of people and goods. The success of the efforts is best demonstrated in the map (Fig. 49) showing the major air routes regularly flown in the United States.

These routes are in contrast with those of the railroad or early waterways in that the connected trade centers are fewer and are practically all of the major class. Intermediate points usually act as emergency landing fields, or as service stations for owners of single planes. On the regularly constituted commercial routes we can hardly say as yet that there is a local service.

Exploration and Mapping.—While public interest in aviation has been centered largely upon purely commercial and to some extent military aspects, one of the highly significant attainments of this new mode of transport lies in its service to exploration and to surveying. These services with respect to trade centers are especially interesting.

Many trade centers which are now planning both their immediate and future projects are employing aerial photography to secure accurate maps quickly, as well as to obtain valuable views of their physical structure, that is their physiognomy. Such photographs are unexcelled for revealing the relationship between a trade center and its immediate environs, the weak elements within its political limits, the quality of its facilities for traffic flow within and without the area, the aesthetic aspects of its physical structure, and numerous space relationships such as density of buildings, width of streets with respect to building heights and percentage of recreational areas to total area.

Aviation and Weather Forecasting.—A by-product of aerial transportation improvement is represented in the contribution which it is making to our knowledge of atmospherics. When commercial aviation was first established in the United States private organizations set up their own weather observatories. However, it was not long until they discovered that they were not properly equipped to maintain that service. As a result, the United States Weather Bureau was urged to take charge of the observing stations.

This request by private business was conveyed to Congress, and the necessary appropriations were made. We should note that, although we have claimed to have developed commercial aviation without government aid, our government has supplied two large subsidies, mail contracts and a weather forecast service, without which commercial aviation would have been almost impossible.

In addition to direct aid given by the Weather Bureau, moneys have been available for privately directed upper-air research. The Guggenheim School of Aeronautics, in association with the Massachusetts Institute of Technology; the Blue Hill Observatory of Harvard University at Hyde Park, Massachusetts; and other organizations have devoted portions of their research funds to investigations of the atmosphere to the end that weather forecasting for aviators may be improved.

As we add to our knowledge of the behavior of cyclonic and anticyclonic movements, learn more about the relation of upper-air movements to those at the surface, and develop so-called air mass analysis we approach much nearer that day when we shall be able to forecast with dependability long periods ahead. If ever the time arrives when we can predict the weather seasons in advance, our entire economic structure will have to be recast. Economic uncertainty owing to weather vagaries will have then been eradicated, and presumably much of the complexity now associated with business will have been eliminated. Where this may lead in the reconstruction of our trade centers no one dare say. But those institutions looking forward to the growth and development of our centers must be alert to this prospective revolution.

The Dirigible.—There is much difference of opinion as to whether or not the dirigible airship will survive as a practical instrument of transportation in competition with the rapidly developing airplane. We can turn to-day to certain facts which are of peculiar interest and worthy of attention.

The Hamburg-American Line, general agents for the German Zeppelin Company, announced on May 6, 1933, the sailing schedule for 1933 of the "Graf Zeppelin." Its service between Germany and South America was first successfully carried out in 1932, and this fact encouraged the company to expand the schedule for 1933 and later for 1934 and 1935 and in 1936 to inaugurate a service to the United States. A copy of a schedule of the latter service is reproduced.

TABLE 9

NORTH ATLANTIC SERVICE
L.Z. 129

SAILING SCHEDULE
(subject to change)

FROM FRANKFURT, GERMANY

May	6
May	16
June	19
June	29
July	10
August	5
August	15
September	17
September	26
October	5

WESTBOUND VOYAGE
ABOUT 3 DAYS

FROM LAKEHURST, N. J.

May	11
May	20
June	23
July	3
July	14
August	9
August	19
September	21
September	30
October	9

EASTBOUND VOYAGE
ABOUT 2½ DAYS

SAILING SCHEDULE OF THE GERMAN ZEPPELIN "HINDENBURG"
BETWEEN GERMANY AND THE U. S. A., 1936

In addition to passengers, mail and freight are carried between Friedrichshafen, Germany, and Rio de Janeiro, Brazil, with a few intermediate stops. Airplane connections at these points link many other trade centers with this trans-Atlantic service. The crossing of the 'Atlantic is reduced from twelve days by steamer to three days by air.

In 1929 the vice-president of what was then known as the Transcontinental Air Transport Company made the following statement: "All long distance passenger hauling will be by airplane, all short-distance passenger hauling will be by motor bus. Railroads will carry no passengers, but will do a continuous business in freight. When we get mail and goods and people in the air we will have a new fast-moving commerce." [1] Whether failure to mention the airship was due to a primary interest in airplanes can not be asserted positively. Apparently this was the case, for even at that time the dirigible was recognized in Germany as a commercial vehicle, although its use was still limited to local areas.

There are men to-day who are largely in accord with the opinion expressed in the above quotation, but who would hold that the airship will also be a long distance carrier to which the airplane will be tributary

[1] Paul Henderson, "Business at Airplane Speed," *Magazine of Business* (February, 1929).

for comparatively short flights, reducing the activity of the motor-bus merely to a highly localized service. Here again, just as trade centers have had to provide landing fields for airplane service and in other ways devoted time and thought to the possible good to be derived from efficient airplane transportation, so attention will soon have to be concentrated upon mechanical and financial provisions for the dirigible. No doubt the activities of these two types of ships will have to be correlated, and the major centers, in particular, will be primarily concerned.

MOTOR TRAIN, SHIP AND BOAT

As a further attempt to gain speed and eliminate time, the motorization of trains, ships, and boats has been going on apace. Each conveyance is associated with the transportation of people and foods from one trade center to another. Each is confronted with the problem of survival in an era of demand for rapid transportation. Progress may be credited to all of them. However, no attempt is made to pronounce the ultimate practical speed which they may attain. That they will contribute to our economic activities in much the same manner, although probably to a lesser degree, as the airplane and motor-bus can not be doubted. It seems reasonable to suppose that they will not be superseded by these other modes but rather integrated with them and the combined services planned with respect to the trade centers which they will serve.

CHAPTER XVIII

LANGUAGE—THE BASIC TRADE ROUTE

Ability to trade implies the means to communicate ideas. Communication of ideas may be accomplished by means of signs, symbols, or by word of mouth. Perhaps a particular method is not a matter of importance so long as the objective, namely, trade, is attained. However, as man has evolved a civilization in which the exchange of ideas has become an increasingly critical factor, he has also evolved a system of verbal expressions which may be recorded and which convey a fixed meaning.

It is doubtful whether large and widely separated trade centers could have come into existence if a system of recording words to communicate ideas had not been invented. Certainly the complex civilization within trade centers and the interrelations of the individuals and corporations located in different centers would probably not have come to pass. Without a system for recording our ideas, we should always have had either to meet in person or to have had a representative meet with the person to whom we wished to transmit our ideas. Clearly, that procedure is cumbersome and impracticable under the type of civilization current in the great nations of to-day.

The bond between language and commerce is strikingly illustrated even locally in our own larger trade centers where the immigrant population has concentrated in settlements. The Italian, Polish, German, Chinese, or other settlement, or the Ghetto are each essentially a piece of a foreign land transplanted. The oneness of language is the tie that binds perhaps more even than traditions or loyalty to the home country. Inability to speak the language of their newly adopted land invites group isolation which, in turn, fosters perpetuation of language. These groups establish their own commercial institutions and so far as possible patronize them. They make a contribution to the trade center as a whole through the introduction of their favorite commodities, as well as through ideas which they have brought with them from regions historically and culturally different. On the other hand, their linguistic differences often present within a trade center difficult social. as well as commercial, problems, many of which social workers have tried to solve through teaching not only American ways of life but the English language.

In newly settled lands the attraction for each other of peoples speaking the same language has tended to make the large trade centers grow larger. Persons gravitate toward each other in proportion to the elements which they possess in common, and no one of those elements probably exerts a stronger influence than language. A brief review of the relation of language to trade may help us better to appreciate another one of those many factors which have contributed to the rise of the modern trade center.

Silent Languages.—Herodotus described a method of "silent trade" customary among the Carthaginians and which is still known to occur among some groups in the islands of Oceania. The procedure requires the seller to display his wares at an appointed place and immediately to withdraw from sight. The buyer then appears, examines the goods, takes what he desires, and leaves a quantity of his own commodities in their place. The seller reappears, takes an amount of the buyer's goods which he believes represents a fair exchange, and departs. Obviously, such a method has its risks, is slow, laborious, and not one to be recommended for general use. It is not only silent trade but a form of barter.

In many of these barter situations the principals belong to different linguistic groups and in the absence of an interpreter must resort to gestures to drive their bargains. The interpretation of these bodily movements probably introduces elements of doubt, not to say actual errors. If the same groups meet frequently enough, they may eventually learn to understand each other with a satisfactory degree of accuracy.

The use of the fingers growing out of these actions probably led to the first exact indices of quantitative values. Peoples in the Near East often use the fingers in effecting their transactions. It is thought by some that the finger signals, which have long been an important medium for quoting prices in the pits of the grain Boards of Trade, represent a carry-over from primitive methods.

Another possible remnant of an earlier practice, which is with us to-day and is being steadily enlarged, is the symbol or sign which conveys ideas without the use of words. Reference is made to roadway signs for autoists indicating to them crossroads, curves, hills, and other features, usually as precautionary warning. The skull and cross-bones is another type of sign which tells a whole story without words; a red flag or a green light and an ever-increasing number of devices is coming into use, enabling one not only to read quickly but to read no matter what one's native language may be.

Before the days of writing the closing of a transaction among primitive peoples generally involved a ceremonial. The smoking of a pipe of peace among the American Indian traders is one of the better known methods for "signing" a contract. Such devices call for honesty on the part of both buyer and seller, as well as faith in the integrity of the respective groups represented. But again, the method is cumbersome and unsatisfactory.

Diplomatic and Commercial Languages.—The most practical means for conveying ideas is found in direct language, that is, in the spoken word. But this, too, has its weaknesses. In the first place, man has developed a multitude of words which are not universally understood. There are about 5,000 so-called different languages and great numbers of dialects. Perhaps many forms now interpreted as languages should be classified as dialects. Many of these are recorded in different kinds of symbols which are not intelligible to the respective masses of people employing other languages. Furthermore, many languages represent compounds and combinations, such as *lingua franca* of the Mediterranean, Pennsylvania Dutch of Pennsylvania, or Pidgin-English of China.

Historically, certain languages have been recognized in international circles as the diplomatic or commercial languages. As early as 2000 B.C., in southern Asia, Assyrian was accepted as both the diplomatic and commercial language. With the rise of the Greek Empire the Greek language became standard in international negotiations. It was superseded by the Roman or Latin tongue, following the decline of the Greek Empire. The Latin tongue held a dominant position until the Middle Ages, giving way then to its descendant, the Italian, which in turn was widely used until about the seventeenth century. Then French became the universal diplomatic language. While important, too, as a commercial language, other languages were not entirely excluded, particularly Latin, German, and later, English.

One of the most surprising situations has been the slow spread of English as a commercial language, in view of the rapidity with which England expanded her empire and in view of the traveling and colonizing propensities of the English peoples. Perhaps this can be accounted for on the basis of British liberalism. On the other hand, compared with the spread of other languages, the rate has been rapid. The strong impression which English has made among some non-English peoples is evidenced by such dialects as Negro-English in Africa, a Bush-patois in Australia, Pidgin-English in China, already noted, and still other mixtures in the far-flung British Empire. In 1921, upon the occasion of a World Disarmament Conference held in Washington, D. C., at the invitation of the United States Government, English was adopted as the official language. This selection no doubt was a compliment to the United States and incidentally was the first instance in which English was given precedence over French or other languages as the official diplomatic language in a world conference.

The German language has wielded considerable influence in commerce through the aggressiveness of German merchants and the planned expansion of oversea trade dating from the establishment of the empire in 1871. The acquisition of colonies and the emigration of large numbers of Germans to North America, estimated at about five millions during the past century, has aided effectively in transplanting the language. The spirit of German nationalism, deeply imbedded in the breast of every German, assures the perpetuation of the language and even the customs abroad wherever Germans settle. Then too, the literature, music, and scientific attainments of the peoples have stimulated large numbers of professional persons to learn the language in order better to enjoy and appreciate these important cultural contributions.

French continues to be recognized as an important cultural and diplomatic language and, likewise, maintains a significant place in the commercial world. Even the Germans, who as a nation have little sympathy for the French, insist upon a knowledge of the French language, both the ability to speak and read it, as an index of true culture. Most influential German business men, as well as persons in the professions, speak French. This situation is equally true in the more progressive countries of Europe except in the British Isles. In the Far East and in many upper circles of Latin America a knowledge of French is common.

Spanish has received considerable recognition in post-War years in non-Spanish speaking nations because of its extensive use in Latin-America and because of the marked commercial activity in that part of the world. Spanish is the commercial language in all of Latin-America except Brazil where Portuguese predominates, in Haiti, and in a few unimportant localities under the control of non-Spanish speaking powers. However, even in these Latin-American regions both French and English have currency among the leaders in commercial and political circles.

TABLE 10

MAJOR LANGUAGES OF THE EARTH'S POPULATION

LANGUAGE	NUMBER SPEAKING IT
English	185—250 million
German	75— 90
Russian	85—100
Spanish	45— 80
French	45— 60
Italian	45— 50
Portuguese	30— 45
Chinese	350—400
Hindustani	100—250
Japanese	65— 80
Malayan	25— 40
Arabian	55
Polish	30
Turkish	25

In all there are about 5,000 different languages and dialects. The French Academy of Languages computes 2,796 distinct languages. The earth's total population is estimated to be 1,900,000,000.

The table of languages spoken by large groups of the earth's inhabitants reveals the diversity of major tongues and the relatively small percentage of the earth's population which speaks English. The percentage of those who speak French is even smaller, but we must recognize the vast numbers who have knowledge of French, but who do not use it in their daily activities. This is in contrast with users of English, for relatively few persons whose native language is not English deem it necessary to know this language. Certainly they do not consider a knowledge of it essential to their culture. Nevertheless, since the War the numbers who have been attracted by English have grown enormously. The assortment of spoken languages and the large groups associated with each of these tongues presents convincing evidence that the business man interested in world trade and certainly in world affairs can profit from an acquaintance with several languages in addition to his own.

The sensitivity of European peoples with respect to the preservation of the national or group language is well illustrated by Germany's recognition of it, when in pre-War days she planned a United States of Europe. She announced that, whereas German would be the official language of the new country, the respective states such as Belgium, France, Spain, Italy, and others would be permitted to speak their current national tongue. Perhaps it was her hope, subsequent to the establishment of such a nation, slowly to impose her own language through the public school system. By requiring the youth to learn German, this language would some day displace the local one.

Correspondence.—Sapir says "Language is a great force of socialization, probably the greatest that exists.... The mere fact of a common speech serves as a peculiarly potent symbol of social solidarity."[2] He might have added that this social solidarity reacts upon the economic and political solidarity, contributing to the growth and persistence of the spirit of nationalism.

So, when one corresponds with persons in foreign countries, persons who are close friends or acquaintances, one should make certain of language preferences. For example, in Finland both Swedish and Finnish are current, but there are antipathies among many of the people owing to linguistic differences. The Swedish element prefers the Swedish name Helsingfors to the Finnish form Helsinki and Abo to Finnish Turku. While most, if not all, of the better educated people speak both Finnish and Swedish, a Finn does not care to speak Swedish with a Swede nor does a Swede willingly speak Finnish with a Finn. An analogous situation prevails in Czechoslovakia where Germans and Czechs clash. In Brazil Spanish and Portuguese languages are in opposition.

These linguistic friction-points generally are more common in large trade centers than in small ones. However, we can not be too careful to keep these differences in mind, no matter whether we communicate with persons in small or large centers. Diplomacy and tact dictate the advisability of observing these niceties.

The Interpreter.—All persons are not endowed with the ability to learn languages easily. Neither is it possible for all those who would like to gain a knowledge of foreign languages to find time to study them. This is especially true in the case of merchants or manufacturers who become engaged in foreign commerce late in life.

Accordingly, the interpreter has made a niche for himself in international transactions. American travelers, in particular, make considerable use of the interpreter—more, in general, than does the European. The latter, owing to his close proximity to many foreign countries, has been forced as a matter of self-defense to acquire the language of his

[2] E. Sapir, "Language," in *Encyclopedia of the Social Sciences,* Vol. IX.

neighbors and, in turn, seems to have developed a keener appreciation of languages than we have. Hence, his need for an interpreter arises usually only where French, English, or German can not be utilized. Incidentally, we may remark here that radio announcers in Europe must be linguists, particularly in the smaller or less influential countries which are desirous of having their entertainment or announcements understood in neighboring lands. In The Netherlands, for example, the principal station announces in Dutch, French, German, English, and Spanish.

An interpreter is not always a satisfactory medium through which to carry on business. One can not be certain that the meaning conveyed in this manner is being accurately transmitted. Furthermore, in translations the idiomatic expression of an idea is frequently lost and damaging interpretations may originate out of sentences offered in perfectly good faith. Besides all of these objections to the interpreter, we must recognize that the indirect method of conversation may eliminate from the atmosphere of the principals involved, that spirit of cordiality, of good will, and of informality which might arise if there were no third person present.

Universal Languages.—Owing to many inconveniences arising out of diversity of languages, numerous attempts have been made to develop a universal medium for conversation. These experiments have met with a varied degree of success. As early as the sixteenth century consideration was given the organization of some simple language, not too far removed in content from those most commonly used at the time and which all persons might learn in addition to their native tongue. We shall consider here only one of those efforts, one which has made the greatest progress, namely, Esperanto.

Esperanto was devised by a physician of Warszawa named Zamenhof and offered to the world in 1887. The name itself, derived from the Spanish, means "hope," an implication no doubt of the sentiment of its author at the time of its origin. As an indication of the impression which this language has made, its proponents point to nearly 200 periodicals, several thousands of books, and over 100 newspapers which have been printed in Esperanto. In addition, thousands of societies and classes for studying the language have been organized. These promotional groups are in evidence at practically all European trade fairs. Although they occasionally appear at United States business congresses, Europe constitutes by far the most fertile field for their efforts.

TABLE 11

A FEW SAMPLES OF ESPERANTO

Bonan tagon sinjoro.	Good day, Sir.
Kiel vi sanas?	How are you?
Tre bone, sinjoro, mi dankas vin.	Very well, sir, I thank you.
Vi estas tre ĝentila.	You are very kind.
Vi estas prava. Li estas malprava.	You are right. He is wrong.
Ili estas nur tri aŭ kvar.	They are only three or four.
Kia bela domo!	What a beautiful house!
Kiom costas tiu-ĉi objekto?	How much does this object cost?

As desirable as universality of expression may be, it is not likely to come about through the creation of a new language. We face sufficient difficulties in learning languages now in existence. Furthermore, no people are willing to surrender their present language in which much or most of their history is recorded. On the other hand, since the World War there has developed a remarkable trend among peoples the world over toward acquiring an understanding if not a speaking proficiency of the English language.

In consequence, many persons, even among the non-English speaking nations, predict the possibility of English becoming a universal commercial language or language of convenience. However, they do not mean to imply that it will displace other languages. Interest among many continental European nations in having the English-speaking world become acquainted with their economic and cultural activities has led to the issuance in the English language of many of their official, as well as unofficial, documents.[3]

The Metric System and Navigation Signals.—Universality of language has been approached in one sphere and actually realized in another sphere of man's activities. Most countries of the world use the metric system of measurement in both their popular and scientific quantitative records. In the English-speaking countries the English system of measurement is still current in a few branches of science as, for example, in meteorology, climatology, and engineering.

Bills to legalize and even compel the usage of the metric system in all measurements in the United States have been introduced into our Congress on many occasions, but as yet no definite action has resulted,

---

[3] The list of such materials is too long for presentation here, but correspondence with the consulates of these countries, located in New York City, will bring forth full information and copies of any of the literature desired.

although sponsors of these bills are convinced that much progress has been made. That universality in the adoption of the metric system will be attained in the near future seems to be certain. Comparison of this system with others now in use will reveal its practicality and the benefits which its introduction would bestow upon business. For example, in calculating fractional parts of a meter compared with a yard, we can determine more quickly and easily one-tenth of a meter as 10 centimeters than we can one-tenth of a yard as three and six tenths inches. The meter with its component elements divided into one hundred parts affords greater simplicity and accuracy in measurement than the yard divided into thirty-six parts.

On the high seas international agreement has been reached with respect to the kinds of signals to be employed when ships wish to communicate with each other. While these signals do not permit of as rapid or even as fluent conversation as one might carry on by wireless telegraphy and in this sense are not strictly comparable with letters and words of an internationally written and spoken language, nevertheless, they simulate the full quality of a universal language in the particular realm for which they are intended.

Script.—There remains one more item to be considered in association with the subject of language with special reference to commerce, namely, the nature of script forms. Numerous forms have been used since the days of the first hieroglyphs. We recognize among those which have been widely used the Latin form, the Russian, the Greek, the Arabic, and the Chinese and Japanese ideographs. To-day there is a strong tendency toward a world-wide use of Latin script and Arabic numerals as employed by English-speaking nations. Even the Chinese have attempted to set up a thirty-nine letter alphabet similar to our own, the additional letters helping to express certain sounds not possible of representation in our limit of twenty-six letters. The Japanese are to some extent replacing ideographs with Latin script.

Uniformity among the nations in kind of script, whether by hand or by type, aids greatly in accuracy of transmission of messages. It also simplifies the work of one who is desirous of learning several languages. It quickens the work of an interpreter and may some day lead to the establishment of universality in language.

CHAPTER XIX

WIRED TELEGRAPH, CABLE, AND THE TELEPHONE

WIRED TELEGRAPH

When the commercial telegraph was invented in 1837 by Samuel F. B. Morse the general public was not prepared to accept it as a device possessing utility. Many men had worked on the idea of telegraphy as far back as the eighteenth century, but little confidence had been built up in its possible practicability. The customary conservative reception awaited those who sought to secure financial assistance for its commercial development. Failing to find sympathetic support in private capitalistic quarters, resort was made to Congress. Even there reverses were staved off only by the parliamentary ruse of attaching to a wholly unrelated bill a rider calling for an appropriation of $30,000. It was an eleventh-hour attempt just as Congress was preparing to adjourn in 1843.

This appropriation made possible the construction of a line between Baltimore and Washington in 1844. It proved an immediate success. The next year it was extended to New York City and Boston. Private capital came forward to build extensions until to-day we boast of nearly two and one half million miles of wire under private control representing 33 per cent of the world's total.

The objective of the telegraph route obviously was to connect trade centers with as rapid a means of communication as possible. It was not created as an institution apart but rather conceived as an adjunct to the organization of trade centers. In this light, we are interested in tracing its spread among the world's centers and the consequence of that distribution.

World Distribution.—The total mileage of telegraph lines in the United States is far in excess of that in any other country, but the service rendered per unit area is not the greatest. For example, the number of miles of wire per 1,000 square miles of area in the United States is only 477 as compared with 2,377 in Germany. Our huge absolute total is due to the great distances between many trade centers, particularly in the Western parts of the nation. On the other hand, a comparison with individual States or groups of densely populated States presents a better picture. In Ohio, for example, there are 2,250 miles of wire per 1,000 square miles of area. Areas of similar population densities, in the more progressive countries, have a corresponding density of wire per square mile.

The actual use made of the telegraph systems in the United States and European countries reveals an apparently greater interest here than abroad. This, no doubt, is partly due to the general desire of speed so prevalent among us. The difference in usage is also a matter of difference in purchasing power, in spite of the fact that the foreign systems are government owned and charge less per word. The public abroad is rarely urged through advertising campaigns, as we are, to send telegrams. Furthermore, inherent foreign conservatism and economy oppose public indulgence in the luxury of using telegrams for birthday congratulations, Mother's Day, and other similar occasions. Their philosophy suggests that a letter or postal card, both much less costly, will answer the purpose equally well. Thus the difference in per capita use of the respective telegraphic systems is not necessarily an index of differences in commercial activity or even general progressiveness. Neither is the difference due to quality of service.

Telegraph Routes.—Telegraph wires follow in the main, railroads and highways. Occasionally they represent the blazing of a new trail and are located many miles from habitations. Yet, with few exceptions, maps of the telegraph lines of the continents are rough approximations of the pattern of trade center distribution. They are the connecting links between centers, even more completely so than railroads, because in many instances centers have telegraphic communication when they do not have the convenience of a railroad. If, on the other hand, they have a railroad station, they automatically are on a telegraph route.

Mention has been made elsewhere of the telegraphic route across Australia connecting Adelaide with Port Darwin. This is an instance of wires preceding rails. Many examples might be cited of telegraph wires crossing mountains independently of railroads, but in these instances, in contrast with the Australian situation, there is not necessarily a likelihood of railroads being projected along the same routes.

The growth of these lines continues in spite of wireless telegraphy. In fact, contrary to early public opinion, wired telegraphy not only has not been threatened by wireless competition, but the two methods of transmission are becoming closely integrated. In consequence, both continue to grow, the latter, however, making relatively slow progress as an adjunct to overland commercial conversations in contrast with its vigorous growth in oversea trade.

THE CABLE

A somewhat later development of the wired telegraph is the cable. In general two kinds of cables may be recognized, namely, land and sea cables. Since the land cable is a part of the land system we need not give this form special consideration. On the other hand, the undersea cable functions in such an important capacity in international trade that it deserves detailed consideration apart from the land system.

The First Cables.—England was the first among the modern nations to appreciate the value of a cable. This perhaps was a natural response to colonial ownership and to the fact that, as a part of an island area, telegraphic communication with the mainland of Europe was highly desirable. It is therefore not surprising that the first cable was laid under the English Channel in 1851.

Following upon the success of this cable, Cyrus W. Field, an enterprising American, visualized a transatlantic cable. He was unable to interest capital in the United States for the support of his project, probably because at this time we were shifting our economic interest from international channels toward the interior. Capital was supplied primarily by the British and after two unsuccessful cable laying attempts, in 1858 and 1865, the third effort in 1866 was crowned with victory. An English company manufactured and laid the cable.

A Revolutionary Date.—The year 1866 marked a revolution in world exchanges because communication between Europe and the United States was reduced from weeks and even months to minutes.[1] Heretofore, a message and a response from one party to another forwarded by ship involved from three to six weeks for a crossing of the North Atlantic in either direction. Many events could happen in the interim to vitiate the purport of these messages. Such commercial exchanges were necessarily carried on inconveniently, not to say somewhat pre-

---

[1] In a public address, Newton D. Baker, one-time Secretary of War, suggested that this date is one which did not necessarily mark the beginning of a happier era in world relations. He stated that before the cable era sensitive nations, which had been inclined to go to war when offended, had an opportunity "to cool off" while an exchange of notes was taking place via the slow oversea transportation methods. After 1866 the cable allowed of a rapid-fire exchange, encouraging the diplomats to say things to each other which in more leisurely circumstances they might not have said. Thus, the flames of international irritation could be fanned quickly into war.

cariously, as compared with the conditions offered under the new speedy method of telegraphic verbal exchanges.

It is difficult for us to-day to imagine just what that revolutionary device meant to the traders of the middle of the last century. Price quotations, the placement of orders, cancellations, changes in specifications, all became possible instantaneously. This situation, of course, meant that merchants had to readjust their methods. They had to quicken their pace, had to be more alert, were forced to reach decisions more quickly and to improve their judgments which had to be formed more hurriedly than before.

The United States versus England.—In 1881, under the sponsorship of Jay Gould, the first American-owned cable was laid in the name of the American Cable and Telegraph Company. Subsequently, it passed into the control of the Western Union Company. In characteristic United States fashion, our enthusiasm for cables having been aroused, we supported another transatlantic project which was completed in 1884 by John W. Mackay and James Gordon Bennett for the Commercial Cable Co.

The cable was now accepted as an integral part of the world's economic physical mechanism. Although the United States Government did not subsidize cable laying, as Great Britain and other nations did, private enterprise gave considerable support. To-day, that capital controls about 26 per cent of all cables, the British controlling upwards of 50 per cent, the remainder being scattered among other nations.

Distribution of Cables.—The map of the world's cables shows a preponderance in the North Atlantic, as one might anticipate. The countries of large population, industrial leadership, and political dominance border upon this ocean and their demand for inter-communication necessitates multiple transmission lines. Along these coasts the major trade centers are most numerous, and in their hinterland secondary centers are densest.

Great Britain controls nearly half of the cables, with France, Italy, and the United States sharing most of the other half. In addition to the transatlantic cables, many shorter ones penetrate coastal waters of the continents, particularly along the highly indented European coast. Great Britain is the greatest of all cable centers with twenty-two cables connecting with continental Europe and about an equal number of trans-oceanic lines.

The North Pacific Ocean, marked by scarcity of cables, stands out in contrast with the North Atlantic. The other oceans are relatively free

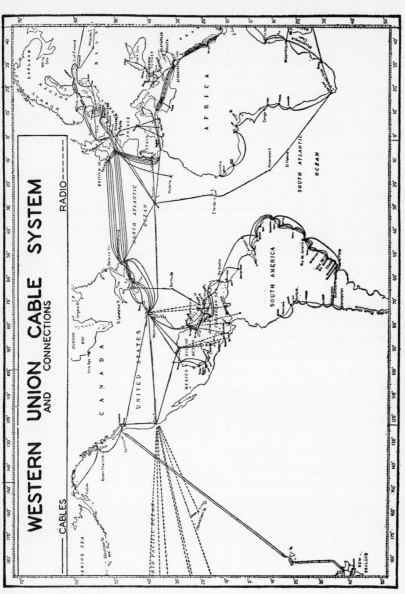

FIG. 57. A PORTION OF THE WORLD'S CABLE NETWORK

The preponderance of cables in the North Atlantic is impressive. The growing importance of transoceanic radio is suggested by this map. Only a few of these cables are under the control of the United States. See text. (Courtesy of the Western Union Telegraph Company.)

from cables except between coastal trade centers of the continents and islands. With such paucity of cables one can readily appreciate the importance of those in existence.

British Leadership.—The reasons for Great Britain's predominance in the cable situation are not far to seek. Besides an early appreciation of their value in the light of her island position, she developed a skill in the manufacture of cable which has not yet been equaled by other nations. Through subsidies the cable manufacturers have been able to survive when business has slackened and, hence, have been available at all times to supply not only British demands but those from many foreign countries, including our own.

Great Britain is the only nation which can transmit messages completely around the earth via her own cables. Since cables still provide an element of secrecy not yet attained in radio telegraph, Great Britain remains the only power which can be assured of secrecy when cabling the parts of the Empire. Codes are not proof against all-comers, and, therefore, the only control of secrecy which can be insured involves complete control of the cable terminals.

United States' Indifference.—The people of the United States, as already indicated, have never shown enthusiasm for cables. Perhaps the reason lies in the fact that not only were cables evolved during the era of our own internal development but the vast size of the country and consequent remoteness from the sea of a large part of the population has militated against our acquiring a cable consciousness. Many business men in trade centers away from the sea have little or no interest in, not to say even slight appreciation of, the significance of sea-cables.

Although cables involve the transmission of trading prices, market quotations, orders for money transfers and goods, and official international conversations, we seem unable to become aroused as to their ownership or operation. In Germany in pre-war days a university professor of geography waxed eloquent over the injustices being done his country by foreign cable control in operation then and predicted that the German people were not in a mood to tolerate that situation much longer. The Germans were just beginning to lay their own cables. His student audience received his remarks with enthusiastic applause. Such expression of interest would not be revealed by American students.

The Future of Cable Communication.—Frequently one hears the question asked, "Are not cables of declining importance as radio develops?" This query is effectively answered by the cable companies when they reveal plans for the laying of more cables. Until radio communication can be controlled in a manner making interception absolutely impossible it will not displace the cable. For ordinary purposes radio transmission does very well as a substitute for cable, although atmospheric interferences are more frequent in the former than in the latter medium. Accordingly, rather than anticipating the elimination of cables, officials associated with the companies operating these lines are convinced of their growing complementary value. Port centers in particular insist upon both services.

The mechanism of cable transmission has been improved by leaps and bounds. For example, the newest transoceanic cables, connecting New York City and Rome via the Azores Islands has a capacity of 50,000,000 words annually, or five times the volume that could be handled on cables owned by the Western Union Company up to this time. The more efficient cables are made, the longer will they hold their own in competition with wireless telegraphy and radiophone and the greater will be their rôle in the exchange of messages among the world's trade centers.

THE TELEPHONE

Although a German (Philipp Reis) claims credit for the invention of the telephone in 1861, the world generally assigns the honor to Alexander Graham Bell whose invention dates from 1876. Much credit goes to Thomas Edison and others for efficient improvements.

Like the telegraph and cable, the telephone has a relatively recent origin. In fact, so recent is it that the man who invented it lived to see the growth of telephone lines from a few feet to thousands of miles in length. A notation about the occasion of the first spanning of the continent is worthy of record:

Mr. Thomas A. Watson, Bell's assistant, relates that it was on March 10, 1867, over a line extending between two rooms in a building at 5 Exeter Place, Boston, that the first complete sentence was ever spoken by Bell and heard by Watson, who recorded it in his note book at the time. It consisted of these words: "Mr. Watson, come here; I want you." Thus the telephone was born.

On January 25, 1915, the transcontinental line, spanning Bell's adopted country from ocean to ocean, was in the presence of dignitaries of state and nation dedicated to the public service. This was a day of triumph for Bell, for, using a reproduction of the original instrument, he once again spoke the memorable words, "Mr. Watson, come here; I want you." But this time Bell was at New York City and Watson, who heard him with perfect ease, was three thousand miles away in San Francisco.[2]

The first long-distance telephone was established between New York City and Boston in 1884. This was followed by a line from New York City to Philadelphia in 1885 and by the first line over a considerable distance, namely, between New York City and Chicago in 1892. Since those days the lines have been extended by millions of miles bringing into telephonic contact most of the earth's largest trade centers.

In the United States in 1935 there were 50.29 per cent of the world's telephones. Europe ranked next with 35.86 per cent. The remaining small percentage emphasizes the relatively few phones used in vast areas, probably due to the public's limited purchasing power.

Per Capita Phones of Nations.—The contrast between the per capita number of telephones in the United States and in European countries frequently calls forth some surprise. In our country it is 50 per cent greater than in Denmark, the nation in Europe having the highest per capita record. The continent of North America has a per capita number over seven times as great as the average for Europe. These striking differences demand some interpretation.

We have already mentioned the cost of living as an important factor influencing the number of telephones in use. In Europe an additional element is the convenient distribution of public telephones in the larger centers and the low charge per call. Public booths are easily accessible upon the public highways and in business establishments. Then too, the service in many respects is not as efficient as in the United States, and therefore, public interest is less. The system is government owned, and, consequently, there is less urging of the public, through advertising channels, to install telephones. Again, the concentration of population within relatively small areas, which we have so often seen as a governing agent in European trade-center activities, makes somewhat less convincing the need for saving time through the use of the telephone.

The mail service being cheap and good, people in foreign lands utilize it frequently as a substitute for the telephone. A postal card, costing but a half cent for local mailing, is far more economical in the minds of many than two and a half cents for a phone call, even though the latter saves time. The foreign psychology that the saving of time is not as important as we in the United States believe it to be has contributed to the reluctance in adopting telephones. Again, this same attitude among business men, combined with the fact that in general

[2] *Science* (Feb. 23, 1923) Vol. XLVII, No. 1469.

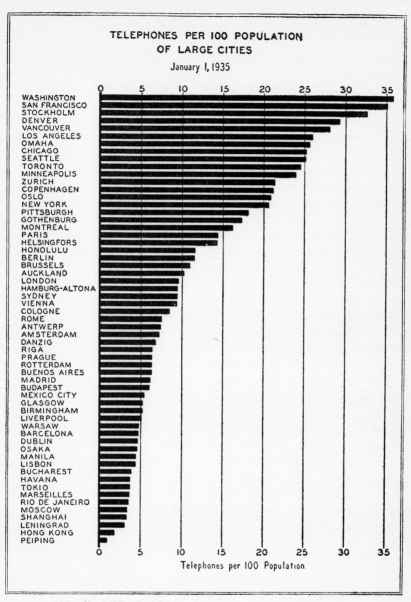

FIG. 58. PER CAPITA NUMBER OF TELEPHONES

(Courtesy of American Telephone and Telegraph Company.)

foreign countries do not develop such large business plants as we do, militates further against extensive installations.

Trade Center Telephones.—One may wonder whether this contrast between the United States and European countries means that the latter are backward or that commerce is of decidedly less importance. A glance at the ranking of the principal world trade centers with respect to per capita numbers of telephones answers the query in large part.

In 1935 Stockholm ranked third among all cities, not far behind Washington which ranked first. New York City, considered only in the light of its business activities, we might have supposed would head the list, but it held the surprisingly low position of fifteenth. This low rank is due to a dense population of apartment dwellers whose living conditions approximate those of the slums. Toronto in Canada shows a better rank, and Montreal is not far behind. Among the first twenty-one, ten, exclusive of Honolulu, are foreign and of these seven are European.

This ranking sheds a somewhat more favorable light upon foreign centers. In other words, some of the larger trade centers compare favorably with those in the United States, the low national per capita numbers being accounted for by the small number of telephones in secondary centers and by the limited rural installations. The latter situation is illustrated in the case of Sweden. While its capital trade center ranks third among all world centers and not far below first, the per capita phones in communities of less than 50,000 inhabitants drops the national ranking to fifth place.

Conversations.—Actual usage of telephones should serve as a fair index of the service rendered by this form of communication. Ranking the countries on the basis of total telephone conversations the United States is far in the forefront. Total conversation, however, is not a satisfactory basis for comparison, since the population numbers in the respective countries vary so greatly. Upon a per capita unit basis we find Canada ranking first just ahead of the United States; then follow Denmark and Sweden, each with over 100 conversations per capita. The number of conversations falls rapidly thereafter for other nations.

After one has experienced the poor service in the trade centers of such countries as France and Great Britain, it is not surprising that the per capita number of conversations is so low. Of course, this is not the sole reason. Fewness of telephones is a further factor. An additional basis may possibly lie in the relatively large number of *telegrams* sent in foreign countries, particularly in long-distance communications. For example, whereas we use the telephone about two and one half times as much as the nations of Europe, we sent in 1934 only about 10 per cent more telegrams. (See Appendix.)

Intercontinental Telephones.—With the development of wireless telegraphy, radio telephony has come into its own and has made oversea conversations between certain trade centers practical. Experimental work, begun in 1915 by the American Telephone and Telegraph Company, aided by the U. S. Navy Department and the French Government, culminated in the first successful transmission of speech across the Atlantic on October 21 of the same year. Commercial telephonic service was established between the United States and England January 7, 1927. Thus progress in this field was exceedingly rapid.

To-day wireless telephony is common between England and numerous continental centers. Through these extensions users of telephones in the United States are given a considerably expanded service. At present there are seventy-one oversea countries in telephonic communication with the United States, most of which involve the use of wireless telephony. Twenty-two ocean liners may be reached by telephone.

As compared with cable messages transoceanic telephone conversations are costly, measured in absolute terms. However, many traders maintain there is economy in the conversation because (1) more words can be used in a given time than by cable, (2) the person with whom one is communicating is at once available, and (3) the trend of conversation is under instant control, varying with the responses received to proposals made. Furthermore, the hearing of the voice allows of a more accurate interpretation of the ideas being exchanged and tends to establish greater intimacy between the parties in cases where they have heretofore not met. The psychological effect of elimination of space adds to the economic value of the conference. Thus, as an additional element in the conduct of international exchanges wireless telephony makes a significant contribution.

The Telephone and Trade.—Familiar to most persons is the convenience which the telephone offers. Sky-scrapers would hardly be practicable without telephonic communication. Hence, the entire trade center pattern of to-day would probably be greatly modified were it not for this device. Farming has been made more agreeable and comfortable because the telephone brings the farmer into close touch with his distant neighbors and, especially in time of emergency, enables him to reach friends, physicians, police, or even fire-fighting assistance. The trade-center housewife orders her daily foods from shops anywhere in the locality and makes purchases from department stores in response to specially advertised goods. Retailers are making increased use of the telephone in calling prospective customers' attention to trade opportunities. The ways in which the telephone facilitates the mechanical conduct of trade are numerous. So thoroughly has this device become a part of our trading mechanism that we now look upon it as an indispensable part of both the physical and social organization of our trade centers.

CHAPTER XX

RADIO AND THE MOTION PICTURE

RADIO

When, in 1896, Guglielmo Marconi filed an application for the first British patent for wireless telegraphy the inter-relations of the world's trade centers were destined to take on many new aspects. From this date the mechanics of wireless communication developed with remarkable rapidity. By 1902 the first message was transmitted across the Atlantic Ocean, although in the preceding year the first letter "s" had been successfully flashed from Poldhu, England, to St. John, Newfoundland.

Radio transmission was scheduled to serve as a medium for the entertainment and education of the mass of people and as an advertising channel to entice the public to spend more millions than they had spent in response to other forms of advertising. Only since 1920 when KDKA, the station of the Westinghouse Electric and Manufacturing Company in Pittsburgh, broadcast the first program for entertainment purposes have we seen the development of the commercial aspects of the radio. In other words, within the life of the present generation a theoretical hope for aerial advertising sent direct to almost every home in the United States has become a practical reality.

Unifying Effects.—Probably no other means of communication has come closer to making all the world "kin" than has wireless, more particularly that phase which has reached into the homes of the people. The broadcasting of messages by government officials, talks by noted scientific men, music by great orchestras and individual musicians, and broadcasts of many significant international, national, or local incidents have all contributed to popular education and to a better understanding and appreciation of the world. The cherished dreams of many persons to travel to interesting trade centers in their own or in foreign countries can never be realized. However, they may find much compensation for such disappointment in their reception via radio of the sounds and descriptions of life as it actually is expressed in those centers at specific moments. This reality in itself is difficult for us

251

fully to appreciate as we endeavor to interpret its effect upon a better and more intelligent understanding which may arise among the peoples of widely separated centers.

In Europe and other regions where international boundaries of a number of countries are in close proximity to each other radio waves are not easily restricted to local territories, but practically all of them are international in range. Their free movement means easy reception by great numbers of foreigners. This situation has suggested the desirability of a universal language. So far as the understanding of music is concerned such a language for the radio is hardly essential, but certainly the spoken word conveys no meaning when it can not be understood. To relieve this condition a common language would be a boon. Hence, there is justification in the belief and hope of many people that the day may not be far distant when the urge to understand messages which slip across international boundaries will bring about either a universal language or a standard radio broadcasting language.

A momentous occasion in the annals of radio transmission occurred on February 17, 1932 when a 15,000 word message was broadcast from Geneva, reporting to the world the findings of the League of Nations in the Sino-Japanese dispute. This message was sent by Morse Code in English and was received in every country of the world simultaneously. The use of English was encouraging to those who have dreamed of the day when it will be the universal language. The complete success of the transmission, so clear that it was recorded without a single error by the *New York Times,* again demonstrated the far-reaching possibilities of this medium in international trade—distance having proved no barrier.

Not only has radio had a unifying effect with respect to breaking down distances and giving people increased familiarity with the world about them but it has directed attention to numerous trade centers heretofore only slightly known or not known at all by residents of other trade centers. Broadcasting stations are identified in the minds of many in terms of the center in which they are located, rather than by countries, states, provinces, or other political divisions. Announcers invariably associate the call letters of their stations with the name of the center in which they are located.

Descriptions of public functions, ceremonials of various kinds, sports, and innumerable other events generally include either direct reference to the local landscape, the characteristics of the people, the nature of the climate, the accessibility of the community, or perhaps

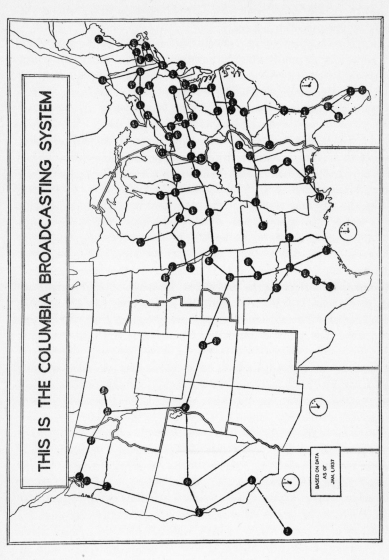

THIS IS THE COLUMBIA BROADCASTING SYSTEM

BASED ON DATA
AS OF
JAN. 1, 1937

FIG. 59. RADIO NETWORK LINES VS. TRADE CENTERS

This network of Broadcasting Stations suggests that "air lanes" may be viewed as trade routes and illustrates their close relation to the distribution of trade centers and population. This map includes only a portion of the total "avenues" in operation. (Courtesy of the Columbia Broadcasting System.)

its remoteness from most avenues of communication. Thus, the listeners involuntarily learn about the geographic qualities of nearby or remote trade centers.

Direct Trade Use.—We have mentioned the advertising use to which radio broadcasting lends itself. That such activity is profitable to the advertisers seems borne out by the tremendous expenditures for this form of publicity. Here we have reference more especially to United States business organizations, inasmuch as broadcasting of advertisements in most other countries is much restricted both in character and the time available. In 1932, a "depression" year, the annual expenditure for radio advertising reached $39,106,776. Imagine what the total sales of products must have been to have compensated the advertisers for their initial expenditure. The number of letters received by one national network of radio stations in the same year was 4,771,000—ample evidence of the serious attention which people pay to the radio programs. This figure may be only one third of the total number of letters written to all stations and direct to advertisers, lecturers, and other broadcasters.

In addition to advertising, the radio functions in the important capacity of disseminator of market reports. These are of critical value to the farmer. No longer need he await the next day's newspaper or, if his location is somewhat remote, have to be content with reports which reach him perhaps once a week. He is apprised at all times of the fluctuations in market prices and can guide his business far more effectively than was possible in pre-radio times. Farm interest in the radio is evidenced by the United States census returns for 1930. Among the total farm families 20.8 per cent owned receiving sets. While this figure may seem to be surprisingly low, examination of the data by states reveals the fact that it is due probably to no lack of desire but to the low purchasing power of our southern farmers. In many of the Northern States the percentage was over fifty, New Jersey leading with 56.6 per cent of the total number of farm families in that state.

Weather Forecasting.—As an exceedingly important by-product of the rapid development of radio broadcasting, much as in the case of that associated with aviation, there have been large expenditures of money for atmospheric investigations. No sooner had broadcasting begun to acquire popularity than the phenomenon known as *static* interfered with satisfactory reception. Manufacturers of receiving sets and owners of broadcasting companies were quick to realize that this condition must be remedied or sales would not increase. Not only was encouragement given to scientists and others interested in solving these disturbing problems but financial support for research was furnished by broadcasting companies. The national government, universities, and other institutions in a position to pursue research in the realm of atmospherics have devoted considerable time to the subject.

Thus, important contributions have been made toward problems associated with long-range forecasting. Again, we emphasize the revolutionary effect which accurate, long-range weather forecasts will have upon trade centers and the whole economic structure.[1] Life in our trade centers will no longer be fraught with present economic hazards. We shall know the crop prospect, the farmer's income, therefore, and the consequent merchandise sales outlook. We shall find it possible to plan and build with confidence and, hence, to eliminate the uncertainties of our present more or less haphazard ways of living.

The Future of Radio.—Forecasting is always more or less treacherous, yet there seems to be substantial reason for believing that carriage of the voice through the air will one day become an accomplishment of every person equipped with a pocket-sized instrument. Each will likewise be in a position to receive messages. Thus we shall no longer be dependent upon the fixed telephone. Transactions, delayed now because of forgotten telephone calls or busy lines, will be only slightly delayed, for one of the parties involved may do his telephoning from any spot of his own choosing. The already swift pace that has been set in the economic and cultural life of our trade centers will be still further quickened.

THE MOTION PICTURE

We have often heard it said that music is the universal language because every listener can understand it, even though interpretations may differ slightly. If this be true, then the silent motion picture has certainly functioned as a universal language quite as much, for every person, without knowing the language, can interpret the actions he sees according to his own experiences. Although the talking feature has

---

[1] Blue Hill Meteorological Observatory has devised a remarkable instrument known as a radio-meteorograph which is sent aloft attached to a small balloon. Heights of nearly fourteen miles have been reached. Radio signals are sent out by the instrument every 30 seconds and recorded at the base stations on a chronograph developed for this purpose. Upper air observations are thus conveniently accessible and when the cost of securing them by these means is greatly reduced, the prospect of increased accuracy in forecasting will be very bright.

greatly changed the character of the presentation, the picture being not so easily translated as the silent one, nevertheless, those unable to understand the spoken words may still derive a fairly comprehensive idea of the meaning intended to be conveyed.

When George Eastman, pioneer in photographic film production, in 1889 produced a flexible film, he paved the way for Thomas Edison's realization of a dream to record motion as he had succeeded in record-

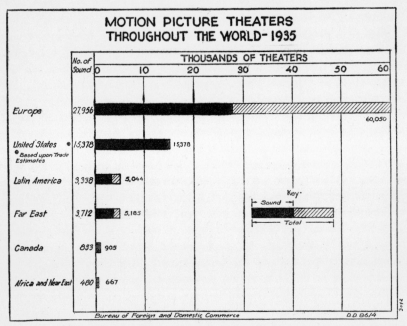

FIG. 60. REGIONS RANKED ACCORDING TO NUMBER OF MOTION PICTURE THEATERS

When comparing the number of theaters in Europe and the United States we must not lose sight of seating capacity. Probably there is little difference in the total seating capacity of the respective regions and there is some probability that it is greater for the United States than for Europe. Data are uncertain.

ing sound. In the same year Edison's kinetoscope appeared, the forerunner of the modern motion picture, awaiting a propitious time for its commercial introduction to the world. Another revolution in industry, trade, and education had dawned. Edison had invested about $34,000 in his inventive efforts, a sum dwarfed into insignificance by the estimated recent investment in the entire industry of somewhere in the neighborhood of $3,000,000,000.

We are not concerned here with the financial aspects of the industry, but rather with the part played by the finished product in facilitating the distribution and exchange of ideas and with its service as a medium for drawing trade centers closer together and eliminating the sharp lines of cleavage which formerly distinguished urban and rural folk.

The average picture shown for amusement purposes reveals much of the detailed equipment for the home, the office, or industrial plant. It also emphasizes style in clothing and suggests indirectly various forms of entertainment. The mass of people who are more or less regular theater patrons are easily impressed by these striking portrayals. Whether they be residents of a center of a million citizens or farmers who have "come to town" for the day or evening, their reaction is much the same—receptive.

The farmer and his family see in action the conveniences of life in widespread use in the larger trade centers. They are stimulated to desire the comforts that urban life supposedly offers. And in so far as the farmer can introduce them into his home or on the farm proper, he does so. No longer is the farmer less familiar with "worldly things" than the urban man.

The "big trade center" man learns about farm life, just as the farmer becomes familiar with urban activities. No longer is the "city" man in almost total ignorance of rural life; nor does he feel himself apart from and perhaps above his countryman "back on the farm." The farm ceases to be *back*. Although we can hardly attribute all of this reformation in concepts and attitudes to the motion picture, this medium has contributed enormously toward alleviating many false notions entertained by both urban and rural residents, respectively, with regard to each other.

In Foreign Relations.—The effectiveness of the film in international relations is somewhat humorously revealed by a story which emanates from reliable sources to the effect that the male population of Sweden appealed to the government to prohibit the showing of our films on the grounds that they were disrupting the home. It seems that Swedish women had been impressed by the luxury in which our women live. The picture showing chauffeurs driving American women to afternoon teas implied, of course, an abundance of leisure as well as wealth. Swedish women wished to be able to indulge likewise in these luxuries. Since Swedish men in general are unable to provide a life of ease which our films erroneously made Swedish ladies believe was commonplace among us, dissatisfaction arose in the Scandinavian homes which led to the men's appeal.

Probably no other medium offers such facilities for acquainting the peoples of different nations with the economic activities, the customs, the styles, habits, and other elements in the lives of humankind. While the radio provides opportunity for verbal description, its effectiveness can not equal that of the visual impression. It lacks the element of visual motion possessed by the motion picture.

As in radio broadcasting where the spoken word is used, the problem of translation presents serious obstacles. The cost of translating the talking feature into one or more languages increases the cost of production. This militates against the interchange of films among the nations. Dialects are so different in parts of many countries that although a film may be accompanied by the national language it may not be understood in many localities. In one motion picture marketing organization thirty-seven languages are used in translating the titles and advertisements. Because of the prohibitive cost, the talking feature is rarely translated into languages other than the French or German, but instead the titles, as in former silent pictures, are introduced and the spoken words allowed to run along in the original language. Herein lies a limitation to the influence and utilization of the picture as a medium for the transmission of ideas along international channels, but it is not so serious as to threaten in any sense the discontinuance of exchanges.

The News Reel.—The news reel is not only valuable as a supplement to the daily press and radio news broadcasts but it brings to the audience views which frequently do not appear in print and can not yet be shown by radio. It presents to the illiterate, current news which, in part or whole, would not otherwise reach him. Besides, it makes the public familiar with living conditions in numerous widely scattered centers and advertises to that public modern machines, styles, architecture, transportation vehicles, landscape designs, and a thousand other elements which constitute a part of the world's total human activities. Claims have been made by some persons that the news reel has "done more to introduce American products into the outside world than any other single influence." Perhaps it is equally true that the foreign film or the American film portraying foreign scenes has been effective in creating a demand in the United States for foreign products and to some extent in the adoption among us of foreign habits and customs. It has been said on good authority that the cradle type of telephone instrument, commonly used in Europe for many years, was introduced into the United States in consequence of its appeal to the American public through the motion picture.

The Audience.—The number of persons reached by the film may be approximated in the light of the fact that about 60,000,000 admissions are collected weekly in the United States. Figuring conservatively that habitués visit the theater twice weekly, the number of different individuals involved may total 30,000,000. If we calculate still more conservatively and figure only 25,000,000, this number represents about one fifth of the nation's population and a somewhat higher percentage of the buying population. Add to this number those in foreign countries who visit the "movies" and the figures approach staggering proportions. The world's weekly attendance is estimated to be 175,000,000. It is estimated that in 1935 there were 87,229 theaters the world over, of which about 15,378 are in the United States, and 60,050 in Europe.[2]

The theater is not the only agency through which this device effectively conveys ideas. In the case of industrial or other equipment which can not be transported easily or to which prospective purchasers can not be brought, the motion picture has served as a most effective substitute for both the still picture of the dull catalog and the material presence of the object itself. So, to-day we find the traveling salesman both in domestic and foreign localities carrying as his catalog several reels of film and a portable projector for demonstrating logging machinery, steam engines, elevators, derricks, and many other bulky commodities.

Although audiences represent essentially group gatherings and receive their impressions as such, the effects of the pictures are not of necessity exclusively mass effects. Individuals are stirred by the story or landscape or other aspect portrayed by a reel. They may be moved to travel in consequence of what they observe or to inquire further into the characteristics of another part of their country or of a foreign territory. As individuals they are made conscious of another world than their own neighborhood, trade center, or political subdivision. They are led to compare and contrast their own setting with that of other centers.

All of these reactions lead ultimately to a gravitational effect in terms at least of ideas and general world knowledge among the people of the world's trade centers. The greater the awareness of the people of the manner in which each group survives and solves the problems

[2] Bureau of Foreign and Domestic Commerce (Washington, D. C., 1935).

of life, the more certainly are their differences modified or even eliminated. The physical characteristics of their respective communities tend to grow alike. The widespread use of the skyscraper, straightline architecture, paved streets, traffic lights, suburban homes, and many other features of trade centers scattered far and wide over the earth evidence this tendency.

CHAPTER XXI

THE PUBLIC PRESS AND THE POSTAL SERVICE

One of the most effective media for the spread and exchange of ideas is the public press. As an agency for facilitating the distribution of the press the postal service has been indispensable.

Under the term "public press" are newspapers issued daily, weekly, or monthly, and magazines and journals usually printed weekly, monthly, or at longer intervals. In the present discussion we shall consider only the daily newspaper and the magazine, the latter including the trade journal. We focus attention upon these publications because of their direct association with the cultural activities in inter- and intra-trade center relations. The Postal Service is discussed in the succeeding section.

THE DAILY NEWSPAPER

Slightly more than one third of the world's daily newspapers are published in the United States and nearly another third in the British Isles. This means that practically two thirds of all daily newspapers are printed in the English language. However, the number of papers published is not an index to the number of readers. In some countries, as for example in central Europe, papers circulate according to a type of coöperative or neighborhood plan. A given subscriber, after reading the paper, passes it on to his neighbor, who in turn does likewise until perhaps a half dozen families have read the same issue. Generally, only the first family pays for the paper but subscriptions may be rotated.

In many countries cafés play a conspicuous part in the daily lives of the people. The drinking of afternoon coffee or tea is for most persons in foreign lands regular practice, and great numbers take this repast in a café. Café proprietors long ago sensed their opportunity and provided not only music to entice patronage and capitalize the longing for afternoon refreshment but introduced newspapers and magazines for the patrons' convenience. The public quickly responded to this courtesy. Under such conditions circulation statistics based upon subscriptions appear small, but reader statistics, if available, would in many instances reveal a circulation equivalent to those in countries where the people have been accustomed to make individual purchases.

Informational Function.—Newspapers carry advertisements which make their appeal direct to consumers and distributing agents. Those who have commodities for sale, stores or homes for rent, articles for exchange, or services to offer find the newspaper to be the best medium for reaching an extensive market at a low cost. Returns seem to be more immediate than from advertisements in most other media.

All trade announcements are not solely for the purpose of sales. The newspaper performs an important function in its citations of market quotations, business consolidations, reorganizations, failures and in a discussion of general business conditions, future prospects, and the status of business in foreign lands. Thus, the publication may be informative without being colored by direct sales objectives. A financial editor of a prominent newspaper has said, "Aside from the news value, financial news is carried by metropolitan newspapers in order to secure financial advertising. On the other hand, the amount of advertising patronage often determines the amount of financial news printed." True as this may be, the fact remains that many persons subscribe for certain newspapers because of their financial information and without reference to the amount, kind, or quality of advertising carried.

The circulation of a newspaper plays a large part not only in the quantity of advertising space which can be sold but in the charge which can be made for that space. Consequently, the reader's interest can not be ignored by the publisher. This informational aspect provides a service (not otherwise readily available) to all persons interested in trade. It is safe to say that, were the public press suddenly to find itself unable to continue in business, the general public would immediately subsidize some type of publication that would perform a similar informational function. Our present economic activities are so complex that we can no longer carry on without the newspaper form of communication. This is particularly true in trade centers of a size which do not make it possible for each citizen to keep informed about local affairs through personal contacts.

In addition to those items possessing a direct commercial bearing, the news columns disseminate much data for the enlightening of the reader. All papers naturally do not print an equal amount of news nor news of similar scope or quality. Here again, financial support gained from the sale of advertising space governs largely these news elements. In the larger trade centers the press usually carries a greater amount of national and foreign news than does the press in the smaller centers. Such publications are available to most persons either through direct subscription or through the facilities of the public library. As in the case of financial news, so in this instance the public would not be content to live without its daily contact with the press, albeit that same public at times roundly condemns the press for the inferior quality of its news. The daily newspaper is indispensable as a factor in keeping the public informed with respect to local, national, and international affairs and frequently plays a significant part in the guidance of the public welfare.

Another field served by the daily press is that involving an exchange of ideas. Increasing amounts of space are being generously given by the publishers to letters and articles written by the general public. In sections of the paper headed "The Mail Bag" or "Letters From the Public" or "The Open Court" or still other indicators of a public forum readers are afforded an opportunity to express themselves publicly and to exchange thoughts publicly. No charge is made for these insertions. Here is an effective avenue for the spread and exchange of ideas which occasionally bear fruit.

Public Opinion.—Arguments are presented pro and con upon the effect of the press upon public opinion. It is a matter hardly demonstrable statistically. One writer has said, "Most sociologists agree that the press does produce changes in opinion but through distortion, omissions, condensations and coloration of facts in news columns rather than by direct editorial exhortation." [1] That the press does affect public opinion can not be gainsaid when one considers the fact that its survival is dependent upon advertising space sold; that the latter would not be sold if the public did not read it; and that the public is evidently moved by its reading, else it would not make the purchases which are necessary to bring profitable returns to the advertisers and in turn warrant them in continuing to buy advertising space and thereby to sustain the newspapers. If the reading of advertising copy causes people to take direct action it is inconceivable that editorials or news accounts have no effect upon the public mind.

A degree of faith has grown up among some classes in the infallibility of the public press. Not uncommonly one hears those of limited experience insist that because a statement appeared in the newspaper

[1] Julian Woodward, *Foreign News in American Morning Newspapers* (Columbia University Press, New York).

of necessity it must be true. The "paper says this or that" is frequently uttered by individuals. Probably none appreciate the "power of the press" more than the press itself. In political campaigns, in local civic policies, in association with community fund drives, in the fostering of trade-center planning, and in connection with numerous activities of a purely non-political or non-commercial character the press may wield a tremendous influence. Accordingly, in the light of its integral part in local and national affairs the press as a medium for communication may prove to be a factor for evil or for good.

In foreign lands the power of the press upon public opinion is recognized by the fact of its frequent suppression. When a political régime discovers some newspaper or magazine in opposition to its policies and the circulation of that publication widespread its sale may be ordered discontinued for a limited period or entirely suppressed. Again, recognition of the press's influence is reflected in the quasi-official character of certain papers. Governments often send out "feelers" through certain publications known by the public as within the favor of the régime. The government seeks to get the sentiment of the public before taking definite action. When the reception of the "rumors" is unfavorable the proposal may be abandoned, delayed, or changed in accordance with the public attitude. Such procedure would be impossible if the public gave little heed to the press.

Potentialities.—No mechanical means of communication approaches so closely to the minimum purchasing power of peoples the world over than does the daily newspaper. Probably no form of current literature possesses the potential influence of this division of the public press. As a channel for the movement of ideas and as a path over which exchanges of almost every kind may be effected, nothing approaches the daily newspaper. In many respects it is no longer an exclusively private undertaking. Its position of influence in public activities is now so impressive that we may consider it essentially a public utility. Our present civilization would be unthinkable without it, and the possibilities of its even larger share in this civilization, particularly as a public aid, are so vast that the day can not be far distant when we shall be interested not only in preserving the "Freedom of the Press" but in enforcing the publication of all the facts in the press to the end that the public shall be accurately informed and also that it shall be free to utilize the press even more so than at present to reveal its attitude upon economic and cultural phases of current life.

Without the press the present integration of the public in our trade centers would be virtually impossible. Radio broadcasting has relieved the press to a slight degree of its responsibility, but so slight as to play a negligible part in this particular function. The daily newspaper distributes news with a certain element of uniformity throughout a community. The individual has an opportunity to read leisurely, to reread, to ponder, and sometimes to verify. News is made available in tangible form, as it were, and public attention is attracted by that form.

The press, as we have seen, is not confined to local circles. National publications and local papers which find their way into the markets of numerous trade centers bring these centers into closer proximity. They help to mold inter-trade center points of view. Without them there would be a serious gap in the relationships of these communities to each other, not merely among trade centers within a given nation but among those in all parts of the world.

The trade center and the public press are integral parts of an economic and cultural unit. While the former could exist without the latter, it could not exist in its present form.

THE POSTAL SERVICE

The extent to which the citizens of a nation employ the postal service may be taken as an index of their stage of civilization and level of their economic status. Fluctuations in amount of mail handled generally are indicators of fluctuating economic activities. A decline in postal receipts usually means that trade is depressed. Exceptions to this may occur when postal rates rise. Then momentarily correspondence is reduced to only most urgent matters. If the new rates become permanent a state of equilibrium eventually follows. If the change is temporary, a return to the former rate generally results in resumption of the former levels. Thus, postal statistics may constitute an excellent economic barometer as well as a basis for judging something of the relative economic activities both within and among trade centers.

Among the Nations.—A table of statistics showing postal data for selected countries brings to light some important comparative situations. Countries with a high percentage of literacy, of course, show the largest numbers of pieces of mail per capita. However, those which are in the upper portions of the list, with one exception, are countries we would hardly anticipate as ranking so high. Argentina heads the entire list and following it are the United States, Australia, and

New Zealand. Those countries which rank highest are recently settled regions. (See Appendix.)

All of the countries in the upper ranges have a relatively high purchasing power. Italy's low rank stands out in contrast with most of the countries of western Europe. No doubt under the new government, which seems interested in improving both the literacy and economic status of the citizens, its position will be greatly improved in the near future.

A Trade Medium.—We who are accustomed to an efficient mail service are likely to take for granted the advantages which we enjoy. Rarely do we stop to recall the enormous handicaps under which we would operate if the service were curtailed or the practical impossibility of conducting inter- and intra-trade center affairs if it were entirely wiped out. On the other hand, we have come more or less unconsciously to view the mail as almost sacred. Penalties for illegal interference with the operation are most severe. Protection, such as few activities receive, is afforded the movement of commodities and other items in the postal service.

In addition to the data in the table on page 302 which shows the enormity of the number of pieces of mail handled in various countries, figures bearing upon the use of the mail by a single mail-order house in some respects cast even more impressive light on this subject. In 1929 this firm handled nearly 14,000,000 pieces of parcel-post matter alone. The postage bill in the same year for all mail totaled over $11,250,000 or not quite 2 per cent of the entire postage sales in the United States. The amount of mail is so heavy that this organization, as well as a few others of similar size, operates a branch United States post office to handle its own mail.

Besides the value of the service rendered by the post office to distributors of commodities, the service has been of inestimable value to the public press. The government early appreciated the value of quick and low cost dissemination of news, and, hence, at one time not only set up low rates for newspapers but authorized also the free exchange of papers. The latter is no longer allowed, although rates continue to be lower than the standard charge paid by an individual who mails a single newspaper. Thus, preferential rates not only facilitate the distribution of the press but its effectiveness is increased by virtue of the increased radius of circulation and number of subscribers.

There is hardly a trade center of the literate world which is not reached by mail to-day. Whether in metropolitan center or at the out-

FIG. 61. THE BEGINNING OF A TRADE ROUTE IN A GREAT MERCANTILE ESTABLISHMENT

Distributing room in a branch of the U. S. Post Office to care for the correspondence and parcel post of a single mail order house. (Courtesy of Sears, Roebuck and Company, Chicago.)

posts of civilization, the arrival of the mail is always an important moment in the affairs of the individual or the corporation. Ideas, announcements, orders, moneys, and a hundred and one other items may be contained in the small envelope or package which has traveled perhaps thousands of miles at only a few cents cost.

Rise of the Postal Service.—The idea of delivering messages quickly over long distances without the necessity of the senders traveling with them dates back to the era of the Incas of Peru and to the runners of the early Mediterranean civilization. The relay race of the modern day is but an inheritance from the original postal service, although this service was not at first official in character. The Romans marked the relay points with *posts,* hence the expression "post office."

A variety of arrangements was made in the early revolution of the postal service. The first general service in the present sense was established in the fifteenth century by Emperors Maximilian I and Karl V of Germany but was supported by private funds of certain nobles. Many of the universities of Europe established systems involving the use of relay runners. That associated with the University of Paris in the thirteenth century was the first system in France. The Hanseatic League owned a private service. However, not until 1840 was the first regular government post office operated which assessed a fixed fee for letters and packages according to "weight and distance conveyed." In that year the British Parliament adopted the penny per ounce post plan, as suggested by Rowland Hill in 1837, for deliveries throughout the Empire.

A post route was established on the North American Continent as early as 1672 when Governor Lovelace of New York issued an order requiring that a post should "go monthly between New York and Boston." It was an intermittent and undependable service. The route itself was the forerunner of the present heavily congested Boston Post Road. Just as this service blazed a trail for the present day overland trade route, so many other highways and even some railways mark the mail routes established by hardy pioneers.

In consequence of the activities of the post office, international trade routes, both overland and overseas, have been effected. The same high regard for the sanctity of mail, shown in domestic circles, has developed in the international service. Many governments extend mail contracts to railroad lines and subsidize steamship companies to insure a dependable and efficient postal service. As exploration of the earth has been followed by settlement, the latter has been encouraged through assurance of mail connections with the home country no matter how infrequent. In the wake of this mail distribution has followed increased settlement and the rise of trade centers.

We have endeavored to show in earlier chapters the many factors which affect the origin, rise, or decline of trade centers. While perhaps no single one of these elements is exclusively deterministic, yet we may safely say that in the era of the development of transportation, centers with a faulty mail service are enormously handicapped. Even when all other conditions are favorable for growth, inability to communicate satisfactorily, either within or without the trade center, slows down the rate of growth. In the same proportion, probably the more efficient the postal service and the more frequently centers may exchange communications, the more rapidly are they likely to grow.

The instance we have cited of the single corporation owning a post office is evidence of the appreciation of that organization of the relationship between a highly coördinated, quick-serving post office and its own welfare. The principle has equal validity when applied to trade centers in their entirety. Once again we have occasion to recognize the reciprocal relations between an avenue of communication and a trade center.

Air Mail.—Until recently we have associated the mails only with water and land surfaces. But now the air is coming to serve indispensably as a route for postal activities. While most nations offer some form of air mail service, the United States has gone farthest in its development and has the most extensive and complete system. The value of aerial communication in mail deliveries was quickly sensed, and hence subsidies, otherwise known as mail contracts, for aviation were secured without difficulty. Encouragement thus given to aviation has been fundamental in the rapid establishment of major and minor routes, both within the countries and across international boundaries.

The aerial postal service has rendered invaluable assistance in knitting the world's trade centers by fostering a means which reduces the time factor. Not only has it shrunk the earth by making possible communication between individuals at negligible cost but it has made distances less formidable and isolation less real by reducing the element of time from weeks to days or days to hours.

Financial Service.—As the post office departments of the nations have demonstrated their dependability, particularly with regard to the delivery of their service to small remote trade centers often unsafe for individuals to approach, public confidence has grown and imposed further responsibilities upon them. So, we find a money-order service, involving the shipment of funds to all parts of the world. For thousands of people who carry no bank checking accounts it is invaluable in domestic transactions. Without this medium of transportation we would find international payments by individuals most cumbersome and difficult.

In many foreign countries, particularly in continental Europe, where the telegraph and telephone systems are owned and operated by national governments, the respective post office departments have jurisdiction. Hence, the functions of the postoffices are greatly enlarged and are coördinated with those other channels of exchange whose worth we have already discussed.

A SELECTED BIBLIOGRAPHY OF WORKS IN ENGLISH

Adams, J. Q., "The North Kansas City Urban District," *Economic Geography* (Worcester, Mass., 1932) Vol. 8, pp. 409-425.

Adams, Thomas, *The Regional Plan of New York and Environs* (Russell Sage Foundation, New York, 1929) 416 pp.

——————, *Recent Advance in Town Planning* (The Macmillan Company, New York, 1932) 400 pp.

——————, *Outline of Town and City Planning* (Russell Sage Foundation, New York, 1937) 368 pp.

Alderson, W., *Advertising for Community Promotion,* Department of Commerce Series No. 21 (Government Printing Office, Washington, D. C., 1928) 36 pp.

Ahlmann, H. W., "Geographical Study of Settlements," *The Geographical Review* (New York, 1928) pp. 93-128.

Allix, André, "Geography of Fairs," *The Geographical Review* (New York, 1922) pp. 532-569.

Anderson, Wroe, *Advertising for Community Promotion,* Department of Commerce Series No. 21 (Government Printing Office, Washington, D. C., 1928) 47 pp.

Appleton, J. B., *A Field Map for a Geographical Study of an Urban Industrial Area* (Illinois State Academy of Science, Springfield, Illinois, 1926) Vol. 19, pp. 308-314.

Aronovici, Carol, "Architectural Harmony for the Small City Civic Center," *The American City* (New York, 1931) Vol. 44, No. 2, pp. 123-124.

——————, "Let the Cities Perish," *Survey* (New York, 1932) Vol. 68, pp. 437-440.

——————, "Planner's Five-foot Shelf," *Survey* (New York, 1932) Vol. 68, pp. 476-479.

——————, "Space-time Planning and Mindedness," *American City* (New York, 1930) Vol. 42, No. 2, pp. 104-106.

——————, "Zoning and the Home," *Annals of the American Academy of Political and Social Science* (Philadelphia, 1931) Vol. 155, pt. 2, pp. 145-153.

Aurousseau, M., "Recent Contributions to Urban Geography—A Review," *The Geographical Review* (New York, 1924) Vol. 14, pp. 444-455.

——————, "Urban Geography: A Study of German Towns," *The Geographical Review* (New York, 1921) Vol. 11, pp. 614-617.

Baker, O. E., "Rural-Urban Migration and the National Welfare," *Annals Association of American Geographers* (Cambridge, Mass., 1933) Vol. 23, No. 2, pp. 59-126.

Bartholomew, Harland, *Urban Land Uses* (Harvard University Press, Cambridge, 1932) 174 pp.

Bassett, Edward M., *Zoning* (Russell Sage Foundation, New York, 1937) 275 pp.

Beckles, Willson, "Paris Press and French Public Opinion," *Living Age* (1926) Vol. 328, pp. 7-14.

Black, R. Van Nest, *Planning for the Small American City*, Public Administration Service, Publication 32 (Chicago, Ill., 1933) 90 pp.

Bleyer, Willard Grosvenor, *Main Currents in the History of American Journalism* (Houghton Mifflin Company, Boston, 1927) 464 pp.

Boyington, Gladys, "Newspaper as a Force in the Changing World," *Addresses and Proc. of National Education Association* (Washington, D. C., 1929) Vol. 67, pp. 639-640.

Bromehead, C. E. N., "The Influence of its Geography on the Growth of London," *Geographical Journal* (London, 1922) Vol. 60, pp. 125-135.

Burgess, E. W., *The Urban Community* (University of Chicago Press, Chicago, 1926) 268 pp.

Chambers, W. T., "Geographic Areas of Cities," *Economic Geography* (Worcester, Mass., 1931) Vol. 7, pp. 177-188.

Chatterton, E. K., *On the High Seas* (J. B. Lippincott Company, Philadelphia, 1929) 319 pp.

City Planning Primer, Advisory Committee on Zoning, Department of Commerce (Government Printing Office, Washington, D. C., 1928) 18 pp.

Clerget, P. C., *Urbanism; A Historic, Geographic, and Economic Study*, Report of Smithsonian Institution (Washington, D. C., 1912) pp. 653-667.

Colby, C. C., "Centrifugal and Centripetal Forces in Urban Geography," *Annals of the Assoc. of American Geographers* (Cambridge, Mass., 1933) Vol. XXIII, No. 1, pp. 1-20.

Creamer, Daniel B., *Is Industry Decentralizing* (University of Pennsylvania Press, Philadelphia, 1935) 105 pp.

Davis, D. H., "Urban Development in the Kentucky Mountains," *Annals of the Assoc. of American Geographers* (Cambridge, Mass., 1925) Vol. 15, pp. 92-99.

Dealey, G. B., "The Newspaper as a City Builder," *The American City* (New York, Sept., 1930) Vol. 43, pp. 129-130.

De Geer, Sten, "Greater Stockholm: A Geographic Interpretation," *The Geographical Review* (New York, 1923) Vol. 13, pp. 497-506.

Dickinson, R. E., "The Metropolitan Regions of the United States," *The Geographical Review* (New York, 1934) Vol. 24, No. 2, pp. 278-291.

Dorau, H. B., and Hinman, A. G., *Urban Land Economics* (The Macmillan Co., New York, 1928) 570 pp.

Duffus, R. L., *Mastering a Metropolis* (Harper & Brothers, New York, 1930) 302 pp.

Douglass, Harlan Paul, *The Suburban Trend* (The Century Company, New York, 1925) 340 pp.

"Town and City Planning" in *Encyclopedia Brittanica,* 14th Edition (New York, 1936), Vol. 22, pp. 332-335.

Fawcett, C. B., "Distribution of the Urban Population in Great Britain," *The Geographic Journal* (London, 1932) Vol. 79, pp. 100-116.

Fead, Margaret I., "Notes on the Development of the Cartographic Representation of Cities," *The Geographical Review,* (New York, 1933) Vol. 23, pp. 441-456.

Ferriss, Hugh, *The Metropolis of Tomorrow* (Ives Washburn, Inc., New York, 1929) 142 pp.

First Annual Report, National Land-Use Planning Committee, U. S. Department of Agriculture Publication No. V (U. S. Government Printing Office, Washington, D. C., 1933).

Fleure, H. J., "Some Types of Cities in Temperate Europe," *The Geographical Review* (New York, 1920) Vol. 10, pp. 357-374.

Gallois, Lucien, "The Origin and Growth of Paris," *The Geographical Review* (New York, 1923) Vol. 13, pp. 345-367.

Gist, Noel P., and Halbert, L. A., *Urban Society* (Thomas Y. Crowell Company, New York, 1933) 724 pp.

Goodrich, E. P., "Airports as a Factor in City Planning," *Supplements to National Municipal Review* (1928) Vol. 17, No. 3, pp. 181-194.

Graves, William B., *Readings in Public Opinion* (D. Appleton and Company, New York, 1928) 1281 pp.

Hanks, Col. Stedman S., *International Airports* (The Ronald Press Company, New York, 1929) 195 pp.

Hartshorne, Richard, "The Twin City District—A Unique Form of Urban Landscape," *The Geographical Review* (New York, 1932) Vol. 22, pp. 431-442.

Houser, G. C., "How Accurately Can Engineers Predict Future Population Growth of Cities?" *The American City* (New York, Sept. 1928) Vol. 39, pp. 124-126.

Howe, Frederic C., *The City, The Hope of Democracy* (Charles Scribner's Sons, New York, 1905) 319 pp.

—————, *The Modern City and Its Problems* (Charles Scribner's Sons, New York, 1915) 390 pp.

Hoyt, Homer, *One Hundred Years of Land Values in Chicago* (University of Chicago Press, Chicago, 1933) 519 pp.

Hubbard, H. V., McClintock, M., and Williams, F. B., *The Airport and the City Plan—Part I of Airports,* Harvard City Planning Series No. 1 (Harvard University Press, Cambridge), pp. 1-43.

Hubbard, H. V., "The Influence of Topography on the Layout of Subdivisions," *Landscape Architecture* (Harrisburg, Pa., April, 1928) Vol. 18, pp. 188-199.

Hubbard, Mrs. Theodora, and Hubbard, Henry Vincent, *Our Cities of To-day and Tomorrow* (Harvard University Press, Cambridge, 1929) 389 pp.

Hughes, T. H., and Lamborn, E. A. G., *Towns and Town Planning—Ancient and Modern* (Oxford University Press, American Branch, New York, 1923) 156 pp.

Ihlder, J., "The City of Tomorrow," *The Nation's Business* (Washington, D. C., Sept. 1928) Vol. 16, pp. 18-20.

International Communications and the International Telegraph Convention —1923, U. S. Bureau of Foreign and Domestic Commerce, Miscellaneous Series No. 121 (Government Printing Office, Washington, D. C.).

James, H. F., *The Urban Geography of India*, Bulletin of the Geographical Society of Philadelphia (1930) Vol. 28, pp. 101-122.

James, Preston E., "Vicksburg—A Study in Urban Geography," *The Geographical Review* (New York, 1931) Vol. 21, pp. 234-243.

Jefferson, Mark, "Distribution of British Cities, and the Empire," *The Geographical Review* (New York, 1917) Vol. 4, pp. 387-394.

————————, "Distribution of the World's City Folk," *The Geographical Review* (New York, 1931) Vol. 21, pp. 446-465.

————————, "Great Cities of 1930 in the United States with a Comparison of New York and London," *The Geographical Review* (New York, 1933) Vol. 23, pp. 90-100.

————————, "Great Cities of the United States, 1920," *The Geographical Review* (New York, 1921), Vol. 11, pp. 437-441.

————————, *How American Cities Grow*, Bulletin of the American Geographical Society (New York, 1915) Vol. 47, No. 1, pp. 19-37.

Klein, J., "Motion Picture in Its Economic and Social Aspects," *Annals of the American Academy of Political and Social Science* (Philadelphia, 1928) Vol. 128, pp. 79-83.

Lasker, B., "What Constitutes a City Plan?" *Survey* (New York, Feb. 1921), Vol. 45, p. 734.

Leighly, John S., *The Towns of Malardalen in Sweden, A Study in Urban Morphology* (University of California Publications, Berkeley, 1928-1930) Vol. 3, pp. 1-134.

Lewis, Howard T., *The Motion Picture Industry* (D. Van Nostrand Company, Inc., New York, 1933) 454 pp.

Lohmann, K. B., *Principles of City Planning* (McGraw-Hill Book Company, New York, 1931) 395 pp.

Lynd, R. S., and Lynd, H. M., *Middletown* (Harcourt, Brace and Company, New York, 1929) 550 pp.

Mackaye, Benton, *The New Exploration, A Philosophy of Regional Planning* (Harcourt, Brace and Company, New York, 1928) 235 pp.

McKenzie, R. D., *The Metropolitan Community* (McGraw-Hill Book Company, New York, 1933) 352 pp.

McMichael, S. L., and Bingham, R. F., *City Growth Essentials* (The Stanley McMichael Publishing Organization, Cleveland, Ohio, 1928) 430 pp.

Martin, Codel, *Radio and Its Future* (Harper & Brothers, New York, 1930) 349 pp.

Miller, Paul D., "How Does the City Look from the Air?" *The American City* (New York, Nov. 1930) Vol. 43, pp. 125-127.

Morrison, Paul C., "A Morphological Study of Worthington, Ohio," *Ohio Journal of Science* (Columbus, Ohio, 1934) Vol. 34, pp. 31-45.

Mowry, Don E., *Community Advertising* (The Cantwell Press, Madison, Wis., 1924) 456 pp.

Nolen, John, *City Planning* (D. Appleton and Company, New York, 1924) 447 pp.

Park, R. E., *Immigrant Press and Its Control* (Harper & Brothers, New York, 1922) 487 pp.

Park, Robert E., Burgess, Ernest W., and McKenzie, R. D., *The City* (The University of Chicago Press, Chicago, 1925) 239 pp.

Parkins, A. E., "Profiles of the Retail Business Section of Nashville, Tenn. and their Interpretation," *Annals Association of American Geographers* (Cambridge, Mass., 1930) Vol. 20, pp. 164-175.

Peake, H. J. E., *The English Village* (Benn Brothers, London, 1922) 251 pp.

Pike, Alfred T., "England's First Planned Town—Letchworth, the Vision and the Reality," *The American City* (New York, 1930) Vol. 43, No. 2, pp. 105-107.

"Planning for City, State, Region and Nation," *Proceedings of the Joint Conference on Planning,* The American Society of Planning Officials (Chicago, 1936) 170 pp.

Propper, H. M., "A New Town Planned for the Motor Age," *The American City* (New York, Feb. 1928) Vol. 38, pp. 152-154.

Purdom, C. B., *The Building of Satellite Towns* (J. M. Dent & Sons, Ltd., London, 1930) 368 pp.

Recreation, Publication of Playground Association of America (New York).

Regional Factors in National Planning and Development, National Resources Committee (U. S. Government Printing Office, Washington, D. C., 1935) 223 pp.

Regional Plan of New York, Regional Plan Association (New York, 1933) 142 pp.

Ridgley, D. C., "Geographic Principles in the Study of Cities," *Journal of Geography* (Chicago, Ill., 1923) Vol. 24, pp. 66-78.

Roswell, C. F., *Influence of Press on Social Relations,* National Conference of Social Work, 56th Annual Meeting (University of Chicago Press, Chicago, 1930) pp. 29-45.

Schneider, Herman, "Letter of Transmittal, June 1927," *Resource Survey of the Commercial Club of Cincinnati* (University of Cincinnati Institute of Scientific Research) series 2, number 1, 15 pp.

Some Recent References (Since 1928) on National and State Planning in the United States (National Resources Committee, Washington D. C., 1935) 24 pp.

Stephenson, C., "Borough and Town, A Study of Urban Origins," The Mediaeval Academy of America (Cambridge, Mass., 1933) 236 pp.

Strabolgi, Kenworthy, and Strabolgi, Ajoung, Freedom of the Seas (Horace Liveright, New York, 1928) 283 pp.

Taylor, G. R., Satellite Cities, A Study of Industrial Suburbs (D. Appleton and Company, New York, 1915) 333 pp.

The Heart of a Great State, Columbus Chamber of Commerce (Columbus, Ohio, 1930) 48 pp.

The Survey (Survey Association, Inc., New York, 1897).

The Survey Graphic, Graphic Number (New York, May 1, 1925) Vol. LIV, No. 3.

Thomas, Lewis F., The Localization of Business Activities in Metropolitan St. Louis, Social and Philosophical Sciences, New Series, No. 1, Washington University Studies (1927), pp. 109-112.

——————, "The Sequence of Areal Occupance in a Section of St. Louis, Mo.," Annals of the Association of American Geographers (Cambridge, Mass., 1931) Vol. 21, pp. 75-90.

Thompson, Tracy E., "The Industrial Expansion Movement," American Federationist (Washington, D. C., 1933) Vol. 40, No. 1-6, pp. 590-593.

Thornthwaite, C. W., Internal Migration in the United States (University of Pennsylvania Press, Philadelphia, 1934) 52 pp.

Van Cleef, Eugene, "The Urban Profile," Annals of the Assoc. of American Geographers (Cambridge, Mass., 1932) Vol. 22, pp. 237-241.

Visher, Stephen, "Chief Urban Centers of the World," Journal of Geography (Chicago, Ill., 1929) Vol. 28, pp. 252-258.

Walenty, Winid, "The Distribution of Urban Settlements of Over 10,000 Inhabitants in the United States in 1930," Scottish Geographical Magazine (Edinburgh, 1932) Vol. 48, pp. 197-210.

Weber, Adna F., Growth of Cities in the Nineteenth Century (Macmillan Company, New York, 1899) 495 pp.

Weber, Alfred, Alfred Weber's Theory of the Location of Industries (University of Chicago Press, Chicago, 1929) 256 pp.

"Wholesale Distribution of Motion Picture Films," 15th Census of the U. S. Census of Distribution, Bureau of Census (Government Printing Office, Washington, D. C., 1932).

Whitbeck, J. R., "Geographic Factors Affecting the Growth of American Cities—A Synopsis," Journal of Geography (Chicago, Ill., 1922) Vol. 21, pp. 205-207.

Zierer, C. M., "Scranton's Industrial Integrity," Economic Geography (Worcester, Mass., 1929) Vol. 5, pp. 70-86.

APPENDIX

Population of Ninety-Six Metropolitan Areas of the
United States *

AREA	POPULATION 1930	LAND AREA IN SQ.MI.	POPULATION PER SQ.MI.
Akron, Ohio			
Metropolitan District	346,681	242.78	1,428.0
Akron City	255,040	37.60	6,783.0
Albany-Schenectady-Troy, N. Y.			
Metropolitan District	425,259	472.45	900.1
In central cities	295,867	38.54	7,676.9
Albany city	127,412	18.87	6,752.1
Schenectady city	95,692	10.35	9,245.6
Troy city	72,763	9.32	7,807.2
Allentown-Bethlehem-Easton, Pa.			
Metropolitan District	322,172	334.53	962.8
In central cities	184,923	32.13	5,755.5
Allentown city	92,563	11.41	8,112.4
Bethlehem city	57,892	17.46	3,315.7
Easton city	34,468	3.26	10,573.0
Altoona, Pa.			
Metropolitan District	114,232	133.06	858.5
Altoona city	82,054	8.64	9,497.0
Atlanta, Ga.			
Metropolitan District	370,920	221.31	1,676.0
Atlanta city	270,366	34.79	7,771.4
Atlantic City, N. J.			
Metropolitan District	102,024	52.77	1,933.4
Atlantic City	66,198	11.50	5,756.4
Baltimore, Md.			
Metropolitan District	949,247	558.51	1,699.6
Baltimore city	804,874	78.72	10,224.5

* Data from Metropolitan Districts, U. S. Bureau of the Census, 1933.

AREA	POPULATION 1930	LAND AREA IN SQ.MI.	POPULATION PER SQ.MI.
Binghamton, N. Y.			
Metropolitan District	130,005	183.19	709.7
Binghamton city	76,662	9.29	8,252.1
Birmingham, Ala.			
Metropolitan District	382,792	307.86	1,243.4
Birmingham city	259,678	50.26	5,166.7
Boston, Mass.			
Metropolitan District	2,307,897	1,022.60	2,256.9
Boston city	781,188	43.90	17,794.7
Bridgeport, Conn.			
Metropolitan District	203,969	169.33	1,204.6
Bridgeport city	146,716	14.64	10,021.6
Buffalo-Niagara, N. Y.			
Metropolitan District	820,573	458.85	1,778.3
In central cities	648,536	51.57	12,575.8
Buffalo city	573,076	38.90	14,732.0
Niagara Falls city	75,460	12.67	5,955.8
Canton, Ohio			
Metropolitan District	191,231	238.38	802.2
Canton city	104,906	13.62	7,702.3
Charleston, W. Va.			
Metropolitan District	108,160	276.78	390.8
Charleston city	60,408	7.69	7,855.4
Chattanooga, Tenn.			
Metropolitan District	168,589	489.72	344.3
Chattanooga city	119,798	16.17	7,408.7
Chicago, Ill.			
Metropolitan District	4,364,755	1,119.29	3,899.6
Chicago city	3,376,438	201.90	16,723.3
Cincinnati, Ohio			
Metropolitan District	759,464	519.56	1,461.7
Cincinnati city	451,160	71.41	6,317.9
Cleveland, Ohio			
Metropolitan District	1,194,989	310.20	3,852.3
Cleveland city	900.429	70.76	12,725.1
Columbus, Ohio			
Metropolitan District	340,400	219.17	1,553.1
Columbus city	290,564	38.46	7,555.0
Dallas, Tex.			
Metropolitan District	309,658	504.42	613.9
Dallas city	260,475	41.78	6,234.4

AREA	POPULATION 1930	LAND AREA IN SQ.MI.	POPULATION PER SQ.MI.
Davenport, Iowa			
Metropolitan District	154,491	126.55	1,220.8
Davenport city	60,751	18.07	3,362.0
Dayton, Ohio			
Metropolitan District	251,928	180.12	1,398.7
Dayton city	200,982	18.13	11,085.6
Denver, Colo.			
Metropolitan District	330,761	305.09	1,084.1
Denver city	287,861	57.95	4,967.4
Des Moines, Iowa			
Metropolitan District	160,963	203.07	792.6
Des Moines city	142,559	54.00	2,640.0
Detroit, Mich.			
Metropolitan District	2,104,764	746.52	2,819.4
Detroit city	1,568,662	137.90	11,375.4
Duluth, Minn.			
Metropolitan District	155,390	443.65	350.3
Duluth city	101,463	62.34	1,627.6
El Paso, Tex.			
Metropolitan District	118,461	290.82	407.3
El Paso city	102,421	13.50	7,586.7
Erie, Pa.			
Metropolitan District	129,817	89.00	1,458.6
Erie city	115,967	19.25	6,024.3
Evansville, Ind.			
Metropolitan District	123,130	148.60	828.6
Evansville city	102,249	8.71	11,739.3
Flint, Mich.			
Metropolitan District	179,949	141.44	1,272.2
Flint city	156,492	29.67	5,274.4
Fort Wayne, Ind.			
Metropolitan District	126,558	138.58	913.2
Fort Wayne city	114,946	17.19	6,686.8
Fort Worth, Tex.			
Metropolitan District	174,575	170.60	1,023.3
Forth Worth city	163,447	46.40	3,522.6
Grand Rapids, Mich.			
Metropolitan District	207,154	136.35	1,519.3
Grand Rapids city	168,592	23.02	7,323.7
Harrisburg, Pa.			
Metropolitan District	161,672	129.52	1,248.2
Harrisburg city	80,339	6.19	12,978.8

AREA	POPULATION 1930	LAND AREA IN SQ.MI.	POPULATION PER SQ.MI.
Hartford, Conn.			
Metropolitan District	471,185	565.05	833.9
Hartford city	164,072	15.88	10,332.0
Houston, Tex.			
Metropolitan District	339,216	799.20	424.4
Houston city	292,352	71.79	4,072.3
Huntington, W. Va.-Ashland, Ky.			
Metropolitan District	163,367	264.27	618.2
In central cities	104,646	23.77	4,402.4
Huntington city	75,572	16.27	4,644.9
Ashland city	29,074	7.50	3,876.5
Indianapolis, Ind.			
Metropolitan District	417,685	311.75	1,339.8
Indianapolis city	364,161	54.15	6,725.0
Jacksonville, Fla.			
Metropolitan District	148,713	218.06	682.0
Jacksonville city	129,549	26.38	4,910.9
Johnstown, Pa.			
Metropolitan District	147,611	179.90	820.5
Johnstown city	66,993	5.45	12,292.3
Kansas City, Kans.-			
Kansas City, Mo.			
Metropolitan District	608,186	454.51	1,338.1
In Kansas	143,606	119.27	1,204.0
Kansas City	121,857	20.46	5,955.9
In Missouri	464,580	335.24	1,385.8
Kansas City	399,746	58.55	6,827.4
Knoxville, Tenn.			
Metropolitan District	135,714	192.63	704.5
Knoxville city	105,802	26.40	4,007.7
Lancaster, Pa.			
Metropolitan District	123,156	231.70	531.5
Lancaster city	59,949	3.27	18,333.0
Little Rock, Ark.			
Metropolitan District	113,137	108.99	1,038.0
Little Rock city	81,679	17.75	4,601.6
Los Angeles, Cal.			
Metropolitan District	2,318,526	1,474.34	1,572.6
Los Angeles city	1,238,048	440.32	2,811.7
Louisville, Ky.			
Metropolitan District	404,396	463.92	871.7
Louisville city	307,745	35.98	8,553.2

AREA	POPULATION 1930	LAND AREA IN SQ.MI.	POPULATION PER SQ.MI.
Lowell-Lawrence, Mass.			
Metropolitan District	332,028	292.18	1,136.4
In central cities	185,302	20.13	9,205.3
Lowell city	100,234	13.38	7,491.3
Lawrence city	85,068	6.75	12,602.7
Memphis, Tenn.			
Metropolitan District	276,126	221.16	1,248.5
Memphis city	253,143	45.67	5,542.9
Miami, Fla.			
Metropolitan District	132,189	111.56	1,184.9
Miami city	110,637	43.00	2,573.0
Milwaukee, Wis.			
Metropolitan District	743,414	241.70	3,075.8
Milwaukee city	578,249	41.14	14,055.6
Minneapolis-St. Paul, Minn.			
Metropolitan District	832,258	525.37	1,584.1
In central cities	735,962	107.55	6,843.0
Minneapolis city	464,356	55.38	8,384.9
St. Paul City	271,606	52.17	5,206.2
Nashville, Tenn.			
Metropolitan District	209,422	323.36	647.6
Nashville city	153,866	25.97	5,924.8
New Haven, Conn.			
Metropolitan District	293,724	249.07	1,179.3
New Haven city	162,655	17.91	9,081.8
New Orleans, La.			
Metropolitan District	494,877	287.02	1,724.2
New Orleans city	458,762	196.00	2,340.6
New York-Northeastern New Jersey			
Metropolitan District	10,901,424	2,514.11	4,336.1
New York Division	7,986,368	1,354.27	5,897.2
New York City	6,930,446	299.00	23,178.7
New Jersey Division	2,915,056	1,159.84	2,513.3
In central cities	1,012,154	54.36	18,619.5
Elizabeth city	114,589	9.73	11,776.9
Jersey City	316,715	13.00	24,362.7
Newark city	442,337	23.57	18,767.0
Paterson city	138,513	8.06	17,185.2

AREA	POPULATION 1930	LAND AREA IN SQ.MI.	POPULATION PER SQ.MI.
Norfolk-Portsmouth-			
Newport News, Va.			
Metropolitan District	273,233	468.59	583.1
In central cities	209,831	37.00	5,671.1
Norfolk city	129,710	28.00	4,632.5
Portsmouth city	45,704	5.00	9,140.1
Newport News city	34,417	4.00	8,604.3
Oklahoma City, Okla.			
Metropolitan District	202,163	181.78	1,112.1
Oklahoma city	185,389	30.35	6,108.4
Omaha, Neb.-Council Bluffs,			
Iowa			
Metropolitan District	273,851	204.98	1,336.0
In central cities	256,054	52.80	4,849.5
Omaha city	214,006	39.10	5,473.3
Council Bluffs city	42,048	13.70	3,069.2
Peoria, Ill.			
Metropolitan District	144,732	105.54	1,371.3
Peoria city	104,969	12.28	8,548.0
Philadelphia, Pa.			
Metropolitan District	2,847,148	993.89	2,864.7
Philadelphia city	1,950,961	128.00	15,241.9
Pittsburgh, Pa.			
Metropolitan District	1,953,668	1,626.05	1,201.5
Pittsburgh city	669,817	51.30	13,056.9
Portland, Ore.			
Metropolitan District	378,728	277.46	1,365.0
Portland city	301,815	63.45	4,756.7
Providence, R. I.-Fall River-			
New Bedford, Mass.			
Metropolitan District	963,686	817.83	1,178.3
In central cities	480,852	69.72	6,896.9
Providence city	252,981	17.83	14,188.5
Fall River city	115,274	32.90	3,503.8
New Bedford city	112,597	18.99	5,929.3
Racine-Kenosha, Wis.			
Metropolitan District	133,463	185.20	720.6
In central cities	117,804	15.99	7,367.4
Racine city	67,542	8.61	7,844.6
Kenosha city	50,262	7.38	6,810.6
Reading, Pa.			
Metropolitan District	170,486	157.07	1,085.4
Reading city	111,171	9.52	11,677.6

AREA	POPULATION 1930	LAND AREA IN SQ.MI.	POPULATION PER SQ.MI.
Richmond, Va.			
Metropolitan District	220,513	334.60	659.0
Richmond city	182,929	24.00	7,622.0
Roanoke, Va.			
Metropolitan District	103,120	231.00	446.4
Roanoke city	69,206	10.00	6,920.6
Rochester, N. Y.			
Metropolitan District	398,591	304.24	1,310.1
Rochester city	328,132	34.23	9,586.1
Rockford, Ill.			
Metropolitan District	103,204	138.77	743.7
Rockford city	85,864	11.74	7,313.8
Sacramento, Cal.			
Metropolitan District	126,995	462.02	274.9
Sacramento city	93,750	13.71	6,838.1
St. Louis, Mo.			
Metropolitan District	1,293,516	821.54	1,574.5
In Missouri	1,039,823	441.37	2,355.9
St. Louis city	821,960	61.00	13,474.8
In Illinois	253,693	380.17	667.3
East St. Louis city	74,347	13.31	5,585.8
Salt Lake City, Utah			
Metropolitan District	184,451	450.85	409.1
Salt Lake city	140,267	52.04	2,695.4
San Antonio, Tex.			
Metropolitan District	279,271	467.34	597.6
San Antonio city	231,542	35.72	6,482.1
San Diego, Cal.			
Metropolitan District	181,020	332.37	544.6
San Diego city	147,995	93.64	1,580.5
San Francisco-Oakland, Cal.			
Metropolitan District	1,290,094	825.60	1,562.6
In central cities	918,457	95.16	9,651.7
San Francisco city	634,394	42.00	15,104.6
Oakland city	284,063	53.16	5,343.5
San Jose, Cal.			
Metropolitan District	103,428	210.39	491.6
San Jose city	57,651	7.75	7,438.8
Savannah, Ga.			
Metropolitan District	105,431	370.01	284.9
Savannah city	85,024	7.60	11,187.4

AREA	POPULATION 1930	LAND AREA IN SQ.MI.	POPULATION PER SQ.MI.
Scranton-Wilkes-Barre, Pa.			
Metropolitan District	652,312	394.73	1,652.6
In central cities	230,059	26.27	8,757.5
Scranton city	143,433	19.32	7,424.1
Wilkes-Barre city	86,626	6.95	12,464.2
Seattle, Wash.			
Metropolitan District	420,663	209.90	2,004.1
Seattle city	365,583	68.50	5,337.0
South Bend, Ind.			
Metropolitan District	146,569	153.60	954.2
South Bend city	104,193	16.86	6,179.9
Spokane, Wash.			
Metropolitan District	128,798	270.25	476.6
Spokane city	115,514	40.37	2,861.4
Springfield-Holyoke, Mass.			
Metropolitan District	398,991	518.69	769.2
In central cities	206,437	52.86	3,905.4
Springfield city	149,900	31.70	4,728.7
Holyoke city	56,537	21.16	2,671.9
Syracuse, N. Y.			
Metropolitan District	245,015	139.73	1,753.5
Syracuse city	209,326	25.34	8,260.7
Tacoma, Wash.			
Metropolitan District	146,771	190.67	769.8
Tacoma city	106,817	46.35	2,304.6
Tampa-St. Petersburg, Fla.			
Metropolitan District	169,010	266.18	634.9
In central cities	141,586	71.58	1,978.0
Tampa city	101,161	19.00	5,324.3
St. Petersburg city	40,425	52.58	768.8
Toledo, Ohio			
Metropolitan District	346,530	204.36	1,695.7
Toledo city	290,718	32.97	8,817.7
Trenton, N. J.			
Metropolitan District	190,219	172.97	1,099.7
Trenton city	123,356	7.23	17,061.7
Tulsa, Okla.			
Metropolitan District	183,207	391.40	468.1
Tulsa city	141,258	21.60	6,539.7
Utica, N. Y.			
Metropolitan District	190,918	358.15	533.1
Utica city	101,740	21.20	4,799.1

AREA	POPULATION 1930	LAND AREA IN SQ.MI.	POPULATION PER SQ.MI.
Washington, D. C.			
Metropolitan District	621,059	484.99	1,280.6
Washington city	486,869	62.00	7,852.7
Waterbury, Conn.			
Metropolitan District	140,575	206.66	680.2
Waterbury city	99,902	28.10	3,555.2
Wheeling, W. Va.			
Metropolitan District	190,623	399.31	477.4
Wheeling city	61,659	9.00	6,851.0
Wichita, Kans.			
Metropolitan District	119,174	142.97	833.6
Wichita city	111,110	20.71	5,365.0
Wilmington, Del.			
Metropolitan District	163,592	228.64	715.5
Wilmington city	106,597	7.19	14,825.7
Worcester, Mass.			
Metropolitan District	305,293	399.56	764.1
Worcester city	195,311	37.20	5,250.3
Youngstown, Ohio			
Metropolitan District	364,560	363.47	1,003.0
Youngstown city	170,002	33.84	5,023.7

AREA AND DENSITY OF POPULATION OF ELEVEN AMERICAN AND EUROPEAN CITIES AND THE CORRESPONDING METROPOLITAN DISTRICTS *

CITY [1]	AREA IN SQUARE MILES		POPULATION PER SQUARE MILE	
	CITY	METRO. DIST.	CITY	METRO. DIST.
New York	299.0	2,514.11	23,178.7	4,336.1
Chicago	201.9	1,119.29	16,723.3	3,899.6
Philadelphia	128.0	993.89	15,241.9	2,864.7
Los Angeles	440.32	1,474.34	2,811.7	1,572.6
Detroit	137.9	746.52	11,375.4	2,819.4
Boston	43.9	1,022.6	17,794.7	2,256.9
St. Louis	61.0	821.54	13,474.8	1,574.5
Cleveland	70.76	310.2	12,725.1	3,852.3
Paris (1920)	30.0	185.0	96.866.0	24,324.0
Berlin (1920)	29.0	339.0	75,862.0	11,222.0
London (1931)	117.0	693.0	37,579.7	11,837.0

* Data for American cities from *Metropolitan Districts*, U. S. Bureau of the Census, 1930; data for Paris and Berlin from McMichael and Bingham, *City Growth and Values*, p. 355.

[1] Adapted from N. P. Gist and L. A. Halbert, Urban Society (Thomas Crowell Company, New York, 1933), p. 129.

TRANSPORTATION AND COMMUNICATION *

RAILWAYS: Operating Statistics

NOTE.—Methods of reporting railway statistics vary in the different countries therefore figures in the table are not on a wholly comparable basis. Data are for the years specified or nearest year thereto, however, all items shown are for the same year for the individual country. The total length of line for countries specified in the table amounts to 750,446 miles, of which 319,097 miles were in North America; 67,134 in South America, including Central America and the West Indies; 249,466 in Europe; 83,834 in Asia; 30,915 in Oceania and 21,684 in Africa. For some countries an additional length of line is included which is not shown in the railway tables of the individual countries in Part I. Figures of ton-mileage are based on metric tons of 2,204.6 pounds. Except as indicated, pre-war figures are based on boundaries as then existing.

Country	Length of line, 1930			Passengers (thousands)		Freight (1,000 metric tons)		Freight (million ton-miles), 1930	Gross receipts ($1,000,000), 1930
	Total	Per 10,000 inhabitants	Per 1,000 square miles	1913	1930	1913	1930		
North America:									
United States	260,440	20.9	88.9	1,043,603	707,987	1,072,796	1,220,134	385,815	5,356.5
Alaska	800	135.6	1.4		59		92	10	1.1
Hawaii	369	9.7	57.6	1,475	613	1,124	2,260		
Canada	42,075	40.6	11.9	46,186	34,698	97,063	104,535	26,857	454.2
Newfoundland	974	35.2	22.8		250		397		3.2
Mexico	14,439	8.7	19.0	[1] 8,666	[1] 10,162	[1] 5,931	[1] 7,175	[1] 1,908	[1] 50.6
Central America—									
British Honduras	25	4.9	2.9						
Costa Rica	430	8.1	18.7		279		121	6	.6
Guatemala [2]	509	2.3	12.0	976	1,956	408	439		4.0
Honduras	1,060	12.3	22.9						
Nicaragua	147	2.0	3.0						
Panama	295	6.3	10.3		[3] 494		[3] 325	[3] 12	[3] 5.6
El Salvador	375	2.6	28.5		[4] 553		[4] 149		
West Indies—									
Cuba	3,040	7.7	68.8	5,506	11,890	6,919	18,256	510	24.2
Dominican Republic	149	1.2	7.7		21		49		.3
Haiti	158	.6	15.5						.2
Puerto Rico	306	2.0	89.1						
West Indies, British	469	2.4	37.2		2,902		702		2.5
South America:									
Guiana, British	79	2.5	.9	300	988	70	79		.3
Surinam (Netherland Guiana)	83	5.4	1.5						
Colombia	1,621	1.9	3.7	1,351	9,117	384	2,234		23.7
Venezuela	587	1.8	1.5	545	2,888	283	411		2.5
Argentina	24,805	21.3	23.0	80,280	158,085	43,038	40,444		144.8
Brazil	20,182	4.9	6.1	52,358	157,266	11,807	24,995	2,908	106.0
Paraguay	632	7.4	3.6	[5] 533	[5] 582	[5] 155	[5] 137		[5] 9
Uruguay	1,717	8.9	23.8		[6] 4,313		[6] 1,722	[6] 214	[6] 11.4
Bolivia	1,400	4.6	2.7		[7] 121		[7] 220		
Chile	5,553	12.8	19.4	[8] 27,684	17,524	10,793	26,836	899	43.9
Ecuador	702	2.8	6.4						
Peru	2,810	4.5	5.4	4,294	5,399	1,701	2,503		9.2
Europe:									
Sweden	10,445	17.0	65.9	67,188	69,555	41,000	41,998	2,644	89.9
Norway	2,407	8.6	20.2	17,835	17,629	7,218	8,320	341	20.2
Denmark	3,291	9.2	198.5	32,520	34,440	8,812	9,679		37.2
Great Britain	20,403	4.6	23.0	1,549,791	1,684,686	[9] 370,277	[9] 309,250	18,079	869.5
Irish Free State	3,027	10.2	113.8	28,205	21,052		[9] 3,753		22.6
Belgium [10]	2,997	3.7	255.0	202,541	211,532	66,542	69,523	3,746	85.9
France	39,725	9.5	186.7	547,886	811,936	217,329	369,934	29,270	629.7
Netherlands	2,286	2.8	172.9	54,072	59,038	[9] 20,183	[9] 22,666		70.6
Austria	4,157	6.2	128.4	301,915	100,963	158,818	27,223	2,369	91.6
Czechoslovakia	6,880	4.6	126.9		235,455		64,667		
Hungary	5,390	6.2	150.2	166,097	87,053	87,175	28,812		50.1
Germany [11]	33,466	5.2	184.9	1,577,000	1,580,000	399,000	325,500	31,817	791.3

[1] National Railways of Mexico.
[2] International Railways of Central America, Guatemala Division.
[3] Panama Railway Company.
[4] International Railways of Central America, El Salvador Division.
[5] Paraguay Central Railway.
[6] Central Uruguay Railway.
[7] Bolivian Section of Antofagasta (Chile) and Bolivia Railway.
[8] Including passengers carried on 2 electric lines.
[9] Not including livestock.
[10] The National Society of Belgian Railways.
[11] 1913 figures are for present boundaries.

* *Commerce Yearbook,* U. S. Department of Commerce (Government Printing Office, Washington, D. C., 1932), Vol. 2, pp. 701-702.

RAILWAYS: Operating Statistics—Continued.

Country	Length of line, 1930			Passengers (thousands)		Freight (1,000 metric tons)		Freight (million ton-miles), 1930	Gross receipts ($1,000,000), 1930
	Total	Per 10,000 inhabitants	Per 1,000 square miles	1913	1930	1913	1930		
Europe—Continued.									
Switzerland	3,354	8.2	210.4	128,779	178,069	18,778	25,513	1,372	97.4
Estonia	1,180	10.5	64.3	----	6,008	----	2,616	171	4.1
Finland	3,196	8.7	24.1	18,310	22,033	4,933	9,574	989	19.9
Latvia	1,712	8.9	67.4	----	13,986	----	3,097	.248	7.5
Lithuania	1,056	4.4	49.1	----	5,115	----	1,787	190	4.5
Poland	12,179	3.8	81.2	----	154,126	----	69,514	12,331	163.7
U. S. S. R. (Russia) (including Asiatic)	50,269	3.1	6.1	244,000	721,500	158,200	254,900	92,833	----
Italy	13,653	3.5	114.0	93,792	104,338	[9] 37,427	[9] 53,476	[9] 7,649	241.1
Portugal	2,128	3.4	61.5	18,939	32,858	5,609	8,084	----	14.3
Spain	9,671	4.0	49.8	57,511	114,550	31,526	49,868	----	139.8
Bulgaria	1,825	3.0	45.8	[12] 1,885	10,219	[13] 788	5,129	[12] 547	9.4
Greece	1,557	2.4	31.0	----	3,779	----	1,245	77	4.6
Rumania	6,917	3.8	60.7	12,054	35,849	8,778	17,857	2,112	69.4
Yugoslavia	6,296	4.5	65.6	----	47,643	----	21,683	1,481	46.7
Asia:									
Turkey (including European)	3,305	2.3	11.2	----	14,733	----	[9] 2,388	----	11.4
Syria	604	1.9	7.8						
Palestine	656	6.3	73.9	----	1,319	----	546	----	2.5
Iraq	751	2.3	5.3	----	841	----	497	103	3.0
Persia	230	.2	.4						
India, British	42,281	1.3	23.2	457,718	601,452	83,940	112,420	20,734	383.8
Ceylon	951	1.8	37.5	11,282	18,009	1,001	1,257	----	10.8
Netherland India	4,634	.8	6.3	103,244	134,989	10,246	15,737	----	44.3
Indo-China, French	1,488	.7	5.2	6,421	10,886	682	1,065	87	4.1
Philippine Islands	840	.7	7.3	7,433	10,704	1,184	1,965	----	5.8
Siam	1,778	1.5	8.9	3,200	6,303	294	1,423	----	8.6
China	9,497	[13] .2	[13] 5.0	[14] 26,025	[14] 34,425	[14] 15,910	[14] 17,524	[14] 1,552	[14] 48.6
Japan (proper)	13,420	2.1	91.0	193,009	1,252,296	36,734	89,208	7,173	288.3
Chosen	1,779	.8	20.9	4,399	20,649	1,123	5,936	----	19.0
Taiwan	549	1.2	39.7	4,650	18,316	1,123	5,040	----	19.6
Malaya, British [15]	1,071	6.3	38.7	----	11,773	----	2,195	----	10.8
Oceania:									
Australia	27,477	42.1	9.2	249,856	363,833	27,413	31,600	3,612	222.8
New Zealand	3,438	22.6	33.2	22,311	22,814	6,346	7,078	475	33.0
Africa:									
Algeria	2,997	4.6	13.5	6,173	9,171	5,079	6,765	----	15.3
Tunisia	1,258	5.7	26.0	2,919	4,389	4,246	5,280	----	6.9
Morocco, French	1,432	2.8	8.8	----	2,796	----	3,517	----	5.9
Egypt	2,072	1.4	5.4	28,574	26,937	[9] 4,492	[9] 5,498	----	34.8
Union of South Africa	13,459	16.6	28.5	43,208	76,287	[9] 11,252	20,077	4,338	118.4
Madagascar	466	1.2	2.0	93	1,062	68	322	32	1.2

[9] Not including livestock.
[12] Standard gauge only.
[13] Exclusive of Senkiang, Mongolia, and Tibet.
[14] Chinese National Railways; 1930 data are for lines reporting only.
[15] Federated Malay States only.

Source: Bureau of Foreign and Domestic Commerce, Department of Commerce, compiled from official statistical publications of the individual countries.

MERCHANT MARINE: Steam and Motor Vessels; Distinguishing Oil Burners, Motor Ships, and Tankers. *

NOTE.—Total steam and motor vessels include vessels of 100 tons and over; steamers, motor ships, and tankers include vessels of 500 tons and over. See also headnote to table "Merchant marine of principal countries."

Class and country of ownership	Number of vessels					Thousands of tons				
	1914	1920	1932	1933	1934	1914	1920	1932	1933	1934
Total steam and motor vessels:										
World total	24,444	26,513	29,932	29,515	28,964	45,404	53,905	68,368	66,628	64,358
United States	1,757	4,110	3,351	3,287	3,218	4,330	14,574	12,820	12,660	12,382
British	10,123	9,779	9,772	9,513	9,280	20,523	20,143	22,632	21,565	20,607
Oil burners, steam:										
World total	441	1,731	3,908	3,895	3,865	1,528	8,346	20,135	20,053	19,858
United States	231	1,254	1,590	1,585	1,565	646	5,930	8,134	8,133	8,014
British	111	282	1,098	1,098	1,073	527	1,665	6,138	6,133	5,997
Motor ships (oil engines):										
World total	60	290	3,100	3,271	3,488	194	693	9,760	9,914	10,315
United States	8	80	329	328	330	10	141	722	715	718
British	10	53	732	761	814	30	158	2,805	2,814	2,919
Tankers:										
World total	320	582	1,458	1,442	1,420	1,352	2,930	8,809	8,757	8,338
United States	26	243	393	389	385	94	1,363	2,519	2,502	2,480
British	181	243	442	437	423	816	1,225	2,584	2,602	2,530

Source: Bureau of Navigation, Department of Commerce, and Lloyd's Register.

ROAD MILEAGE: Jan. 1, 1935 *

Country	Total	Per 1,000 square miles of area	Country	Total	Per 1,000 square miles of area
North America:			Europe—Continued.		
United States	3,065,254	1,031	Lithuania	2,645	1,230
Canada	409,124	118	Poland	12,371	825
Mexico	56,923	75	U. S. S. R.	1,682,109	204
South America:			Italy	105,810	884
Colombia	17,086	38	Portugal	12,371	348
Argentina	138,000	128	Spain	64,857	334
Brazil	92,441	28	Bulgaria	10,856	273
Uruguay	22,487	312	Rumania	79,811	701
Chile	24,356	85	Yugoslavia	25,170	262
Peru	11,703	24	Asia:		
Europe:			Turkey	23,242	79
Sweden	84,045	531	Malaya, British	5,868	110
Norway	24,101	202	Ceylon	17,002	671
Denmark	32,211	1,943	Netherland India	35,900	49
United Kingdom	177,347	1,881	Indochina, French	19,884	70
Irish Free State	48,054	1,806	China	51,056	12
Belgium	18,936	1,611	Japan (proper)	594,626	4,028
France	406,090	1,909	Chosen (Korea)	15,435	181
Netherland	15,845	1,175	Oceania:		
Austria	23,370	691	Australia	468,251	157
Czechoslovakia	43,169	796	New Zealand	50,930	490
Hungary	33,666	938	Africa:		
Germany	216,674	1,197	Algeria	32,736	147
Switzerland	9,792	614	Tunisia	7,143	148
Estonia	14,565	793	Morocco, French	3,961	24
Finland	37,495	279	Union of South Africa	111,336	236
Latvia	20,259	942			

Foreign Commerce Yearbook, U. S. Department of Commerce, Bureau of Foreign and Domestic Commerce (Government Printing Office, Washington, D. C., 1935), p. 366.

MOTOR VEHICLES IN USE, 1936 *

AFRICA

Country	Automobiles	Cars	Trucks	Buses	Motorcycles
Algeria	60,750	52,000	6,800	1,950	4,500
Angola	3,000	1,200	1,800	....	....
Belgian Congo	4,527	2,339	2,188	....	1,387
British East Africa	19,665	13,210	6,455	....	3,300
British West Africa	12,112	4,495	7,617	....	1,820
Canary Islands	4,000	2,250	1,750	....	110
Egypt	22,850	19,300	2,500	1,050	3,000
Ethiopia	205	165	40	....	50
French Equatorial Africa	1,265	527	738	....	225
French West Africa	9,186	3,968	5,218	....	585
Liberia	104	52	52	....	9
Madagascar and Reunion	4,900	4,900	....	....	....
Madeira	1,001	675	155	180	25
Mauritius	2,278	1,850	311	117	193
Morocco	29,132	21,463	7,669	....	1,845
Nyasaland	1,312	764	548	....	628
Port. East Africa	3,625	2,200	1,425	....	625
Rhodesia	15,150	12,200	2,950	....	1,060
Seychelles	90	....	....	....	85
Somalilands and Eritrea	900	550	350	....	....
South West Africa	2,300	1,700	800	....	100
Sudan	3,370	....	....	....	275
Tangier	1,000	775	225	....	170
Tripolitania	1,025	475	550	....	170
Tunisia	16,100	13,600	2,200	300	1,800
Union of South Africa	238,855	239,926	28,929	....	33,148
Total 1936	**458,911**	**⊙370,584**	**⊙81,270**	**⊙3,597**	**⊙54,940**

⊙Not complete for all territories

ASIA

Country	Automobiles	Cars	Trucks	Buses	Motorcycles
Afghanistan	2,500	2,150	350	....	....
Arabia	1,500	....	....	....	....
British Malaya	37,000	26,998	10,002	....	4,174
Brunei	180	90	60	30	40
Ceylon	23,650	17,592	3,588	2,470	3,091
China	44,650	30,250	15,400	....	....
Chosen	7,360	2,212	2,688	2,460	960
Cyprus	1,850	....	....	....	300
French Indo China	14,800	11,500	1,100	2,200	1,200
Hongkong	4,100	3,075	825	200	325
India	164,706	112,932	15,548	36,226	13,142
Iran (Persia)	7,800	3,500	4,000	300	500
Iraq	5,350	4,200	1,150	....	90
Japan	130,118	58,132	46,476	25,500	51,500
Manchukuo	7,000	....	....	....	800
Netherlands East Indies	57,214	41,239	9,435	6,540	13,438
Palestine	9,050	5,100	3,950	....	750
Philippine Islands	43,838	27,381	16,547	....	524
Siam	9,000	6,000	3,000	....	300
Syria	12,300	9,500	2,800	....	....
Trans-Jordan	496	268	161	34	6
Turkey	6,500	3,000	3,500	....	600
Total 1936	**590,935**	**⊙365,119**	**⊙140,580**	**⊙75,960**	**⊙91,640**

⊙Not complete for all territories

AMERICA

Country	Automobiles	Cars	Trucks	Buses	Motorcycles
Alaska	3,100	2,200	900	....	6
Argentina	290,553	220,392	62,661	7,500	....
Bahamas	985	835	150	....	40
Barbados	2,315	1,800	375	140	1,350
Bermuda	47	....	....	....	....
Bolivia	2,200	950	1,250	....	....
Brazil	145,000	98,000	47,000	....	....
British Honduras	214	140	74	....	2
Canada	1,161,002	986,605	174,397	....	10,463
Chile	32,950	23,250	9,700	....	700
Colombia	15,950	10,250	5,700	....	....
Costa Rica	2,234	1,672	548	114	132
Cuba	34,381	20,324	11,984	2,073	358
Dominican Republic	2,625	1,850	775	....	157
Ecuador	3,058	1,625	1,038	395	8
Grenada	420	305	115	....	....
Guadeloupe	3,105	....	....	....	....
Guatemala	3,035	1,825	850	360	207
Guiana	2,030	1,550	480	....	....
Haiti	2,679	2,173	506	....	39
Honduras	1,503	1,050	450	3	30
Jamaica	9,612	7,507	1,985	120	533
Martinique	2,500	2,000	500	....	100
Mexico	97,500	66,000	23,900	7,600	1,200
Netherlands West Indies	2,879	1,775	750	354	434
Newfoundland	3,685	2,984	689	12	141
Nicaragua	775	575	200	....	70
Panama	10,050	8,924	586	540	53
Paraguay	1,350	500	850	....	....
Peru	15,000	9,500	5,000	500	150
Puerto Rico	15,920	12,912	3,008	....	180
Salvador	2,550	1,950	600	....	....
St. Pierre and Miquelon	125	50	75	....	....
Trinidad and Tobago	6,250	4,250	1,550	450	1,000
United States	26,167,107	22,589,660	3,511,061	66,386	95,633
Uruguay	29,968	23,890	6,078	....	....
Venezuela	17,180	11,600	5,580	....	75
Virgin Islands	400	300	100	....	....
West Indies	1,056	840	152	64	135
Total 1936	**28,093,338**	**⊙24,122,013**	**⊙3,877,167**	**⊙86,611**	**⊙112,896**
†Total 1936	**1,926,231**	**⊙1,532,353**	**⊙366,106**	**⊙20,225**	**⊙17,263**

⊙Not complete for all territories
†Not including United States.

EUROPE

Country	Automobiles	Cars	Trucks	Buses	Motorcycles
Albania	900	300	450	150	20
Austria	44,941	26,810	15,673	2,458	55,809
Azores	839	712	44	83	113
Belgium	162,450	103,750	58,700	....	....
Bulgaria	3,944	1,928	866	1,150	560
Czechoslovakia	90,000	70,000	20,000	....	40,000
Danzig Free City	2,795	1,975	765	55	2,200
Denmark	130,599	91,533	39,066	....	26,347
Estonia	3,705	2,060	1,438	207	1,180
Faroe Islands	100	29	48	23	....
Finland	35,129	20,846	12,399	1,884	5,425
France	2,182,138	1,713,430	468,708	....	....
Germany	1,104,000	840,000	250,000	14,000	1,053,556
Gibraltar	1,050	875	125	50	1,075
Great Britain	1,990,650	1,490,665	414,760	85,225	499,712
Greece	14,300	7,400	4,600	1,900	550
Holland	143,920	93,250	46,880	3,790	47,390
Hungary	15,200	10,950	4,250	....	9,500
Iceland	1,550	600	950	....	....
Irish Free State	52,518	42,961	8,744	813	4,035
Italy	391,709	277,841	104,407	9,461	114,542
Latvia	3,955	2,115	1,594	246	1,800
Lithuania	2,180	1,360	490	330	1,250
Luxemburg	5,300	3,100	2,200	....	....
Malta	3,989	2,700	719	579	549
Monaco	1,607	1,327	180	100	250
Northern Ireland	37,470	28,940	7,750	780	5,100
Norway	60,540	35,600	24,940	....	7,600
Poland	25,212	18,721	4,881	1,520	8,777
Portugal	34,900	25,200	8,300	1,400	3,200
Rumania	28,700	20,600	6,200	2,500	2,300
Spain	179,500	130,700	48,800	....	14,000
Sweden	154,800	106,400	44,600	3,800	46,000
Switzerland	90,500	70,000	19,000	1,500	35,000
U. S. S. R. (Russia)	245,600	44,100	201,500	....	....
Yugoslavia	10,400	7,150	2,525	725	2,850
Total 1936	**7,257,099**	**⊙5,295,328**	**⊙1,826,552**	**⊙134,729**	**⊙1,990,391**

⊙Not complete for all territories

OCEANIA

Country	Automobiles	Cars	Trucks	Buses	Motorcycles
Australia	631,854	473,992	157,862	....	76,279
Fiji Islands	1,260	775	210	275	125
French Oceania	600	425	175	....	25
Hawaii	49,146	39,652	9,163	331	456
New Guinea	339	255	83	1	24
New Zealand	190,876	149,112	41,205	559	22,392
Other Oceania	600	....	....	....	....
Samoa	306	163	143	....	....
Total 1936	**874,981**	**⊙664,374**	**⊙208,841**	**⊙1,166**	**⊙99,301**

⊙Not complete for all territories

* The American Automobile (Overseas Edition), New York, U. S. A., copyright 1936.

TELEPHONE DEVELOPMENT OF THE WORLD BY COUNTRIES
January 1, 1935 [1]

Countries	MILES OF TELEPHONE WIRE			MILES OF TELEGRAPH WIRE			NUMBER OF TELEPHONES		
	Number of Miles	Per Cent of Total World	Per 100 Population	Number of Miles	Per Cent of Total World	Per 100 Population	Total	Per Cent of Total World	Telephones Per 100 Population
NORTH AMERICA:									
United States	86,800,000	55.88	68.73	2,270,000	32.40	1.80	16,868,955	50.29	13.36
Canada	5,134,000	3.30	47.32	367,000	5.24	3.38	1,193,729	3.56	11.00
Central America	61,000	.04	0.89	20,000	.28	0.29	25,669	.08	0.37
Mexico	557,000	.36	3.17	90,000	1.28	0.51	108,652	.32	0.62
West Indies—									
Cuba	275,000	.18	6.62	14,000	.20	0.34	32,994	.10	0.79
Puerto Rico	33,000	.02	1.98	2,000	.03	0.12	12,066	.04	0.72
SOUTH AMERICA:									
Argentina	1,250,000	.80	10.42	200,000	2.85	1.67	322,873	.96	2.69
Bolivia	5,500	.004	0.17	5,000	.07	0.16	2,218	.01	0.07
Brail	683,000	.44	1.46	110,000	1.57	0.24	192,666	.57	0.41
Chile	201,000	.13	4.48	55,000	.79	1.23	50,360	.15	1.12
Colombia	130,000	.08	1.36	20,000	.29	0.21	32,784	.10	0.34
Ecuador	9,000	.01	0.36	4,000	.06	0.16	6,371	.02	0.25
Paraguay	7,000	.005	0.78	3,000	.04	0.33	2,996	.01	0.33
Peru	60,000	.04	0.92	12,000	.17	0.18	20,985	.06	0.32
Uruguay	105,000	.07	5.21	8,000	.11	0.40	32,183	.09	1.60
Venezuela	78,000	.05	2.34	7,000	.10	0.21	19,285	.06	0.58
EUROPE:									
Austria	670,000	.43	9.89	49,000	.70	0.72	258,748	.77	3.82
Belgium †	1,831,000	1.18	22.12	35,000	.50	0.42	323,423	.96	3.91
Bulgaria	67,000	.04	1.10	7,000	.10	0.15	20,646	.06	0.34
Czechoslovakia	601,000	.39	3.95	82,000	1.17	0.54	171,646	.51	1.13
Denmark ‡	1,249,000	.80	34.10	13,000	.19	0.35	377,565	1.13	10.31

Finland	350,000	.22	9.30	18,000	.26	0.48	141,067	.42	3.75
France ‡	5,160,000	3.32	12.16	521,000	7.44	1.23	1,399,869	4.17	3.30
Germany ‡	15,850,000	10.20	23.73	130,000	1.85	0.20	3,134,103	9.34	4.69
Great Britain & No. Ireland ‡	11,670,000	7.51	24.98	252,000	3.60	0.54	2,366,311	7.06	5.06
Greece	76,000	.05	1.13	35,000	.50	0.52	26,712	.08	0.40
Hungary	400,000	.26	4.50	45,000	.64	0.51	121,802	.36	1.37
Irish Free State ‡	125,000	.08	4.17	22,000	.31	0.73	34,799	.11	1.16
Italy	1,600,000	1.03	3.69	266,000	3.80	0.61	516,075	1.54	1.19
Jugo-Slavia	145,000	.09	0.99	58,000	.83	0.39	49,846	.15	0.34
Latvia ‡	276,000	.18	14.15	5,000	.07	0.26	65,345	.20	3.35
Netherlands	1,150,000	.74	13.70	16,000	.23	0.19	352,741	1.05	4.20
Norway *	602,000	.39	20.98	28,000	.40	0.98	199,684	.60	6.96
Poland	1,056,000	.68	3.15	48,000	.68	0.14	211,334	.63	0.63
Portugal	134,000	.09	1.89	18,000	.26	0.26	49,466	.15	0.70
Russia §	1,300,000	.84	0.75	600,000	8.56	0.35	739,381	2.20	0.43
Spain	1,220,000	.79	4.98	92,000	1.31	0.38	312,719	.93	1.28
Sweden	2,275,000	1.46	36.50	27,000	.38	0.43	616,947	1.84	9.90
Switzerland	1,362,000	.88	32.86	15,000	.21	0.36	383,289	1.14	9.25
ASIA:									
British India ‡	424,000	.27	0.12	427,000	6.09	0.12	64,448	.19	0.02
China	520,000	.33	0.04	130,000	1.86	0.03	164,000	.49	0.04
Japan ‡	3,834,000	2.47	5.58	233,000	3.33	0.34	1,068,244	3.19	1.56
AFRICA:									
Egypt	263,000	.17	1.23	35,000	.50	0.16	49,765	.15	0.23
Union of South Africa ‡	576,000	.37	6.73	31,000	.44	0.36	140,349	.42	1.64
OCEANIA:									
Australia *	2,581,000	1.66	38.66	98,000	1.40	1.47	501,402	1.49	7.51
Netherland India	254,000	.16	0.38	22,000	.31	0.03	41,048	.12	0.06
Hawaii	89,000	.06	23.73	0	.00	0.00	23,857	.07	6.36
New Zealand ‡	588,000	.38	37.69	26,000	.37	1.67	159,170	.48	10.20
Philippine Islands	66,000	.04	0.48	11,000	.16	0.08	26,358	.08	0.19

1 Courtesy, American Telephone and Telegraph Co.
Telephone service is operated by Governments, except in the United States and Canada.
* June 30, 1934.   † February 28, 1935.   ‡ March 31, 1935.   § U.S.S.R. including Siberia and Associated Republics.
|| Includes approximately 15,560,000 automatic or "Dial" telephones, of which about 45 per cent are in the United States.

TELEPHONE DEVELOPMENT OF LARGE CITIES
JANUARY 1, 1935 [1]

Country and City (or Exchange Area)	Number of Telephones	Telephones per 100 Population
ARGENTINA:		
Buenos Aires	188,528	6.28
AUSTRALIA:		
Adelaide	28,949	9.22
Brisbane	26,707	8.76
Melbourne	103,137	10.31
Sydney	117,759	9.43
AUSTRIA:		
Graz	10,784	7.05
Vienna	175,947	9.38
BELGIUM: †		
Antwerp	39,228	7.40
Brussels	105,654	10.95
Liege	23,695	5.59
BRAZIL:		
Rio de Janeiro	64,046	3.56
CANADA:		
Montreal	164,594	16.19
Ottawa	35,441	18.85
Toronto	188,287	24.57
Vancouver	52,549	28.03
CHINA:		
Canton	8,056	0.76
Hong Kong	14,845	1.75
Peiping	12,948	0.84
Shanghai ‖	54,861	3.32
CUBA:		
Havana	25,899	3.70
CZECHOSLOVAKIA:		
Prague	57,725	6.32

[1] Courtesy American Telephone and Telegraph Co.
† February 28, 1935.
‡ March 31, 1935.
‖ International Settlement and French Concession.

Country and City (or Exchange Area)	Number of Telephones	Telephones per 100 Population
DANZIG:		
Free City of Danzig	17,964	6.78
DENMARK:		
Copenhagen	173,372	21.14
FINLAND:		
Helsingfors	38,653	14.32
FRANCE:		
Bordeaux	20,348	7.59
Lille	17,346	8.59
Lyons	35,317	5.27
Marseilles	34,165	3.67
Paris	416,870	14.35
GERMANY: ‡		
Berlin	488,244	11.49
Breslau	42,185	6.70
Cologne	64,935	8.49
Dresden	60,899	8.29
Dortmund	23,958	4.10
Essen	30,254	4.55
Frankfort-on-Main	61,968	9.46
Hamburg-Altona	155,826	9.44
Leipzig	65,038	8.39
Munich	79,219	10.63
GREAT BRITAIN AND NO. IRELAND: ‡		
Belfast	19,280	4.65
Birmingham	62,147	5.14
Bristol	22,711	5.45
Edinburgh	34,565	7.78
Glasgow	61,747	5.17
Leeds	25,922	5.04
Liverpool	60,131	5.01
London	891,725	9.59
Manchester	67,336	6.10
Newcastle	20,558	4.36
Sheffield	21,202	4.08
HAWAII:		
Honolulu	15,942	**11.55**

‡ March 31, 1935.

Country and City (or Exchange Area)	Number of Telephones	Telephones per 100 Population
HUNGARY:		
Budapest	81,886	6.02
Szeged	2,100	1.52
IRISH FREE STATE: ‡		
Dublin	19,920	4.64
ITALY:		
Milan	88,701	8.33
Naples	27,098	3.08
Rome	86,393	7.51
JAPAN: ‡		
Kobe	34,700	4.06
Kyoto	42,408	4.03
Nagoya	34,846	3.42
Osaka	124,883	4.59
Tokio	209,605	3.70
LATVIA: ‡		
Riga	24,437	6.35
MEXICO:		
Mexico City	61,969	5.39
NETHERLANDS:		
Amsterdam	56,468	7.22
Haarlem	12,775	7.89
Rotterdam	38,808	6.30
The Hague	48,939	9.45
NEW ZEALAND: ‡		
Auckland	22,236	10.20
NORWAY: *		
Oslo	52,198	20.88
PHILIPPINE ISLANDS:		
Manila	17,328	4.40
POLAND:		
Lodz	14,356	1.60
Warsaw	59,842	4.75
PORTUGAL:		
Lisbon	28,470	4.37

* June 30, 1934.
‡ March 31, 1935.

Country and City (or Exchange Area)	Number of Telephones	Telephones per 100 Population
ROUMANIA:		
Bucharest	24,718	3.86
RUSSIA:		
Leningrad	91,023	3.03
Moscow	134,440	3.36
SPAIN:		
Barcelona:	51,014	4.72
Madrid	61,017	6.10
SWEDEN:		
Gothenburg	44,228	17.32
Malmö	21,591	15.56
Stockholm	144,011	32.64
SWITZERLAND:		
Basel	32,441	21.48
Berne	24,992	21.92
Geneva	27,235	18.53
Zurich	57,330	21.39
UNITED STATES:		
New York	1,493,374	20.61
Chicago	824,293	25.21
Los Angeles	341,221	25.95
Pittsburgh	183,761	18.09
Milwaukee	135,963	17.81
San Francisco	242,026	35.08
Washington	189,017	35.80
Minneapolis	121,123	23.98
Seattle	105,087	25.19
Denver	87,755	29.25
Omaha	61,186	25.64
Hartford	53,224	22.43

TELEPHONE CONVERSATIONS AND TELEGRAMS, YEAR 1934 [1]

Country	Number of Telephone Conversations	Number of Telegrams	Per Cent of Total Wire Communications Telephone Conversations	Per Cent of Total Wire Communications Telegrams	Wire Communications Per Capita Telephone Conversations	Wire Communications Per Capita Telegrams	Wire Communications Per Capita Total
Australia	428,000,000	14,051,000	96.8	3.2	64.3	2.1	66.4
Austria	600,000,000	1,689,000	99.7	0.3	88.7	0.2	88.9
Belgium	245,424,000	5,312,000	97.9	2.1	29.7	0.7	30.4
Canada	2,298,508,000	9,857,000	99.6	0.4	213.4	0.9	214.3
Czechoslovakia	270,000,000	3,860,000	98.6	1.4	17.8	0.3	18.1
Denmark	611,395,000	1,684,000	99.7	0.3	167.2	0.5	167.7
Finland	225,000,000	730,000	99.7	0.3	60.0	0.2	60.2
France	888,065,000	27,943,000	96.9	3.1	21.0	0.7	21.7
Germany	2,288,596,000	17,233,000	99.3	0.7	34.3	0.3	34.6
Great Britain and Northern Ireland	1,720,000,000	43,926,000	97.5	2.5	36.9	0.9	37.8
Hungary	146,000,000	1,873,000	98.7	1.3	16.5	0.2	16.7
Japan	4,051,000,000	54,571,000	98.7	1.3	59.4	0.8	60.2
Netherlands	407,000,000	3,126,000	99.2	0.8	48.8	0.4	49.2
Norway	226,000,000	2,806,000	98.8	1.2	78.9	1.0	79.9
Poland	526,000,000	3,164,000	99.4	0.6	15.8	0.1	15.9
Spain	735,000,000	24,393,000	96.8	3.2	30.2	1.0	31.2
Sweden	900,000,000	3,592,000	99.6	0.4	144.6	0.6	145.2
Switzerland	278,335,000	1,857,000	99.3	0.7	67.3	0.5	67.8
Union of South Africa	247,000,000	5,529,000	97.8	2.2	29.0	0.7	29.7
United States	24,250,000,000	160,000,000	99.3	0.7	192.4	1.3	193.7

Telephone conversations represent completed local and toll or long distance messages. Telegrams include inland and outgoing international messages.

[1] Courtesy American Telephone and Telegraph Co.

RADIO RECEIVING SETS AND BROADCASTERS BY PRINCIPAL COUNTRIES **

NUMBER OF STATIONS

The numbers of long and medium wave broadcasting stations given herein are accurate, subject to recent changes as yet unreported, but with regard to short wave stations attention is called to the many factors as yet existing in this field by which the identity of many stations as "broadcasters" is uncertain. So far as it has been possible in the light of available data, those stations were selected which intentionally cater to the broadcast listener, on the frequencies above 1,500 kilocycles, irrespective of official classifications.

CLASSIFICATION OF BROADCASTING STATIONS

Long......Wavelength from 2,000 to 550 meters; frequency from 150 to 545 kilocycles.

Broadcast..Wavelength from 550 to 180 meters; frequency from 545 to 1,666 kilocycles.

Short......Wavelength below 180 meters; frequency above 1,666 kilocycles. Shortwave classifications are indefinite and many are providing more or less broadcasting service although distinctly otherwise classified officially. Those accounted here are of official classification indicating broadcasting to be the principal activity.

Total......Stations wiht dual waves in different ranges are counted once in each range.

	Number of Receiving Sets in Use	Number of Radio Broadcasting Stations Operating			
		Long [1]	Broadcast [1]	Short [1]	Total [1]
North America					
Alaska	1,500	..	3	..	3
Bahamas	1,000	..	..	..	..
Bermuda	2,813*	..	..	..	..
Canada	812,335	..	67	2	69
Costa Rica	3,000	..	6	1	7
Cuba	30,000	..	56	3	59
Dominican Republic ..	3,000	..	1	..	1
Honduras	3,000	..	1	1	2
Mexico	130,000	..	57	1	58
Newfoundland & Lab..	8,000*	..	5	..	5
Puerto Rico	15,000	..	3	..	3
United States	25,551,569	..	644	16	660
South America					
Argentina	650,000	..	38	..	38
Bolivia	20,000*	..	2	2	4

** U. S. Dept. of Commerce, Washington, D. C.
* As of December 31, 1935, or subsequently.
[1] See note at head of table.

| | Number of Receiving Sets in Use | Number of Radio Broadcasting Stations Operating | | |
		Long [1]	Broad-cast [1]	Short [1]	Total [1]
Brazil	250,000*	..	58	..	58
Chile	50,000	..	52	4	56
Colombia	25,000	..	10	23	33
Ecuador	4,000	..	..	13	13
Paraguay	6,000*	..	8	2	10
Peru	8,500	..	10	3	13
Uruguay	100,000	..	36	..	36
Venezuela	47,000*	..	4	7	11
Europe					
Austria	560,120*	..	8	2	10
Belgium	746,345*	..	14	1	15
Bulgaria	17,213*	..	..	..	..
Czechoslovakia	847,955*	..	7	1	8
Danzig	29,000*	..	1	..	1
Denmark	609,226*	1	1	1	3
Estonia	24,193*	..	2	..	2
Finland	143,986*	1	7	..	8
France	2,625,677*	2	24	1	27
Germany	7,192,952*	..	24	12	36
Greece	6,317*	..	..	..	..
Hungary	352,907*	..	6	7	13
Irish Free State	78,627*	..	3	..	3
Italy	530,000*	..	16	5	21
Latvia	82,175*	..	4	..	4
Lithuania	26,763*	1	..	..	1
Netherlands	946,844*	1	3	2	6
Norway	191,378*	1	14	5	20
Poland	491,823*	1	6	..	7
Portugal	40,409*	1	19	1	21
Rumania	127,041*	..	2	1	3
Spain	303,983*	1	65	5	71
Sweden	843,143*	2	29	..	31
Switzerland	418,499*	1	5	2	8
United Kingdom	7,403,139*	..	10	15	25
Yugoslavia	81,385*	..	3	..	3

* As of December 31, 1935, or subsequently.
[1] See note at head of Table on page 298.

	Number of Receiving Sets in Use	Number of Radio Broadcasting Stations Operating			
		Long [1]	Broad-cast [1]	Short [1]	Total [1]
European Asia					
Russia ‖	2,000,000	32	41	15	88
Turkey ‖	6,175*	2	..	..	2
Asia					
British India	15,000	..	5	2	7
British Malaya	2,574‡	..	..	3†	3†
Ceylon	2,829	..	1	..	1
China	200,000§	..	100	1	101
Chosen	50,047*	..	..	..	..
Hong Kong	4,200	..	2	..	2
Iran (Persia)	1,500*	..	..	..	..
Iraq	3,500*	..	..	..	..
Japan (proper)	2,025,000	..	31	..	31
Netherland India	17,875	..	9	17	26
North Manchuria	11,000	..	..	..	..
Palestine	12,200*	..	..	..	..
Philippine Islands	24,231*	..	3	1	4
Siam	27,288	..	2	1	3
Taiwan	19,122	..	..	..	..
Oceania					
Australia	744,507	..	98	1	99
Hawaii	20,000	..	3	..	3
New Zealand	165,000	..	30	..	30
Africa					
Algeria	41,344*	..	1	..	1
Egypt	41,370*	..	2	1	3
Ethiopia	25	..	..	..	..
French Morocco	23,079*	..	2	1	3
Southern Rhodesia ...	1,405	..	..	..	..
Tunisia	13,500*	..	1	..	1
Union of South Africa	131,434*	..	7	1	8

[1] See note at head of table on page 298.
* As of December 31, 1935 or subsequently.
† Straits Settlements, 2; Federated Malay States, 1.
† "homes"—additional sets may be operated by licensee without additional license.
‡ Straits Settlements, 1,160; Federated Malay States, 1,136; Kedah, 64; Johore, 189; Kelantan, 17; Trengganu, 8.
‖ Separate statistics for European and Asiatic Russia and Turkey not available.
§ Estimated at from 100,000 to 300,000....Registrations, 70,000.

TOTAL FOR EACH CONTINENT, INCLUDING AREAS NOT LISTED HERE

	Number of Receiving Sets in Use	Number of Radio Broadcasting Stations Operating			
		Long [1]	Broad-cast [1]	Short [1]	Total [1]
North America	26,579,696	..	850	32	882
South America	1,161,142	..	218	54	272
Europe	24,755,203	15	273	62	350
Europe-Asia	2,006,175	34	41	15	90
Asia	2,436,608	..	154	25	179
Oceania	929,949	..	133	2	135
Africa	262,836	..	14	5	19
WORLD	58,131,609	49	1,683	195	1,927

POSTAL SERVICE: Number of Offices and Pieces of Mail *

NOTE.—Data for 1913 are not adjusted to conform to present boundaries; data are for the year specified or the nearest year thereto.

Country	Offices, 1930	Pieces of mail (1,000) 1913	Pieces of mail (1,000) 1930
Total countries specified	337,655		80,329,715
North America:			
United States	48,544	18,587,445	26,544,000
Alaska	174		
Hawaii ¹	93	91	238
Canada	12,409	1,478,504	1,400,000
Newfoundland	923	7,100	19,200
Mexico	3,153	101,920	219,270
Central America—			
British Honduras	26	555	935
Costa Rica	203		4,746
Guatemala	305	13,238	31,804
Honduras	336	1,617	2,610
Nicaragua	116		802
Panama	113	1,676	5,000
El Salvador	201	4,705	12,317
West Indies—			
Cuba	826	38,288	99,231
Dominican Republic	134		11,575
Haiti	92		3,131
Puerto Rico	94		
Bermuda	19		5,020
British West Indies	515		35,416
South America:			
Guiana, British	70	3,200	3,497
Guiana, French	22		521
Surinam (Netherland Guiana)	14		1,193
Colombia	1,216	6,961	21,132
Venezuela	441	17,766	78,308
Argentina	3,872	899,954	2,300,000
Brazil	4,870	634,003	930,541
Paraguay	264		5,866
Uruguay	995	117,661	136,446
Bolivia	454	7,341	7,109
Chile	898	75,436	101,231
Ecuador	311	5,333	9,215
Peru	994	31,648	44,895
Europe:			
Sweden	3,808	490,007	842,000
Norway	4,192	244,456	311,374
Denmark	1,429	358,947	532,736
United Kingdom	22,710	5,608,200	6,636,900
Irish Free State	2,205		398,662
Belgium	1,703	933,736	1,192,000
France	16,814	3,396,827	6,281,180
Netherlands	1,314	630,714	1,045,984

Country	Offices, 1930	Pieces of mail (1,000) 1913	Pieces of mail (1,000) 1930
Europe—Continued:			
Austria	2,753	²2,049,923	985,860
Czechoslovakia	3,724		1,110,849
Hungary	2,386	(²)	385,960
Germany	56,440	9,802,255	10,000,000
Switzerland	4,012	565,900	759,500
Estonia	127		66,063
Finland	3,231	134,308	303,526
Latvia	1,449		84,775
Lithuania	581		92,753
Poland	4,017		1,193,838
U. S. S. R. (Russia) including Asiatic	15,902	1,885,241	1,040,130
Italy	10,867	1,478,160	2,400,000
Portugal	1,254		159,843
Spain	10,456	459,024	753,135
Bulgaria	578	72,456	90,364
Greece	1,230	47,660	145,620
Rumania	6,390	179,808	411,913
Yugoslavia	4,012		470,781
Asia:			
Turkey (including European)	818		130,745
Syria and Lebanon	112		27,860
Palestine	42		18,814
Iraq	102		7,725
Persia	230		15,400
India, British	24,175	1,014,788	1,299,692
Ceylon	844	46,847	113,088
Netherland India	618	³46,177	117,560
Indo-China, French	395	15,131	46,365
Philippine Islands	989	618	3,332
Siam	841	6,667	15,888
China	12,523	635,624	796,018
Japan (proper)	9,690	1,659,544	5,160,262
Chosen	721	135,799	508,114
Taiwan	175	31,269	66,921
Malaya, British ⁴	179	17,700	40,172
Oceania:			
Australia	8,607	737,989	1,138,839
New Zealand	1,773	338,400	278,083
Africa:			
Algeria	744	79,548	125,230
Tunisia	174	81,901	128,666
Morocco, French	269	9,994	88,990
Egypt	3,819	86,295	180,218
Union of South Africa	3,260	216,656	276,480
Madagascar	184		8,258

¹ Honolulu only.
² Former territory of Austria includes that of Hungary.
³ Inland mails only.
⁴ Figures are for the Federated Malay States only.

Source: Bureau of Foreign and Domestic Commerce. Compiled from official statistical publications of the individual countries.

124691—33——46

* Commerce Yearbook, U. S. Department of Commerce (Government Printing Office, Washington, D. C., 1932), Vol. 2, p. 715.

INDEX

(Illustrations are indicated by bold-faced type.)

303